An Uncommon Union

An Uncommon Union

HENRY B. STANTON AND THE EMANCIPATION OF ELIZABETH CADY

LINDA C. FRANK

UPSTATE NY HISTORY
AUBURN, NEW YORK

Published by Upstate NY History
Auburn, New York
www.UpstateNYHistory.com

Printed in the United States of America
First edition 2016

Book Design: Brightman House Graphics

Publisher's Cataloging-in-Publication Data

Frank, Linda C.,
    An uncommon union : Henry B. Stanton and the emancipation
    of Elizabeth Cady / Linda C. Frank
    p. cm.
    Includes bibliographical references and index.
    ISBN 978-1-945161-00-1 (paper)
    ISBN 978-1-945161-01-8 (eBook)
1. Stanton, Elizabeth Cady, 1815-1902.
2. Stanton, Henry B. (Henry Brewster), 1805-1887.
3. Women's rights—New York (State)—Seneca Falls—History.
4. Antislavery movements—United States—History—19th century.
I. Title
    HQ1413.S67 F73 2016   305.42092—dc22
    Library of Congress Control Number: 2016904072

For my parents, Pauline W. Frank and Edward R. Frank,

my very dear friend Harry Rice,

my son, Matthew Telesky,

and for Susanna Brewster Stanton

CONTENTS

ACKNOWLEDGMENTS

I could never repay the debt of gratitude I owe to historian Ellen Carol DuBois. Not only has Ellen been incredibly generous with her time and knowledge, she has modeled both scholarship and mentorship at every turn of my graduate and post-graduate careers. Ellen's unflagging support of my work has sustained me many times over the past decade. It was Ellen's work that initially inspired me to pursue a doctorate, and it was through her guidance that I learned how to be a historian. She has been a mentor in every sense of the word.

This book could not have been written without the work of historian and editor Ann D. Gordon. From the magisterial microfilm collection of Elizabeth Cady Stanton's papers, to the serious scholarship of the six-volume edited works of Stanton and Anthony, every scholar of women's rights owes her a great debt.

I would also like to thank the many librarians and archivists who always went the extra mile to insure my access to their holdings, despite my often very tight time constraints. The staff at the William L. Clements Library at the University of Michigan could not have been more gracious or helpful, and the Price Visiting Research Fellowship gave me the luxury of time to consult their important collections. The librarians at the Library of Congress and National Archives in Washington, DC, worked tirelessly to make the most of my week-long visit. I would especially like to thank the Boston Public Library

Special Collections librarians for allowing me to condense a month-long visit into four days. My visit to the BPL was made all the more meaningful by access to Elizabeth Cady Stanton's commonplace book. The volume traveled with Stanton to the Troy Female Seminary and later to the World's Antislavery Convention in London, and looking through her journal was the highlight of my research experience.

The professionalism and kindness of Mary Huth, longtime librarian at the University of Rochester Special Collections, welcomed me into the Rochester women's history network. The encouragement of the staff and volunteers at the Susan B. Anthony House in Rochester was also much appreciated.

The staff at Women's Rights National Historical Park in Seneca Falls, in particular, Dr. Andrea DeKoter, Jamie Wolfe, Dr. Jessica Queener, John Stoudt, Marie Queener, and the late Dave Malone, made my tenure as a park guide an enriching and enjoyable experience. The Park's cultural resources team, Dr. Anne Derousie and Dr. Vivien Rose, gave generously of their time and resources. I know Dave Malone would have loved to read this book.

The Seneca Falls Historical Society helped with this project on many occasions, and I don't believe a more beautiful reading room exists than their facility. Thanks too to the Thomas Stanton Society for their kind words about this project.

Coline Jenkins, the great-great-granddaughter of Henry and Elizabeth Stanton, was always encouraging, gracious, and helpful. Her generosity in sharing her family's photographs and stories helped to make this project come to life. I'd also like to thank Theodore Stanton of Paris, France, for connecting across the ocean when I was having a particularly bad day.

Rev. Lou Harper, former minister at the First Presbyterian Church of Griswold, shared not only the church's records and history, but his friendship and warmth were almost as inspirational as his devotion to all that is good in the world. After hearing her story, Rev. Lou arranged for an official public apology to Susanna Stanton for her unjust excommunication 185 years earlier, in the same building that it originally happened.

Bonnie Linck and the entire staff of the Connecticut State Library's History and Genealogy Unit in Hartford heroically helped me search through several boxes of material one snowy Saturday morning before the library closed.

Although I am sometimes critical of previous scholars of Stanton and the Seneca Falls Convention in this work, I want to acknowledge my tremendous respect for these authors and the body of work they produced. Many of these historians engaged with previously unexplored aspects of our history and conducted their painstaking research before the plethora of online databases and internet searches became commonplace. This work would not have been possible without their pioneering and significant efforts.

My co-workers at the Cayuga County Historian's office, Jessica Armstrong and Nancy Assmann, are two of the best historians I've ever worked with, and they make our office a fantastic place to learn about history. Cayuga County Clerk Sue Dwyer has been a model of kindness and professionalism since I first stepped into her office.

Last, but certainly not least, I am grateful for the support of my friends Erika Lopez and Lisa Burks who listened tirelessly for over a decade as this project took shape and whose love and support helped me finish. I'm so grateful to have had Erika Lopez as "my person" for more than three decades, and Lisa Burks has been with me every step of the way during the many bumps in the road. Harry Rice was always available as a treasured friend, scholar, and generally wonderful person. My mother and best friend, Pauline Frank, first taught me about civil rights and women's history when I was just a child, and she has sustained me in every way imaginable in the years since.

PREFACE

"Mr. Stanton said that he was in favor of woman suffrage;
indeed he did not know whether he would be
permitted to live in his own house unless he were." [1]

Following a speech before a constitutional convention in Lincoln, Nebraska, in the spring of 1875, Elizabeth Cady Stanton fielded a question from a man in the audience. Stanton later described the man as possessing "an unusually small head" and a "diminutive form," and when he began his question, it was obvious to her that his intention was to disrupt the otherwise serious question and answer period. The man asked whether or not Stanton agreed with him that "the best thing a woman can do is to perform well in her part in the role of wife and mother?" He continued, "My wife has presented me with eight beautiful children; is not this a better life-work than that of exercising the right of suffrage?"

Sizing up her audience's displeasure at this mocking question, Elizabeth Cady Stanton decided to respond with an answer "not soon to be forgotten." As she slowly and deliberately glanced up and down the man's body, she replied, "I have met few men, in my life, worth repeating eight times." One such man was Elizabeth's husband of 47 years, Henry Brewster Stanton. [2]

This book is more than the history of a marriage. It is the story of a small group of people who ignited a revolution for equality in the United States that still continues today. It is the story of men and women who challenged the prevailing cultural and political institutions in nineteenth century America, and lost—at least in the short term.

This revolution, ultimately transforming the rights of over half of the population of the United States with the passage of the Nineteenth Amendment, is rooted in the early years of a marriage between an up-and-coming reformer and the daughter of a wealthy lawyer. Despite the profound impact their work had on our nation going forward, their story is a story that most of us have never heard.

The marriage of the Stantons—Henry Brewster and Elizabeth Smith Cady—not only offers a window into the determination and talent of antebellum reformers, but their marriage also provides the missing piece in the historical narrative needed to fully understand the most significant way in which the abolition movement influenced the women's rights movement: the quest for voting rights.

Henry Stanton became an abolitionist in the early 1830s, and like many others, he was inspired by the religious revivals of the Second Great Awakening. Motivated by the revivals, many Americans sought to use their "free moral agency" to achieve perfection on earth, and many of them saw chattel slavery as the nation's greatest sin. The strategy of the early abolition movement was initially based on the premise that others would be brought into the movement by the use of moral-based arguments against slavery. However, within the movement's first decade, many within the antislavery ranks realized that without exercising their political power, they could never succeed.

Beginning in 1840, this relatively small group of politically minded abolitionists changed the outcome of virtually every presidential election for the next twenty years. Along the way, they formed two political parties, attempted to infiltrate another, and eventually succeeded in establishing a significant antislavery voting coalition with the founding of the Republican Party. In 1860, this new political party won the White House, and with it, a new definition of freedom in the United States.

Although this period and these reform movements have been chronicled in many previous works, no historian has examined the transformative influence that Henry Stanton exerted on his wife's reform career, nor have they explored the ways in which political abolitionism impacted the women's rights movement.

More often than not, the early histories of the women's rights movement in the United States emphasized the victimhood of female reformers and heroicized their small victories. From the Grimké sisters being publicly chided for daring to lecture before mixed audiences of men and women, to the women of the antislavery movement being denied their full right to participate alongside their male counterparts, seldom in the early historical narratives do we read of women who, despite the rigid roles imposed by society, fought against these roles, not as victims, but as agents of change. Oftentimes, more recent historians relied too heavily on the early histories without seriously considering the skill and political adroitness of their subjects.

Certainly these women faced victimization, and it was in keeping with the era in which the early histories were written that authors focused attention on the powerlessness women faced within the larger society. However, we cannot forget that many of the women agitating for women's rights and suffrage became skilled political organizers, devising strategies for success, and working within the confines of the society in which they lived. An example of such a strategy is Susan B. Anthony's arrest and subsequent trial for voting in 1872. Although Anthony was found guilty and fined for illegally voting, she skillfully brought the issue of equal protection and the meaning of citizenship to a national audience—hardly the act of a victim.

We do our foremothers a disservice by emphasizing their helplessness, rather than their long list of achievements, despite their restricted platform. We also minimize their accomplishments and efforts in social reform by explaining their reformism as originating only in repression, and not by seeing their work—like that of their male counterparts—as an outgrowth of their well-reasoned perceptions of society and the resulting desire to correct the inequalities within that society.

An Uncommon Union explores this intersection of power and victimization and argues that far from being an oppressed wife, Elizabeth Cady Stanton's marriage put her squarely within the heart of antebellum reform, and it provided her with the tools, encouragement, and connections within which to develop her own intellect and reform agenda. The marriage freed Stanton from her conservative family of origin, and it freed her mind from the dictates of her time.

This project began as a study of the egalitarian nature of reformers' marriages in the nineteenth century. Based on the scanty but always dismissive historical portraits of the Stantons' marriage in previous works, they were to be my contrasting example—the couple going against the tradition of a supportive and sympathetic union among reformers. I began by reading the surviving letters between Henry and Elizabeth, and I was shocked by what I found. An established "fact" within women's history is that Henry Stanton was an absent, disengaged, political opportunist who also oppressed his wife and was opposed to women's rights. However, the more I read their letters, the more it was clear that many other historians had not done so. Without exploring Elizabeth Stanton's relationship with her husband, writers were left with no other explanation as to why the leader of the women's suffrage movement worked for women's rights in the first place; and more often than not, they incorrectly assumed that she herself was oppressed within her intimate life, and out of that oppression, came her passion for change.

It's a tidy story—one that was so relatable that it continued for over a century without substantiation or challenge. Over time, I came to believe, at least when it came to Elizabeth Cady Stanton, that a broader pattern of over-reliance on previously published sources was responsible for the continued perpetuation of the incorrect legend. The early feminist histories were written in a different era and for a different audience, and because the authors were struggling to insert women into the history of our country, these writers often added a heroic bent to their subjects, much like the legend of George Washington chopping down the cherry tree.

For the most part, Elizabeth Cady Stanton's more modern biographers have not substantively questioned these early accounts, including Elizabeth's late life autobiographical recollections.[3] Further, in many instances, Stanton's biographers have also added their own unsubstantiated embellishments to the early narrative, thus building one false claim on another, until the entire narrative is suspect and the truth is obscured.

The reality of what happened, however, is quite different. Unlike Elizabeth Cady's family of origin, nearly every member of Henry Stanton's family was a reformer in his or her own right. The addition of the extended Stanton family into the history of women's rights offers an intriguing way in which to enlarge the somewhat mythological inspiration for the suffrage resolution introduced in Seneca Falls, and also helps to explain why Elizabeth Cady Stanton fought so hard for the suffrage resolution's inclusion and passage at the convention.

Elizabeth Cady Stanton's late life account of the origins of the Seneca Falls Convention had its roots in the shadow of the Civil War, and she constructed it in large part to secure her own place within the founding history of the movement. While the addition of female reformers in her martial family certainly does not fully explain Elizabeth Cady Stanton's development as a reformer, it does perhaps allow the consideration of something more fundamental and more important. If Elizabeth Cady Stanton was championing women's rights not as an oppressed wife, but as part of a family of reformers, while enjoying a supportive and egalitarian marriage, the foundation upon which much of women's history is based is also decidedly altered.

An Uncommon Union seeks to redefine the pivotal moments in the first decade of the Cady-Stanton marriage to better understand the many reasons, causes, and inspirations that led to Elizabeth Stanton's leadership at the Seneca Falls Convention in particular and the woman suffrage movement in general.

Elizabeth Cady was born into a wealthy and conservative family in Johnstown, New York, and surprisingly, she became one of America's most radical female leaders. By family tradition, it was understood that she would marry well and spend her days as women of her era and class were expected: in the trappings of what her future husband referred to as "fashionable follies." Yet over the objections of her father and extended family, she married a young reformer well below her social and economic status and entirely changed the trajectory of her life.

While not a traditional biography of Elizabeth Cady Stanton or her husband, this book offers an important and previously unexplored account of Elizabeth's transformation from débutante to radical reformer by bringing her husband back into her life story. By understanding Henry's background, character, and reformism—both before they met and throughout the first decade of their marriage—it becomes clear that Henry Stanton, his extended family, and the example he provided of a politically based reform agenda greatly impacted his wife's understanding of women's rights and the importance of suffrage to securing those rights. I hope to provide an original and under-appreciated context within which to understand Elizabeth Cady Stanton's development as a reformer.

The second primary focus that this book explores is the connection between political abolitionism and the antebellum women's rights movement, and more specifically, the demand for woman suffrage. While historians generally recognize the connection between American abolitionism and the women's rights movement, the traditional narrative emphasizes the role of Garrisonian moral-based persuasion as the arm of the abolition movement that served as the cornerstone of and the inspiration for the emerging women's rights movement.[4]

Although William Lloyd Garrison had long supported women's rights within antislavery organizations, and he made substantial contributions to raising awareness of gender inequality within American society, beginning in 1837, his rigid adherence to the doctrine of non-resistance which called for "no human government" changed everything. Garrison's complete rejection of political participation runs counter to the shift in emphasis within the women's rights movement—spearheaded by Elizabeth Cady Stanton—toward woman suffrage following the 1848 Seneca Falls Convention.[5]

Those abolitionists opposed to non-resistance, including Henry Stanton, began to focus on political agitation at the close of the 1830s. These political abolitionists sought to redirect the abolition movement away from morally persuasive rhetoric alone and toward a more pragmatic strategy utilizing political and legislative tactics to end slavery in America.

The political abolitionists initially attempted to work with Garrison and the existing antislavery organizations. However, Garrison's dogmatic adherence to non-resistance was completely incompatible with political participation, causing the political abolitionists to leave the early organization and to form the nation's first antislavery political party, the Liberty Party, in 1840. Although often characterized by historians as staid and anti-women's rights, Liberty Party members demonstrated a long history of advocacy toward gender and racial equality in their reform efforts before and during the period in which they were active as a political party.[6]

Henry Stanton and Elizabeth Cady married only two weeks before the formal break within the abolition movement. Between their marriage in 1840 and the Seneca Falls Convention in 1848, Henry Stanton was a leading organizer and proponent of the Liberty and Free Soil parties—both formed with the expressed purpose of utilizing the electoral system to end slavery in America.[7] The Cady-Stanton marriage thus provides a unique point of contact between the two most significant reform movements of the nineteenth century. Further, this marriage offers the opportunity to examine the influence and example provided by the political abolitionists to the women's rights movement that has not previously been considered.

In most respects, the Stantons were an uncommon couple in their own time, even among their group of radical reformers. Particularly in the later years of their marriage, they openly disagreed on political issues, reform strategies, and religion, yet unlike most marriages in the nineteenth century, from the time they first met, Elizabeth was free to express herself publicly through her reform work, speeches, and writings, without the censorship of her husband. In fact, during the 1850s and 1860s when Henry was actively pursuing a political career, Elizabeth's very public radical views hurt his chances for elected office and nearly prevented him from receiving the only political appointment of his career during the Lincoln administration.

To be clear, this work does not challenge Elizabeth Cady Stanton's significance as a reformer or the foundational importance of the Seneca Falls Convention on the movement going forward. If there is an element of myth in the narrative of Elizabeth Cady Stanton's life story or of the convention itself, it is found within her own mythologized intimate life and not within her contributions to or leadership within the movement. The inclusion of Henry and his family to Elizabeth's life story allows us to fully understand how she arrived at the podium in Seneca Falls in 1848 and to better appreciate her development as a reformer in the years to come.

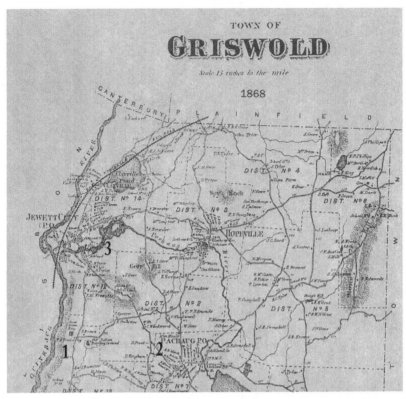

1868 Map of Griswold, Connecticut, and surrounding areas

1) Location of Simon Brewster homestead

2) Birthplace of Henry B. Stanton and the location of the First Congregational Church

3) Location of the Fanning Cotton Manufacturing Company and Scholfield Woolen Mill.

ONE

THE RIGHT TO DETERMINE
FOR HERSELF

"Learning is like gold.
Those who get it the hardest generally keep it,
while from those to whom it comes
without the asking, it is liable to slip away."[1]

Henry Brewster Stanton was born in a rambling federal-style home in the heart of the tiny hamlet of Pachaug, Connecticut, on June 27, 1805. The second child of Joseph and Susanna Stanton, Henry was the eldest son of a marriage that united two politically and religiously prominent New England families.

Henry's mother, Susanna Brewster, was born on February 18, 1781, and she was raised in the home that her father built shortly after his marriage in 1770. Susanna was a direct descendant of William Brewster, who arrived on the *Mayflower* and became the religious leader of Plymouth Colony. Henry's maternal grandfather, Simon Brewster, was a local magistrate and one of the defenders of Fort Griswold during the Revolutionary War. The vast Brewster farm was located about two miles from the center of the Pachaug, then a part of the town of Preston, Connecticut, in the southeastern part of the state. The Brewster family was well established in Preston, and Susanna's aunts, uncles, and grandparents were an important part of the family's social and political network.

On his father's side, Henry descended from Thomas Stanton who arrived in Massachusetts in 1635. After mastering several dialects of the local Native American tribes, Thomas Stanton was appointed chief interpreter and negotiator of the region. Henry's paternal grandfather,

Lodowick Stanton, also served as an officer in the Revolutionary War, and the extended Stanton clan included naval hero Oliver Hazard Perry. Lodowick was a farmer, and he raised, bred, and boarded horses at his coastal Rhode Island farm located just east of the Connecticut border. Henry's father, Joseph Stanton, was born in 1780, and as a young man of 21, he left his birthplace of Charleston, Rhode Island, to partner with an established shopkeeper, James Treat, in a mercantile enterprise in Pachaug, Connecticut. The firm of Treat & Stanton carried "a general assortment of European, East and West India goods," and the store was located in a prime downtown spot, near the town's North Society Meeting House.[2]

Joseph Stanton and Susanna Brewster married on January 25, 1803, at the First Congregational Church in Pachaug, where Susanna was a full member. Within two months of their marriage, Joseph purchased the Pachaug store, together with the surrounding land, and he dissolved the partnership with Treat to form a new enterprise with his father and father-in-law. The new firm of Joseph Stanton & Co. operated at the same location as his previous partnership and advertised the same imported goods.

In his autobiography, *Random Recollections*, Henry Stanton described his father as "an enterprising country merchant." However, life as a country merchant was not easy, enterprising or not. During the winter of 1812, an editorial appeared in a local newspaper charging that Stanton's gin was so watered down that he added soapsuds to the mixture in order to produce a head. Ever mindful of his reputation, Stanton fired back by placing an editorial in the same paper, written not under his own name, but under the name of his accuser, and fully recanting the earlier story. The forged editorial also stated that the original charges lobbed against Stanton and his gin were written solely out of "malice and envy." The real accuser, Israel Burton, didn't let the forged editorial stand, despite Joseph's creative attempt at public relations. In the following issue, Burton responded with a lengthy article claiming that the original editorial had been "ironically spoken," and that Stanton was a man "so tenacious of his own feelings" that he had proven to be "absolutely void of pity."[3] This would not be the last time that Joseph Stanton's temper and his need to retaliate against real or presumed slights overcame more practical considerations.

As a merchant specializing in imported goods, Joseph's available merchandise was constantly in flux during the foreign trade embargoes of the Jefferson and Madison administrations. However, these unpopular trade policies did not diminish Joseph's support of the Democratic Party's candidates or principles.

Despite the uncertain economic and political climate of the first decade of the nineteenth century, Joseph Stanton's enterprises prospered. While maintaining his store in Pachaug, Stanton also partnered in two other similar shops within the town of Preston. He invested in speculative land holdings, and he also owned an interest in a blacksmith shop. The revenues from his mercantile businesses allowed Stanton to continue to buy and sell land, and he was financially secure enough to carry mortgages on some of the land parcels he sold.

According to his son, Joseph Stanton was also wealthy enough to own at least one slave. Although unsubstantiated by the 1810 and 1820 census records, Henry recalled being lulled to sleep as a child by the "sweet cadence" of a family slave. The surviving 1810 and 1820 federal census records that include the Stanton family were completed on makeshift forms that were handwritten by the census taker. Perhaps because of the lack of standardized forms, the census reports do not include the columns that designated either slaves or free blacks during either of these census years.

Henry's only mention of his father's slave was tied to another iconic legend of New London County, that of the death of the Narragansett sachem, Miantonomoh. An ally of Uncas and the Mohegans during the Pequot War of 1637, seven years later, Miantonomoh and his Narragansett warriors attacked Uncas after he falsely accused Miantonomoh of an assassination attempt. The Mohegans captured Miantonomoh and surrendered him to the English authorities in Norwich. Not wanting to involve themselves in the dispute, the English magistrates returned Miantonomoh to Uncas for execution. According to Henry, a dirge was composed in the eighteenth century to the memory of Miantonomoh, and it was this lament that was sung to him so memorably by the family's female slave when he was a young boy. "It sank deep into my breast, and moulded [sic] my advancing years," Henry wrote. As an elderly man, the still powerful memory of the lilting dirge commemorating the death of Miantonomoh and sung to him by a slave was credited as the foundation upon which he built his life as a reformer. "Before I reached manhood," Henry explained, "I resolved that I would become the champion of the oppressed colored races of my county. I have kept my vow."[4]

Above: Henry Stanton's birthplace circa 1917 from: *Griswold: A History*. Below: Stanton's birthplace in 2009. The house today is at the head of a busy intersection. (*author's collection*)

Henry Stanton first experienced war as a boy. When the War of 1812 began, Connecticut stubbornly refused to send troops to the federal army. However, when the British blockaded the coastline and began firing upon New London County, the Connecticut state militia rallied to protect the shores. According to Henry, his father spent nearly six months at the front, drilling the volunteers and composing verses to motivate the troops such as, "Brave boys, don't be afraid or skittish, but go and learn to fight the British," and, "If you'll boil a lobster in a stew, he'll look as red and gay as they do."[5] Joseph served as captain in Colonel William Belcher's 8th Connecticut militia company, and after his service, Joseph was frequently referred to as "Capt. Stanton."[6] In addition to Joseph's service in the militia, the War of 1812 marked an important turning point for the Stanton family. Politically, Connecticut in general and Griswold in particular were largely Federalist districts, but Joseph Stanton was an outspoken Jeffersonian Democrat.

The serious partisan differences affected all age groups. Henry recalled being drawn into hair pulling fights in school and he was taught as a young boy to stand on a chair and recite, "the Hartford Convention was hatched in the purlieus of hell." Held in December 1814, the Hartford Convention was a meeting of New England Federalists who met to strategize against the policies of the Madison administration. Although no official minutes were published at the time of the meeting, among the topics discussed were Federalist opposition to trade policies, the war with Britain, and even the secession of New England.[7] While the adults must have enjoyed young Henry's performance, Henry's awareness of the political divides of his childhood had a lasting impact. Throughout his recollections of his childhood, Henry emphasized the patriotism of his extended family and his considerable respect for his father's stubborn adherence to principle, despite the consequences.

Joseph Stanton's political clashes were far more serious. On September 11, 1813, a newly formed militia corps, comprised of local Federalists, attempted to file the required militia enlistment papers with Joseph Stanton who was then serving as town clerk. Joseph responded "in a furious, angry and hostile manner" by donning a military coat, drawing his sword and placing it at the breast of the self-appointed Sergeant, Roger Coit, and ordering him and the others to leave the premises. According to Coit, Stanton "threatened" his life and promised to "shew him the use of said sword."[8]

Three weeks later, on October 7, 1813, Coit filed a complaint against Stanton with the Preston Justice of the Peace. Coit was seeking $1,000 in damages, and his complaint charged that Stanton was "unmindful...of his duties as a publick officer...or as a gentleman [and Stanton] did in a furious angry and hostile manner and with force and arms an assault make in and upon the Body of the Plff."

The New London County Constable was ordered to arrest "the body of Joseph Stanton," and on October 9, Stanton first heard the charges against him at the hearing following his arrest the previous day.[9] Despite the seriousness of the charges and the many witnesses to the altercation willing to testify for Coit, Stanton nevertheless refused to back down or to admit any wrongdoing. At his first court appearance, Joseph Stanton pled "not guilty." However, according to the local magistrate, Joseph "exhibited sufficient evidence of his being probably guilty"—not an enviable position for the accused. The town justice ruled that it was beyond his jurisdiction to give a definitive judgment, and he referred the case to the county courts. Stanton was ordered to post bond to a surety in the amount of $1,200 and to appear in county court in Norwich on December 6.

When the case was heard before the county court in December, the jury found Joseph Stanton guilty as charged, and Stanton was ordered to pay $87 damages to Coit along with court costs. Additionally, the judge ordered Stanton to pay a fine of $25 for "breaking the Peace." Rather than paying the fine, which represented less than one-tenth of the amount of the initial suit, Joseph Stanton continued to assert his innocence, and he filed an appeal at the county superior court.

The following month, the superior court jury also found Stanton guilty as charged, and Joseph Stanton's fine was increased to $200, plus the additional court costs, and the jury upheld the $25 fine for disturbing the peace. Stanton paid the fine on February 2, 1814. Fortunately for the family's finances, following the appeal, Joseph didn't pursue further action.

Henry Stanton's later retelling of the incident was far more heroic than the historical record indicates. To his young son, who was only eight-years-old at the time, the memory of Joseph's arrest and the subsequent trials served as an example of his father's bravery and commitment to his minority political views, and Henry used the incident in his autobiography as evidence of the bitter political divides of the times. Henry claimed that his father "[drove] out of his grounds at Pachaug, sword in hand, a whole company of Federalist militia, who had come there to insult him," without making any reference to Joseph's responsibilities as town clerk.[10] Perhaps Henry was correct in his claim that the group had used the opportunity of filing official paperwork as a means to "insult" Joseph Stanton and his politics; however, the incident also gave Henry, who would later face violent anti-abolitionist mobs, an indelible memory of his father's refusal to bow to political pressure and insults. From his father, Henry learned the importance of tenacious commitment to principle, despite the financial cost and the weight of popular opinion.

It is not known if Joseph Stanton's arrest was directly responsible for the removal of the family from Pachaug to nearby Jewett City, but within two weeks of the final verdict in the assault case, Joseph closed his store and sought payment of all open credit accounts. By the end of May 1814, Joseph announced that his new store in Jewett City was offering imported goods "on as reasonable terms at the times will permit."[11] At the annual Preston town meeting later that year, Joseph was not in attendance, and he was replaced as town clerk. Joseph Stanton never again held public office.

Joseph Stanton's legal difficulties came at a time of change in Preston and in the state of Connecticut. The area encompassing the hamlets of Pachaug and Jewett City, referred to as the North or Second Society, had first petitioned the legislature in 1787 seeking independence from the town of Preston. Part of the reason for the proposed separation was because Preston was geographically large. The size and sprawl of the town required construction of a second church to serve the congregation in the north, and town meetings were switched between northern and southern locations every year.

However, the differences between the two areas were also political. The majority of Preston's Jeffersonian Democrats resided in the southern portions of the town, while the North Society had a decided Federalist majority. Jeffersonians had pushed for the separation for several years in an attempt to forge an electoral district large enough to consolidate as a voting bloc, while the Federalists of the North Society sought the same. In the spring of 1815, 142 members of the North Society once again issued a formal petition to the Connecticut Legislature asking for separation. The petition was granted, and the town of Griswold was formed on October 26, 1815. Neither Joseph Stanton nor his father-in-law, Simon Brewster, signed the petition, and Joseph's move to Jewett City insured that his political views would continue to be unpopular with many of his neighbors and customers.

Joseph Stanton's populist political leanings were also evident in his choice of religious denomination. After moving to Jewett City in 1814, Joseph joined with other town leaders to establish a Protestant Episcopal Church in Jewett City. Stanton was elected treasurer of the new congregation, and he was responsible for purchasing the materials needed for construction of the church building and for collecting all of the subscription fees from members. Stanton also owned two shares of the new church.

The newly independent town of Griswold also held much of the burgeoning industry in the area. In 1810, Englishman John Scholfield settled near Norwich, Connecticut, and he opened the county's first woolen factory. Scholfield opened a second mill in New London County, and within a few years, Joseph Stanton became his partner.[12] By 1814, Joseph Stanton also partnered with his uncle-in-law, Charles Fanning, and two others to form the area's first cotton yarn factory. The Fanning Cotton Manufacturing Company, located near Scholfield's woolen factory, produced cotton yarn for local weavers.

Despite the upheaval of moving his store, Joseph Stanton's financial situation initially stabilized, and he continued to expand his business interests. In addition to his partnership in the two mills, by 1815, the store in Jewett City offered a "good supply of new and fashionable goods" on "liberal credit and at very reduced prices for cash." The cotton yarn produced at the Fanning mill was available at Stanton's store for local weavers, and Stanton offered both cash and goods in exchange for woven cloth.[13]

However, the family's financial success was short-lived, and by early 1816, Stanton's fortunes had changed. Placing a notice in the *Norwich Courier*, Joseph announced that he was leaving Jewett City, and that his merchandise was being sold "very cheap indeed" for cash or "other good pay." Additionally, he cautioned his debtors that they "will do well to call and settle their accounts...as they can settle them cheaper with me than with an attorney."[14] Despite his collection efforts, Stanton was unable to finance a move out of town, and by April, he relocated his family and place of business to another village house in Jewett City, where he continued to sell groceries for cash.[15]

The following year, 1817, was no better, and Joseph Stanton's finances continued in a downward spiral. Although Joseph previously carried paper on numerous parcels of land, by August 1817, he was forced to mortgage his 1/6 share of the Fanning Cotton Manufacturing Company to his brother, New York City merchant George W. Stanton, for $403. Then, just before Christmas, on December 22, 1817, twelve-year-old Henry watched as his father was arrested for the second time—this time, for insolvency.

Although from the mid-eighteenth century forward the linkage between moral character and insolvency was weakening, in 1817, the two were far from completely severed. To many, a business failure was still seen as a failure of character, morals, and work ethic. In addition, there were no federal statues concerning bankruptcy in 1817, leaving a wide disparity of punishments throughout the states. Insolvency laws continued to be administered unevenly by the states until 1898 when a federal bankruptcy statute was finally passed.

Much of the debate surrounding the proper treatment of insolvents was politicized in the nineteenth century. The issue was framed as an economic question between encouraging industrial and commercial expansion on the one hand, while still safeguarding established businesses from reckless speculation on the other.[16] This is illustrated by the wording used in Joseph Stanton's insolvency petition:

> Joseph Stanton...humbly showeth that for fourteen years he has been deeply engaged in the mercantile interest, and the manufacturing of Cotton Goods, has ever been honest and industrious, but by reason of many losses and misfortunes that he could not resist or avoid, he has become insolvent, and unable to pay and discharge his just debts.

When Joseph's insolvency petition was granted, the court noted that Stanton had proven that he "sustains a fair character for probity and industry, and is not justly chargeable with idleness or mismanagement in his affairs." The petition recorded debts amounting to nearly $3,000, many to prominent businessmen and importers in New York City. Joseph Stanton was ordered to turn over all of his remaining real property to the court-ordered commissioners, and the two remaining lots he owned were awarded to his two largest creditors.[17]

Although he lived another decade, following the insolvency proceedings, Joseph Stanton never again owned real property or held an interest in a business enterprise. Throughout his mercantile career, Joseph was frequently mentioned in newspaper advertisements and editorials in the two Norwich newspapers. However, following the final notice to creditors in the spring of 1818, Joseph Stanton disappears from newspaper, church, and municipal records.

It is difficult to know the extent of the chaos and turmoil that the rest of the Stanton family endured in the years following Joseph's insolvency. It is also likely that Joseph's financial support of his family ceased shortly after the filing of his petition for bankruptcy. Further, it is unclear exactly why Joseph Stanton's seemingly prosperous enterprises failed in 1817. However, as a merchant and land speculator, Stanton was especially vulnerable in the years leading up to the nation's first economic crisis, the Panic of 1819. Several of Joseph Stanton's partners also filed for insolvency within six months of Joseph's filing. Additionally, Scholfield's mills failed, as did the Fanning Cotton Manufacturing Company. Fanning partner Christopher Avery was also deemed insolvent in mid-1817, and he went to work as a day laborer at the Slater Mills—the only surviving mill in the once bustling Jewett City.

Perhaps revealing the personal shame still connected to bankruptcy in the 1880s, Henry Stanton omitted his father's insolvency and the ensuing instability from his autobiography. Instead, Henry chose to depict his adolescence as a time full of interesting political events such as his meeting with cousin Oliver Hazard Perry shortly before the Commodore's death in 1819 and Lafayette's tour of Griswold in 1825.

Henry Stanton's only surviving mention of his family's financial troubles came more than two decades later in a letter to his then fiancé, Elizabeth Cady. Writing that from the age of thirteen he had been "thrown entirely upon [his] own resources, especially as to money," Henry did not explain why he was forced to support himself at such an early age. Instead, Henry used the statement to illustrate the foundation upon which he developed his own sense of industriousness and self-reliance. However, in reality, the family unit was forever disrupted by Joseph's financial collapse, and the shame of his insolvency was hidden from many, if not all, members of subsequent generations.

Henry was still several months away from his thirteenth birthday at the time of his father's financial collapse. As the eldest son, but still a child himself, from that time forward, Henry not only provided for his own needs, but also those of two of his younger brothers.[18] Henry later wrote that he spent a great deal of time in his father's mills as a boy. He credited his "close acquaintance" with the machinery for helping him to understand the mechanics of the equipment that would serve him well in his later career as a patent lawyer. However, while Henry may have visited the mills with Joseph as a young child, it is more likely that his knowledge of factory operations came not from visits as the mill owner's son, but learned first-hand during an apprenticeship following his father's financial ruin.

Decades later, Henry's nephew Robert Brewster Stanton composed a lengthy family history for his children, and he was seemingly unaware of the dire financial situation the Stanton family faced during his father's childhood. Robert B. Stanton, son of Henry's brother Robert Lodowick Stanton, noted that "for some reason" his father was forced to leave school at an early age and was apprenticed to a carpet weaver in Jewett City. Robert B. Stanton could not understand why his father was "selected for work" and received such "bad treatment," while his father's brothers were allowed to remain in school. Robert explained that it was a "source of sorrow" to his father that he had been forced to work at the age of seven.[19] It is unlikely that the seven-year-old Robert was singled out and apprenticed; and, taken together with Henry's claim that he was self-supporting from age thirteen, Joseph's insolvency was more than a financial downturn and represented an important turning point in the lives of his family.

While the early pages of Henry's semi-autobiographical work, *Random Recollections*, are laden with heroic stories of his father, in his private correspondence, Henry credited "the ingenuity of a New Englander, trained up by a mother," as the foundation upon which he built his life.[20]

In contrast to her husband, the historical record contains little information about Susanna Stanton. Henry wrote that she was "intelligent, high-spirited and pious," which made her relative powerlessness in the nearly constant financial upheavals of her married life all the more difficult.[21] Susanna gave birth to at least six children: Susan in 1803, Henry in 1805, Frances in 1807, Robert in 1810, Joseph in 1812 and George in 1815, and she was a full member of the First Congregational Church. It was under her membership that all of the children were baptized.

Above: Susanna Stanton's birthplace circa 1908 from: The *Brewster Genealogy*. Below: The home in 2009. The Brewster home stayed in the family until 1996, and it is on the National Register of Historic Places. (*author's collection*)

Other than the record of her marriage and children's baptisms, Susanna Stanton's name does not appear in historical records until July 22, 1823, when she filed a petition with the county court requesting a divorce from her husband of twenty years.[22]

Susanna's complaint stated that Joseph had deserted the family on May 1, 1820, and it further charged that he provided "no support to her or her family," while displaying "a total neglect of duty." Divorce on the grounds of desertion in Connecticut required a three-year period of absence, and Susanna filed her petition only two months after this required waiting period had ended. This suggests that Susanna was aware of the prevailing statutes, and she filed her petition accordingly. Although Susanna's complaint did not specify where Joseph had fled, records from his father's real estate transactions show that Joseph was living with his father in Pittsfield, Massachusetts, by the end of 1820. Three years later, on August 4, 1823, Joseph was served with the divorce complaint in Pittsfield, and he was still there when he agreed to the dissolution of his marriage two months later.[23]

Although the date of the final decree was not recorded on the divorce complaint, minutes of the meetings of the church elders held at the First Congregational Church of Griswold provide the missing information. In November 1823, the records stated that in two consecutive meetings the church elders debated the supposed abstract question: "Can a Husband or a Wife obtain a bill of divorce for any cause but fornication or adultery, without violating the Divine Law?" At the second meeting it was unanimously decided that the church had a "duty to discipline" any members who had obtained a divorce on grounds other than fornication or adultery.

Undoubtedly the questions being debated by the church committee were prompted by an awareness of the Stantons' divorce, and initially church elders attempted to discipline Susanna by consulting with her privately. However, by March 1824, it was clear to the elders that more drastic and formal measures were required in order to "bring [their] sister to a sense of her duty."[24]

On March 3, the elders lodged a formal complaint against Susanna. In the complaint, the elders noted that they had attempted the first two steps required by church doctrine in these situations. The elders explained that they dispatched a committee member to formally notify Susanna of her fault; and secondly, the committee held another meeting with Susanna, this time sending at least two or three others to argue their points. However, despite Susanna's devotion to the church and her strong piety, the firm and persuasive arguments of committee members were received "without effect." Later that month, the rhetoric of the church elders became even stronger. The committee resolved that Susanna was required to make a "penitential confession of her fault," and they demanded that she "remove the legal obstacle she has put in the way of rendering to [Joseph] all the duties of a wife."

On April 6, 1824, the committee met again—this time with Susanna Stanton in attendance—at a meeting specifically called in order for Susanna to answer to the charges brought against her. When questioned, Susanna displayed a radical determination and resolve that would be echoed decades later in the work of her daughter-in-law, Elizabeth Cady Stanton. Susanna pointedly stated that she not only "felt justified" in seeking a divorce on grounds other than fornication and adultery, but further, it is clear from her testimony that she felt entitled and absolved of any transgression of divine law. Citing Joseph's long absence and total lack of financial support, along with other reasons "in her view" that were sufficient to justify her actions, Susanna refused to retreat from her position, despite her strong allegiance to the church and to her religious beliefs.

Susanna Stanton's claims for divorce rested on civil grounds, but then as now, these claims were not necessarily grounds sanctioned by religious orthodoxy. Marriage, viewed as a civil contract, required not only a husband's faithfulness, but also his financial support. Civilly, Joseph had ceased to be a husband by virtue of his lack of financial support of Susanna and their children, and indeed, these were the grounds under which Susanna obtained her legal divorce. Throughout her testimony before the church committees, Susanna continued to argue for the soundness of her position on civil, not religious, grounds and she continually asserted her right to do so.

Although the legal system recognized her right to dissolve her marriage based on no more than proof of Joseph's desertion, the church committee remained unmoved. However, Joseph's role in the demise of the marriage went beyond desertion and lack of support. Never relenting from her belief in the soundness of her position, Susanna revealed more intimate details of her marital life in an attempt to justify her decision to the committee. Susanna explained that Joseph "had often abused her by threats & acts of violence by which she considered, that in view of the Divine Law the bonds of marriage were sundered."

As a result of this abuse, Susanna concluded that she was "freed from any obligation to perform the duties of a wife."[25]

The committee responded to this intimate revelation by challenging Susanna to supply the appropriate ecclesial rule under which she asserted her right to divorce. In a spirited and radical reply, Susanna Stanton simply stated that she "had a right to determine for herself" when her marriage bonds had been sundered. Church records noted that while much was said to convince Susanna of the "error of her thinking," the comments were received "without any apparent effect."[26]

Over the next few weeks, the church continued to send members to talk to Susanna to bring her to an awareness of her "sense of duty." Despite the frequency and firmness of these visits, the reports consistently stated that Susanna "still adhered to [her] sentiments." Finally, an exasperated Susanna told the committee, "It would be useless for the church to deal any further with her." On April 30, 1824, Susanna Brewster Stanton was excommunicated from the church she had attended for nearly 40 years because she refused to relinquish her rights to secure a divorce from her abusive and absent husband.[27]

The divorce was an important turning point in Henry's life, and his mother's insistence on asserting her own rights, as she saw them, forever altered Henry's own views of marriage, organized religion, and fatherhood. Perhaps even more importantly, Susanna Brewster Stanton's unyielding commitment to securing and defending her own right to divorce her absent and abusive husband—rights she fought for on both civil and religious fronts—provided a living example to her own children of what would decades later become the cornerstone of her daughter-in-law's reform agenda.

Historian Nancy Cott's research into marriage and divorce found that not only were divorce rates "minuscule" during this era— comprising less than two divorces per thousand marriages as late as 1870—but far more common than a legal divorce were the so-called "self divorces."[28] In a "self-divorce," the wronged party simply went on with his or her life as though they were legally divorced. Many communities were aware that such marriages were still legally intact, but they still allowed the partners, usually only the wronged party, to remarry without a legal divorce.

Although we cannot know with certainty why Susanna took the important step of securing a legal divorce from Joseph, rather than simply continuing to lead a separate life without formally divorcing, it is nonetheless significant to understand what Susanna Stanton gained by obtaining a divorce.

Nancy Cott explains that throughout most of American history, "the common law turned the married pair legally into one person—the husband. The husband was enlarged…while the wife's giving up her own name and being called by his symbolized her relinquishing her identity."[29] In Susanna's case, being legally subsumed under Joseph, especially following his insolvency, was likely an onerous burden. As a married woman, any wages Susanna might have earned would have become the property of her husband. Likewise, any financial or propertied assistance she received from her father or other family members would have been exposed to the same situation.[30]

Legal scholar Hendrik Hartog found that divorce proceedings were often filed as a means to compel financial support from absent husbands. Oftentimes, simply filing a divorce petition would be enough of an incentive to cause the errant husband to return to the family circle, thereby avoiding the public legal proceedings. However, from the Griswold church records, it was clear that Susanna was firm in her decision, and she did not want to return to the marriage in exchange for financial support.[31]

By securing a legal divorce from Joseph, Susanna removed the net of coverture, and she became an independent agent, both personally and economically. Although she never married again, it is also possible that the freedom to do so was a motivation to secure a legal divorce. No child custody agreement was filed in the courts, but because Joseph had already left Connecticut, it would seem he wanted little to do with his children, and he was probably incapable of providing for them.

In the 21st century, it is perhaps difficult to understand the full significance of Susanna Stanton's divorce and why her choice was such a remarkable one. Not only were divorces exceedingly rare, but by bringing the matter to the courts and later defending her actions in the church, Susanna exposed her private life—a life filled with financial failure, physical and emotional abuse, and desertion—to the community of her birth in the most public way imaginable. She also publicly and steadfastly proclaimed her right to self-determination in an era when women, both married and single, had few rights under either secular or church law, leaving most women in her circumstances to live their lives in quiet desperation.

Following her excommunication, Susanna Stanton's name does not appear in the records of the First Congregational Church of Griswold. However, six months later, in November 1824, she enrolled in the Congregational Church in Riga, New York, and it's doubtful that her new congregation was aware of the proceedings in Connecticut or of Susanna's status as a divorced woman. Although it is clear from her continued desire to be an enrolled member of a congregation that her piety did not waiver following her excommunication, it is equally clear that Susanna believed that her divorce did not violate the tenets of her faith, and she refused to relinquish her right to a divorce in order to satisfy what she believed was an unjust and man-made rule.

The surviving records suggest that Susanna and her three youngest children joined her brother Henry Brewster and her eldest daughter in Riga, leaving Henry and Robert in Jewett City with their great-uncle Charles Fanning. Fanning had re-established his manufacturing enterprises by the early 1820s, and by the time Susanna left Connecticut, he once again owned several mills and businesses. It was in Fanning's mills that Henry and Robert were likely apprenticed.

In stark contrast to the harsh reality of the financial and emotional instability of his early life, Henry Stanton's retelling of his adolescence was packed full of much happier memories than the historical record supports. Carefully avoiding any direct mention or even suggestion of the family's true circumstances, Henry selected stories that highlighted his interest in politics and the larger political issues of the times. Although it is nearly certain that he worked as an apprentice during some of the years after Joseph's insolvency, Henry was also able to continue his education in the town's one-room schoolhouse.

Henry's adolescence was also filled with events that positively shaped his later life in meaningful ways. On July 4, 1824, Henry gave his first impromptu speech at his family's Independence Day celebration. In his address, he praised presidential candidate Henry Clay as the champion of "domestic manufacturers and internal improvements." Although in later years, Henry would not support either Henry Clay or publicly-funded internal improvements, his politically-minded family and the highly charged partisan debates within the community helped to foster Henry's interest in politics, public speaking, and the issues of the times. In 1825, Henry looked on as General Lafayette arrived in Jewett City and greeted his uncle Charles Fanning nearly five decades after they served together in the Revolutionary War.

Joseph Stanton's whereabouts immediately after the divorce are unknown. Joseph's brother, George Stanton, was a successful merchant in Albany, New York, and it was likely through George's influence and aid that Joseph eventually moved to New York City sometime between 1824 and 1827. There, on July 26, 1827, at the age of only 48, Joseph Stanton died. An obituary published in the *New York Evening Post* invited relatives and friends to attend his funeral; however, it is doubtful that word reached any of Joseph's six children or his ex-wife in time for them to attend the services.[32]

Although Henry Stanton was silent on his relationship with his father in the years after Joseph's bankruptcy, from Joseph's public quarrel with Israel Burton, we know that he sold homemade gin in his stores, and from his very public legal cases, it is clear that Joseph was an emotionally excitable and sometimes violent man, especially following the loss of his stores and land in 1817. Although we cannot know for certain, Joseph's increasingly senseless behavior from 1813 until he deserted his family suggests that he might have been drinking excessively. Henry Stanton's first foray into reform was in the temperance movement, and although many young men untouched by an alcoholic family member did the same, Henry's vehemence against "rum sellers," both in reform circles and later as a lawyer, suggests that his fight was perhaps more personal.

In April 1826, twenty-year-old Henry Stanton, together with his younger brother Robert, left Connecticut for the "far west" of Rochester, New York, to join their mother and siblings. The experiences of his childhood, from his father's first arrest when Henry was seven, to his parent's divorce when he was eighteen, had left an indelible impression on the young man. He witnessed violent political clashes, learned the mechanics of the mill industry, helped to support his family while still a child, and he received an education that would serve him well in the years to come. Equally important, before the age of twenty, Henry Stanton had witnessed something very few men of his time had ever seen: a woman, his mother, asserting her right to self-determination.

TWO

THE WORLD OF
FASHIONABLE FOLLIES

*"Our parents were as kind, indulgent, and
considerate as the Puritan ideas of those days
permitted, but fear rather than love,
of God and parents alike, predominated."*[1]

In stark contrast to Henry Stanton's unstable and often chaotic childhood, when she was born more than ten years later on November 12, 1815, Elizabeth Cady's father, Daniel Cady, was a Federalist member of the United States House of Representatives and a very wealthy man.[2]

Daniel Cady was born a British subject on April 29, 1773, in Canaan, New York, and he was the eldest son of Eleazar and Tryphena Beebe Cady. Daniel Cady's father was one of seven sons, and all seven of Daniel's uncles served in the Revolutionary War. In the 1760s, Eleazar and his younger brother Ebenezer married sisters Tryphena and Chloe Beebe, and the two couples settled in Columbia County, New York, just across the border from Massachusetts. Chloe Beebe Cady was perhaps the first female member of the Cady family to become involved in politics. In 1840, at the age of 91, Elizabeth Cady Stanton's great-aunt gave a speech in support of William Henry Harrison for president.[3]

Daniel Cady's third great-grandmother was a daughter of Thomas Stanton and a sister to the direct ancestor of Henry Stanton. Thus, Henry Stanton and Elizabeth Cady were equally descended from Thomas Stanton who arrived in Massachusetts in 1635.

Elizabeth's mother, Margaret Livingston Cady, was born on February 18, 1785, four years to the day after Henry Stanton's mother, to another Revolutionary War veteran, Colonel James Livingston. Margaret was the sixth of nine surviving children born to Elizabeth Simpson and James Livingston, and she was 17 years younger than her eldest sister, Elizabeth.

Margaret's parents were both born in present-day Canada. James Livingston claimed to be the first man in Canada to raise troops and take up arms for the American cause. Because his landholdings were in British territory and Livingston supported the Americans in the conflict, after the Revolutionary War, the British government confiscated all of his land. Livingston had an illustrious career during the war, including being summoned by George Washington to relay his first-hand knowledge of Benedict Arnold's treason. Due to his wartime service and the loss of his Canadian land holdings, Livingston was given land near Johnstown, New York, and it was there that he lived the remainder of his life. While in Johnstown, James Livingston was a farmer and shop owner, and he served in the New York Assembly from 1784-1791. Elizabeth's maternal family was very tight-knit, and many extended family members also lived in Johnstown.[4]

As a young man, Daniel Cady tried a number of potential careers. He farmed alongside his father, but he was eventually apprenticed to a shoemaker. After a short time in his new profession, a cobbling accident left Cady blinded in one eye and ended his career as a cobbler. After spending some time as a schoolteacher, Cady began to study law, and in 1795, at the relatively young age of 22, he was admitted to the bar. In his first recorded case, the young Daniel Cady served as co-counsel with the notorious Aaron Burr.[5]

In 1799, Cady moved about 80 miles west to Johnstown. Two years later, at the age of 28, he married sixteen-year-old Margaret Livingston on July 8, 1801. Marrying into the Livingston family altered the course of Daniel Cady's life in many ways. Although before the marriage he appeared to have a promising career as a lawyer, his financial future and opportunities as an attorney were greatly enhanced by the connections Daniel Cady made through his in-laws.

The most important of these connections came through Margaret Livingston's eldest sister, Elizabeth. In 1792, Elizabeth married Utica, New York, merchant Peter Smith. As a young man, Smith, together with partner John Jacob Astor, established an extensive fur-trading network with several Native American tribes in the Mohawk Valley, and they quickly became two of the wealthiest men in New York

State. Smith maintained a store in Utica that served as the base of the acquisition side of the operation, and the furs were then sent for sale to Astor in New York City. Early in their partnership, Smith began acquiring large tracks of land in central New York, and he eventually amassed holdings in excess of 500,000 acres.[6]

When Elizabeth Livingston Smith died in 1818, Peter Smith decided to sell his personal and business holdings to his second son, Gerrit, and his brother-in-law Daniel Cady. The contract was in the amount of $225,000, and it called for yearly payments spanning a decade. Peter Smith's holdings were valued close to $400,000, and at the time of the transaction, in October 1819, debts amounting to $75,000 were also transferred to the new partnership. The arrangement also included a requirement that Peter Smith would continue to receive the income derived from $125,000 of the assets of the estate, and it was further stipulated that one-half of the remainder of his estate was to be equally divided among his grandchildren. In addition to his new land speculation business with Gerrit Smith, Daniel Cady also continued to practice law. Because of Cady's ties to the Smith family, he eventually began specializing in land patents and mortgages.[7]

Elizabeth Cady's childhood home (left) circa 1860 (*author's collection*)

Politically, Daniel Cady was a Federalist, the party of Washington and Adams. He was elected to the New York State Assembly in 1808, and he served until 1814 when he ran for a seat in the United States House of Representatives. Cady won, but by the slim margin of less than 200 votes out of the approximately 5,000 votes cast, and he took his seat in the Fourteenth Congress in March 1815.[8] While in Congress, Cady served on several committees related to Indian affairs and land claims. He was also appointed to a committee to review a petition from an abolition society seeking stronger penalties for those who kidnapped free blacks. When his term expired in 1816, he did not run for re-election. Cady never again held legislative office, but he did run unsuccessfully for Congress in 1832.[9]

Perhaps the story most often told about Elizabeth's relationship with her father is also the most disparaging. The story first appeared in print in 1868, when Elizabeth was 53 years old, and it was quoted nearly verbatim in every lengthy biographical treatment during her lifetime and also by the majority of her modern biographers. According to Elizabeth's recollection, when her only surviving brother died in 1826, the eleven-year-old Elizabeth tried to comfort her father. She wrote that he had not really noticed she was there, and that he "mechanically" put his arm around her when she sat on his lap. According to his daughter, Daniel Cady then spoke the words that immortalized him as not only a cold, stern, and unsympathetic figure, but a statement that would also serve as the first awakening of Elizabeth's feminist consciousness: her father reportedly lamented, "My daughter, I wish you were a boy."[10]

Although he was forward-looking in his business affairs, in his personal life, Daniel Cady was a man of his time. He held a devout and unshakable religious faith, even in the hour of his greatest trials. The Cady family's faith was often tested. Margaret Cady give birth to eleven children, but only six survived to adulthood, and of these six, Eleazar was the only Cady son to live beyond the age of eight. It was on the occasion of this only surviving son's death that Elizabeth later wrote so poignantly of her father's grief.

Eleazar Livingston Cady was born May 26, 1806, and he died on August 16, 1826, a few months shy of Elizabeth's eleventh birthday, and shortly after his graduation from Union College in Schenectady, New York. At the time of his death, Margaret Cady was pregnant with her last child, a boy, born on January 28, 1827, and named after his deceased brother. The second Eleazar met the fate of so many of his siblings when he died the following year at 20 months of age.[11]

Whether or not Daniel Cady really told his young daughter that he wished she were a boy, in 1826 and arguably even in 1926, it would not have been an unusual or even an unexpected expression. As the Seneca Falls Declaration of Sentiments would later articulate, women's roles during Elizabeth's lifetime were severely limited and rigidly constrained. Taken in this light, perhaps we can consider that Daniel Cady's comment, if it was said, might reflect more than simply a one-dimensional piece of evidence indicating his apparent indifference to his female children. For example, it might perhaps show her father's acknowledgment of Elizabeth's intelligence and potential, combined with the sad realization that with all she possessed, because she was a woman, her talents would likely remain undeveloped.

Although the consensus among Stanton's biographers is that Daniel Cady held little appreciation for his daughter's budding intellect, and he so pointedly preferred sons to daughters, it seems that these same biographers were unmoved by Daniel Cady's patience with his daughter's questions about the law. Elizabeth also wrote repeatedly that her father spent hours explaining the statutes to her pertaining to women's lack of property rights. Had Cady been so unconcerned with Elizabeth's interest in male-dominated subjects and as dismissive of Elizabeth's intellect as her biographers suggest, it seems doubtful he would have, according to Elizabeth, carefully explained the functions of the law to his daughter.

Elizabeth's recollections of her childhood, like those of her future husband, were primarily written in late life and with an agenda and an editorial eye that still confounds modern historians seeking a more balanced and complete narrative. While Henry Stanton's childhood recollections served to explain his lifelong interest in politics, Elizabeth's first extended interview discussing her early life took place as the women's rights movement was splitting into rival organizations. As a result, Elizabeth's narrative emphasized her awakening to gender inequality at a young age in order to establish her credentials as a child activist. When the first biographies were written in the late 1860s, Stanton felt that her leadership of the movement she founded was under siege. In Elizabeth's later recollections of her childhood and early adulthood, nearly every major incident served to reinforce this central theme and lead her inevitably to the Seneca Falls Convention.[12]

Nonetheless, it is possible to consider Daniel Cady in a more intimate and balanced fashion from his surviving correspondence. In a letter written following the loss of the couple's third son at the age of only six months, Cady wrote of his grief to Peter Smith in 1814, the year before Elizabeth's birth:

> It is true that I have lost my youngest child. I thought too much of him…I flattered myself he was formed to contribute largely to my happiness…The death of my boy has robed [*sic*] me of one object of my affections, has dried up one source of my anticipated happiness, but to him, I doubt not, death was gain and had he lived, instead of fulfilling my expectations and contributing to my happiness, he might have covered himself with disgrace and filled me with shame.[13]

This son, named Daniel Cady in honor of his father, was the second son of the same name to die in 1814 at a young age. The first Daniel was Eleazar's twin, the son whose own death occasioned such profound grief fourteen years later.

From this same letter, another side of Daniel Cady emerges, one that is also absent from Elizabeth's later writings. Responding to Peter Smith's unhappiness with his daughter's choice of a husband, Daniel Cady responded in a way that contradicts not only his historical depiction as a tyrannical and unsympathetic ruler of his household, but also in a way that was completely different from his own reaction when faced with a similar situation in 1839:

> If a daughter disobliges an indulgent father and gets a bad husband, God knows she is sufficiently punished without one frown from her Father; but if she happens to get a husband who does every thing in his power to render her happy what then ought to be done? Shall the Father look constantly at the gloomy side of the picture and torment himself by reflecting that he had a loved daughter…Would he not more promote his own happiness by saying, I have done my duty. The happiness of my daughter was my object, and although she has cruelly disappointed me, may

God forgive her, and make that marriage a prosperous
one which promised nothing but misery. Although
my feelings and my honor may not permit me to take
her to my arms nothing shall tempt me to say one
word, or do any act which shall give her pain.[14]

Against her father's misgivings, Peter Smith's daughter Cornelia
married Walter Cochran. The marriage was seemingly a happy one,
lasting until Cornelia's untimely death at age 33 in 1825. The Cochrans
had eight children, including a future Attorney General of New York
State and a close friend of the Stantons, John Cochrane.

Like the recollections of her husband, Elizabeth's writings contain
very little information about her mother. In Elizabeth's autobiography,
the Reverend Simon Hosack receives more attention than Margaret
Cady. In at least one respect, Hosack acted as an intellectual mentor to
Elizabeth, teaching her Greek and encouraging her to study subjects
usually reserved for male students. Unlike her father, according to
Elizabeth, Hosack also claimed to prefer girls to boys.

Despite her father's seemingly stern demeanor, Daniel Cady and
the family's "servant" Peter Teabout dominate Elizabeth's retelling
of her early life. Although he played an integral role in Elizabeth's
childhood, Peter Teabout's contributions are frequently minimized
or omitted altogether by some of Stanton's biographers. Perhaps this
was because Peter's initial presence in the Cady household was as the
property of Daniel Cady.

Slavery in New York State lasted surprisingly far into the
nineteenth century. The 1799 Gradual Manumission Act stated that
children born into slavery after July 4 of that year were born "free,"
but they were forced to serve as indentured servants until the age of
25 for females and 28 for males. The act also stated that slaves born
prior to 1799 would remain slaves for life. Thus, because his 1755 birth
date was well in advance of this date, Peter Teabout's status as a slave
remained unchanged by the legislation. It was not until 1817 and the
passage of the so-called Final Abolition Act that Peter Teabout was
given his freedom. While this second act freed slaves unaffected by the
1799 manumission act, it did not take effect until July 4, 1827—ten
years after the bill's passage and not until Elizabeth was twelve. Thus,
prior to her adolescence, Elizabeth's companion and babysitter was, in
fact, the property of her father.

In addition to being a slave owner, Daniel Cady's legal practice also included slave holding clients. In 1812, Cady represented a fellow Johnstown resident, Andrew Wimple. Cady filed a lawsuit complaining that Wimple had purchased the unexpired term of a female slave who was sold as being "sound in all aspects," but who was, instead, "unsound and lame" in addition to being incontinent and possessing a bad hip. The poor woman died a month later, however, it was her new owner, Wimple, through his attorney Daniel Cady, who claimed to have been "injured" and "hath sustained damage." The ruling in the case is unknown.[15]

After he became a freedman in 1827, Peter Teabout continued to work in the Cady household, and it is likely that freedom did not significantly change the routine of his life. In 1845, long after the Cady children were adults, Teabout was listed in the New York State Census immediately following the Cady household, indicating that he continued in their employ while living nearby in a modest home valued at $100. In the 1850s, in a letter to his sons, Henry Stanton wrote of his departure for Johnstown, noting that "Black Peter" would probably be at the depot to pick him up.[16] In 1860, Teabout was still employed as a "day laborer" at the age of 85. Two years later, after a lifetime of service to the Cady family, Peter Teabout died in Johnstown.[17] These few meager facts are all that remain of Peter Teabout in the historical record, however, his influence on Elizabeth's childhood was immeasurable and far-reaching.

Nearly every moment of childhood joy that Elizabeth recalled in her autobiography was chiefly due to Peter, and in the absence of similar stories about her own parents, his role in her childhood is all the more important. From his violin accompaniment of her dancing, to his preparation of Christmas dinner, and from his storytelling to his rescue of Elizabeth and her sisters from a fast-moving stream, Peter was Elizabeth's protector, her "guardian angel," and likely the person she turned to for nurturing and affection.[18] Curiously, in her autobiography Elizabeth did not mention Peter's status as a slave, and although she spoke highly of him and frequently mentioned his contributions to her health, intellect, and happiness, following the death of her brother Eleazar, Peter disappeared from her narrative.

It is widely acknowledged by historians, based solely on Elizabeth's own recollections, that as a child, she spent a great deal of time in her father's law office, located just next door to the Cady household.

Although the details of her recollections often varied, Elizabeth expressed an early appreciation for the law and a particular interest in her father's law books. According to Elizabeth, the women who visited her father's office for legal help were often unsuccessful because of the inherent unfairness of the legal system as it applied to women. Elizabeth wrote that she decided that the best way to deal with these unfair laws was to cut them out of her father's law books. However, she confided her plan to a potential client, Flora Campbell, and Campbell alerted Daniel Cady to the upcoming assault on his law books before Elizabeth could execute her plan.[19]

In 1940, Stanton biographer Alma Lutz offered new details about Mrs. Campbell. Lutz's additions to the story included a lengthy dialogue between Campbell and Daniel Cady, and she also wrote that the Campbells lived on a farm left to Mrs. Campbell by her late father. According to Lutz, Flora Campbell's visit that day was not to tattle on Elizabeth, but to seek legal help from Elizabeth's father. Without her knowledge, Flora's husband had taken out a mortgage on the property, and the Campbell farm was about to be seized by creditors.[20] Later biographers also added to the event, one bringing an errant son into the story, while citing the same scanty information provided by the aging Elizabeth Cady Stanton.[21]

The story of "dear old Flora Campbell" illustrates the ways in which Stanton's late life autobiography—augmented by the fictional embellishments of later biographers—make it difficult to develop an accurate or meaningful portrait of Elizabeth's childhood. A thorough search of newspaper, census, genealogical and cemetery records, uncovered no record of a "Flora Campbell" at all. The 1830 census lists a "Wid[ow] Ann Campbell" immediately following the Cady family in the census report. In 1830, Ann Campbell was listed as living not with a son, but with a female between the ages of 20 and 30.[22] Further, had the Campbell farm been seized by creditors, an official notification to creditors would have appeared in the newspapers, but no such notice was published. Cemetery records show that Ann Campbell's husband, James, died at the age of 69 on April 17, 1828, when Elizabeth Cady was thirteen years old. Ann Campbell died three years later on July 28, 1831, and she was buried next to her husband.[23]

While Ann might have used the name "Flora," and given that the tale had little impact on Elizabeth's overall life story, the legend of "Flora Campbell" would seem to be of no significance. However, the story illustrates the unquestioned acceptance of the early histories by Stanton's later biographers. For her own part, Elizabeth was often wrong about her birth year and the date of her marriage, and the incidents she later shared about her personal life, especially as a child, were carefully shaped to show not only her awareness of gender inequality, but her willingness to tackle the issue, even as a child. By not interrogating these childhood stories, the bigger and more important legend—that even as a child, Elizabeth was a budding reformer—also went unchallenged.

In her autobiography, Elizabeth discussed Peter Teabout's interest in the law, and she wrote of his bringing her and her sisters to the courthouse, the jail, and the hotel where the lawyers held their conferences. However, the connection between Elizabeth's fascination with the law and Peter's visits with her to court have been largely unexplored.[24] According to Elizabeth's daughter Margaret, it was Peter who would "carefully explain the merits and demerits of the lawsuits to his young charges before entering the courthouse, then with one child on each knee and a third standing beside him, they would sit contentedly and listen."[25]

Margaret no doubt heard this story from her mother, indicating that it was Peter's influence, rather than Daniel Cady's, that first sparked Elizabeth's appreciation for the law. However, because Peter was a slave during much of her childhood, in her own writings, Stanton may have felt uncomfortable sharing this fact about her family. By replacing the importance of Peter's teachings with the legend of "Flora Campbell," Stanton offered her readers a more socially acceptable way to introduce her own awakening to gender inequality, while also providing her with an active role in the process.

As an adult, Elizabeth Cady Stanton was known as an interesting and impressive storyteller, and from an early age, she expressed an interest in debate. It seems logical then, because of his fostering her curiosity about the law and exposing Elizabeth to the art of debate, that Peter Teabout played an important and unacknowledged role in Elizabeth's intellectual development.

Equally important, Peter Teabout also served as an example of someone who was severely restricted by social, political, and cultural conditions, but still possessed an unbounded curiosity and interest in the world around him—a world in which he was also not permitted to take part. It was also with Peter that Elizabeth first experienced an event

Above: The Johnstown Courthouse from Stanton and Blatch, *Elizabeth Cady Stanton…1922* (Vol. 1 - Autobiography)

Below: The same building in 2007. Daniel Cady's portrait still hangs inside, and the Johnstown Courthouse is one of the oldest courthouse buildings still in use in the United States. (*author's collection*)

similar to what she would later encounter at the World's Antislavery Convention in London in 1840. At the Christmas morning services, Elizabeth sat with Peter near the door of the church in what was called "the negro pew."

From the time of the first published biographical sketch of Elizabeth's childhood in 1868, it is clear that she had already assembled a narrative to account for her feminism and interest in reform. The story she crafted was the sort of background story that her readers would have expected. To credit Peter or any man with the development of her keen legal mind or her awareness of oppression would have been entirely unsatisfactory to Stanton's audience. The post-Civil War period was an era of heroic autobiographies in which public figures used their early lives to show a steady progression toward the person they had become as an adult. The vast majority of these autobiographies, including that of Henry Stanton, feature a similar "awakening" as a child to explain the adult reformer.

Elizabeth described her mother as a "tall, queenly looking woman," possessing courage, self-reliance, and being at "ease under all circumstances and in all places."[26] A later biographer noted that Elizabeth was uncomfortable in her mother's presence because of Margaret Cady's air of authority and perhaps even austerity. However, from Elizabeth's late life recollections and the choice of words she used to describe her mother, it is doubtful that the young girl sought out her mother for nurturing and consolation. While Henry Stanton's written memories of his mother were also brief, it seems clear that the choice of emphasis and de-emphasis in the Stantons' autobiographical works allow us to draw different conclusions and meanings.

Henry Stanton's childhood recollections were also carefully constructed with an eye to conceal the family's dire economic conditions, his father's erratic behavior, and his parent's divorce. The public persona that Henry was reinforcing through his autobiography required that his childhood be filled with vivid political images that would explain his lifelong interest in electoral politics. Further, as a man who spent his working life in the largely male-dominated professions of law and journalism, his reading audience would have expected to learn more about his father than his mother.

However, an entirely different conclusion seems fitting in the case of Elizabeth's neglect of her mother in her autobiography. As a women's rights activist, it would seem that if there were memories of her mother pushing her toward male-dominated arenas or even a mother's sympathetic understanding of the frustrations her daughters faced within the limited cultural roles available to them as women, such memories would have dominated Elizabeth's recollections of her childhood. Importantly, other than her sister Margaret, no woman emerges in a sympathetic or encouraging role in Elizabeth's retelling of her childhood. Instead, according to her autobiography, Elizabeth's childhood was dominated by men, and importantly, men who encouraged her intellectual abilities and curiosities, men who allowed her to explore the world in which she lived, and men she sought to emulate in her adulthood.

THREE

THE INFECTED DISTRICT

*"I have seen many sharp political and social contests
in my day, but, viewed in some aspects,
I think the Anti-masonic feuds excelled them all."* [1]

W hen Henry and Robert Stanton arrived in Rochester,
New York, in April 1826, they found a city that had risen
almost overnight. In the nine-year period from 1817 to
1826, Rochester's population had grown from only 700 residents to
ten times that.[2] Although white settlement in western New York had
begun in the late eighteenth century, these early towns were clustered
primarily in the southern part of the state near the Pennsylvania border.
Between 1812 and 1830, what had been "unbroken wilderness," had
already transformed into a thriving city of 10,000.

Rochester's growth was stimulated by water power. Within the
city, the power of the Genesee River was harnessed to run flour mills,
and the Erie Canal brought the flour to markets far beyond the city
limits.[3] Demographic figures for 1830 noted that men, three-quarters
of whom were under the age of thirty, overwhelmingly populated the
new "Flour City." Although Rochester was heavily populated by young
men, the city's residents were also constantly changing. Historian Paul
Johnson's research found that 130 new arrivals reached the city on the
Genesee each day, replacing the 120 residents who left Rochester on
a daily basis.[4]

What drew Henry and Robert Stanton to Rochester was
somewhat out of the ordinary. While they fit the demographic model
of Rochester's new arrivals, they were joining family members who

were early settlers. However, while this pattern of family migration was not unique, the Brewster-Stanton clan was not part of the wealthy landowning Rochester city founders who typified this type of kinship recruitment to the region.[5]

In the Rochester area, the Stanton brothers joined their uncle Henry Brewster, their mother, Susanna, and siblings Susan, Frances, Joseph, and George. By the time Henry and Robert arrived, the rest of the family had already lived in western New York for over three years. Henry's eldest sister, Susan, married Samuel Baldwin in 1823, and the Baldwin and Brewster clans were already well established in political and church circles in the Genesee Valley. The Baldwin and Brewster families were pioneer settlers, but they were not wealthy or particularly influential beyond the confines of their small village. Thus, while many young men flocked to Rochester to work as laborers for a time before moving on, Henry and Robert joined an already established family network in Monroe County.

Within a few months of his arrival, Henry was already close to the center of Rochester politics. His first position was as a clerk in the Rochester canal office. Because the canal office was such a vital part of the city's businesses and the state's economy, Henry also met many of the reigning political leaders of the "Albany Regency" during their visits with the canal commissioner. At the same time, Henry and Robert also worked part-time for a local newspaper, the *Monroe Telegraph*, which was run by an eccentric young publisher, Thurlow Weed. By the time of his acquaintance with the Stanton brothers, Weed had already developed a local and statewide reputation for his keen political insights and his ability to sway large numbers of voters by his somewhat unorthodox personality and editorial practices.[6]

Although Weed was chronically broke and disheveled, he managed to purchase the *Telegraph* from Rochester pioneer settler, Everard Peck in 1825, only a year after he was hired as the paper's editor. Shortly thereafter, Weed partnered with Robert Martin, and they expanded the paper to a semi-weekly by October 1826.[7]

Weed's timing could not have been better. A month earlier, in nearby Canandaigua, New York, itinerant stone worker William Morgan disappeared under suspicious circumstances following his release from the Ontario County jail. The so-called "Morgan Affair" forever changed the face of New York politics and helped propel Thurlow Weed to national prominence.

William Morgan was a member of a Masonic lodge in LeRoy, New York. According to Weed, Morgan fell out with the lodge in LeRoy, prompting a move to nearby Batavia. When the Batavia lodge refused to enroll Morgan, he retaliated by writing a book that revealed the secret rituals of the organization. Through an agent, Morgan approached Weed to publish his book, but Weed declined because his new partner, Robert Martin, was a Mason. Morgan eventually found a Batavia publisher willing to take on the project, and according to Weed, the book was printed in strict secrecy in the dead of night and on Sundays due to its inflammatory content.

Shortly after the exposé was published, word spread that Morgan had made good on his threat to reveal the secret Masonic rituals. Morgan was soon arrested on a likely fabricated charge of theft for allegedly stealing a shirt and tie that he borrowed months earlier, but never returned. After his arrest, Morgan was brought to the Ontario County jail in Canandaigua. Bail was quickly posted, and Morgan was spirited away in a carriage by unknown assailants screaming "Murder" as the carriage drove away. William Morgan was never seen publicly again, dead or alive.

The following month, New York Governor DeWitt Clinton, also a member of the Masons, called for the cooperation of the citizens in apprehending those responsible for Morgan's abduction. By November, four Masons were indicted by a grand jury for the crime of kidnapping—a misdemeanor at the time—and all four received light sentences. Although dozens of other defendants were eventually tried over the course of the next five years, the most important legacy of William Morgan's disappearance was the changes it brought about in New York politics.

While trials and grand juries continued to convene, in March 1827, Canandaigua attorney and legislator Francis Granger proposed a bill in the legislature to double the reward initially offered for the safe return of Morgan or the discovery of his body and the arrest of those responsible. Granger also called for a special committee to investigate the entire Morgan affair.

Politically, Granger represented the John Quincy Adams-Henry Clay wing of the New York State political coalition known as the "Bucktails." His measures were soundly defeated in the Assembly, controlled at that time by the Martin Van Buren wing of the Bucktails known as the Albany Regency. Already sensing the discontent of the supporters of the Granger resolutions, Governor Clinton signed into law two bills that he hoped would silence the growing suspicions and anger aroused by the light sentences given to those convicted in the Morgan affair. One of the bills proposed by Governor Clinton raised the crime of kidnapping to a felony, thereby increasing the penalty of those convicted from to three to fourteen years at hard labor. Clinton also removed the ability of local sheriffs to call grand juries. Clinton hoped that by stiffening the penalties for kidnapping and removing judicial power from local authorities, he could quell the growing cries of corruption and cover-up. However, Clinton's measures accomplished neither.

Thurlow Weed later praised Clinton for his honest handling of the Morgan case. Weed claimed that Clinton obtained a copy of Morgan's manuscript in early September 1826 while chairing a statewide Masonic meeting held in New York City. Understanding the magnitude of Morgan's betrayal, Clinton assigned the manuscript to a special committee for their recommendation. The committee summoned the man who had brought the manuscript to the meeting for further information and clarification. The messenger was none other than Thurlow Weed's partner at the *Telegraph*, Robert Martin. Martin told the committee that the manuscript had been obtained by unscrupulous means. After hearing Martin's report, Clinton ordered the book to be returned from whence it came, and the special committee issued a statement saying that they hoped no further "mischief" would ensue. Weed maintained that Clinton handled the situation in an ethical way. Despite his extraordinary knowledge of the Morgan case, Clinton did not betray the Masonic brotherhood, but as an honest public servant, he also attempted to follow the law in prosecuting those involved in the kidnapping. Clinton died suddenly on February 11, 1828, just as the Anti-Masonic political agitation was in its infancy.[8] He had not been able to calm the growing hysteria in western New York.

Throughout the state, non-Masons began to view the entire "Morgan Affair" as a miscarriage of justice and as evidence that the highly placed fraternal members within Masonry had not only kidnapped and murdered Morgan, but they also purposefully obstructed justice and mishandled the investigation. Masonry was thus seen as incompatible with the very foundations of American citizenship, and non-Masons, especially in the western part of New

York State, passionately believed that the presumed cover-up exposed by the Morgan case had proven that Masonry was a very real threat to the young nation. They further charged that the Masons thought themselves above the law, and that because so many fraternal members were placed in such powerful positions within the state and federal governments, Masonry itself was a threat to the function, stability, and future of the republic.

In his autobiography, Henry Stanton wrote that he witnessed three bitter political eras in his life. The first was the Jeffersonian Democrats versus the Federalists which resulted in his father's altercation with Roger Coit and Joseph's first arrest, and the second was the anti-Masonic excitement. Stanton wrote that he was "a witness to the whole of it," adding that "the Anti-masonic feuds excelled them all."[9]

As a part-time writer for Thurlow Weed's *Telegraph*, Henry Stanton could not have been any closer to the epicenter of the beginnings of the political movement against Masonry. Throughout 1827, outrage in Rochester continued to grow as trial after trial resulted in either the acquittal of the accused or the light sentencing of those convicted in the Morgan conspiracy. However, despite the excitement of the controversy, Henry Stanton's initial foray into politics was not prompted by the anti-Masonic tensions, but by his longtime support of Henry Clay and the administration of John Quincy Adams.

In the mid-1820s, predating the Morgan affair, political power in New York State was bitterly divided into two distinct factions: the Clintonians, followers of then Governor DeWitt Clinton, and Clinton's political enemies, the Albany Regency, headed by Martin Van Buren, supporter of Andrew Jackson. This rather clean distinction in alliances belies the complex splintering within each of these two groups. Within each coalition, a block of voters called themselves "Bucktails," but the Bucktails within each political group supported entirely different candidates and programs. Many Adams-Clay supporters in New York wanted to form a new Republican coalition in the presidential contest, but some former Jeffersonian Bucktails supported Jackson and the Democratic ticket making the idea of unifying the Bucktail groups impossible.

Similar disarray existed within the other, non-Bucktail, portions of the Clintonians and the Albany Regency. Thus, during the last half of the 1820s, within both of the major New York State factions, there were supporters of Adams-Clay and Jackson within each faction.

Complicating an already thorny political landscape, by 1827 DeWitt Clinton changed alliances from the Adams-Clay wing to Martin Van Buren, and thereby Andrew Jackson, creating not only political chaos, but also causing a vacuum in party politics that did not escape the keen eye of Thurlow Weed.

Clinton's defection to Van Buren and Jackson left followers of John Quincy Adams' National Republican Party in New York without a state leader. The timing could not have been worse for the National Republicans. In 1827, the legacy of the charges of the "corrupt bargain" that gave Adams the presidency in 1824 were still powerfully felt throughout New York, serving to further bolster the influence of the Albany Regency under Van Buren.

The presidential contest of 1824 was especially bitter. John Quincy Adams, son of the second president, enjoyed broad support in New England. Much of Adams' support came from bankers, merchants and manufacturers. His opponent, Andrew Jackson, was the popular hero of the Battle of New Orleans at the end of the War of 1812, and his candidacy typified the rise of the "self-made man." Also running in the 1824 contest were Treasury Secretary William H. Crawford of Georgia, and Congressman Henry Clay of Kentucky.

With four candidates in contention, no one candidate was able to secure enough electoral votes to win the presidency. Coming in fourth, Henry Clay was eliminated when the election fell to House of Representatives. Believing that Adams was the most qualified for the presidency, Clay used his considerable influence in Congress to help Adams win the election. When Adams appointed Clay as secretary of state—considered a springboard to the presidency—Jackson's supporters labeled the Adams-Clay maneuvering as a "corrupt bargain." The election and its aftermath were so contentious that it laid the groundwork for the next generation of American political parties. Jackson's supporters coalesced under the banner of the Democratic Party, while a few years later, the Adams-Clay supporters formed the base of the Whig Party.

News of the political chaos and the brewing storm against Masonry quickly reached the national political organizations. In an attempt to clear his name from the controversy, John Quincy Adams wrote to New York political leaders reminding them that he had never been a Mason, and also to point out that his opponent, Andrew Jackson, was a prominent member of the brotherhood. However, as anti-Masonic sentiment began to rise in the western part of New York, already being called "the infected district," the party leaders of the Adams-National Republican organization saw the potential of joining forces with the budding groups against Masonry.

As early as February 1827, only six months after Morgan's kidnapping, meetings were held in several towns in western New York to discuss the handling of Morgan's abduction. Resolutions were passed at these meetings to withhold votes from anyone in the Masonic fraternity. However, coordinated political agitation outside of localized pockets caused by Morgan's kidnapping did not happen immediately. It took eighteen months of Morgan-related trials before groups opposed to Masonry began to organize into a political entity, with Thurlow Weed steering the group by the head.

Whether because of Weed's influence or at his suggestion, the young men of Rochester, "friendly to the National Administration," began to organize well in advance of the presidential election of 1828. At the end of January 1828, the group first met to reaffirm their support of John Quincy Adams and Henry Clay. Meeting minutes noted that their confidence remained "undiminished" by the "unfounded and disproved charges of corruption and corrupt coalition."[10] Henry Stanton attended this meeting, and he was appointed to the standing committee along with a young Rochester merchant, George A. Avery.

By the time the group met again on February 9, the resolutions that were passed were far more anti-Jackson than they were pro-Adams. This change reflected the growing distrust of Masons and their presumed corruption. Charging that Jackson exhibited "a habitual disregard of the constitution and laws of his country," and further that he possessed "a rashness and violence of temper," the group concluded that if Jackson were elected, the event would be "fraught with evil consequences" and "dangerous to the future liberties of the American people." This time, Henry sat on the central committee with the renegade son of Rochester founder, Nathaniel T. Rochester.[11] Thus, during the eighteen months between Morgan's abduction and early 1828, the anti-Jackson and the anti-Mason supporters had coalesced into a coordinated anti-Mason effort.

Henry Stanton's first presidential campaign as an adult, the bitterly contested Adams-Jackson election of 1828, gave him the opportunity to further his already wide network of political acquaintances. In the spring, he gave speeches for Adams in Rochester, and he also served on the standing committee for the Monroe County Republican Party.[12] Perhaps more importantly, Henry attended the statewide convention of Republican "young men" held in Utica on August 15, 1828, where he met the meeting's chairman, a young lawyer from Cayuga County, New York, William Seward. Although they would disagree many times throughout their long careers, the two men were personally warm friends, and their friendship dated from this meeting.

Following the overwhelming defeat of Adams in the November 1828 election, Henry turned his attention elsewhere. In January 1829, he became deputy clerk of Monroe County, and because the clerk lived several miles outside of Rochester, many of the office's daily responsibilities fell to Henry. As Deputy Clerk, Henry officiated in a wide variety of legal situations. From attesting to signatures on Revolutionary War pension requests to recording land deeds, Henry met many influential people in Monroe County, and he also represented the county in many legal contests. It was this function of the position that most intrigued Stanton, and he later wrote that during the three years he held this position, he was, in fact, studying law.

In October 1829, a full ten years before he met Elizabeth Cady, Henry Stanton expanded his attention from partisan politics to include reform when he co-founded the Young Men's Temperance Society of Rochester. The young men's group was formed a year after Rochester's Society for the Promotion of Temperance, and the groups' aims were similar. Despite the bitter political divides of the time, the young men's group included members from both political parties.

Perhaps the most important part of Henry's involvement with the early temperance movement were the strategies he learned as a young reformer. Rochester's temperance societies were affiliated with the Rev. Lyman Beecher's temperance group, and Beecher advocated a strategy of moral suasion to gain converts to the temperance crusade. This tactic would later be employed by antislavery agitators, and it relied on moral-based reasoning to convince imbibers to stop drinking. Temperance groups in this era focused their efforts on the individual, rather than trying to lobby for coercive laws against alcohol. Rochester's civic leaders also believed that the weight and example provided by their involvement in the temperance crusade would serve to further the group's aims. Henry Stanton's position of responsibility in the organization suggests that in only three years, he had distinguished himself enough within the Rochester elite to hold such a position.[13]

Historian Paul Johnson argues that the 1828-1829 Rochester temperance movement was organized not only against the growing problem of high alcohol consumption, but also because city elites hoped to drive a wedge between wage laborers and business owners who often shared a dram of whiskey together at the end of the workday. Also during this time, Rochester was maturing as a city, and as the city elites crusaded against drink by encouraging businessmen and shop owners to prohibit drinking on the job, residential neighborhoods throughout Rochester became increasingly segregated by class and occupation.[14]

By 1830, what began as an isolated crusade against Masons running for local office had matured into a well-organized political movement. Because of Henry's close relationship with Anti-Masonic leader Thurlow Weed, and his involvement with the city's temperance reformers, Stanton was well informed about the aims of this new political organization. In May, Henry served as secretary of the Anti-Masonic Young Men of the Village of Rochester with the sons of many of Rochester's pioneer families. Later that summer, Stanton's leadership within the "young men" was well established, and he chaired many committees at both the local and state levels. In mid-September, Henry and his new friend George Avery attended the Young Men's Anti-Masonic State Convention in Utica as delegates from Monroe County.

THE REVIVAL WINTER

Despite his increasing involvement in reform and politics, any interest Henry might have had in the political arena took a backseat for nearly two decades after he heard the Rev. Charles Grandison Finney preach in Rochester in October 1830. Although Henry was baptized in the Congregational faith as a child in Connecticut, there is no record of his membership as an adult in any denomination until January 1831—or as historian Paul Johnson termed it, "the revival winter."[15]

At the time Stanton first met Finney, he was still serving as deputy clerk of Monroe County, and he seemed well positioned for a future political career. In addition, his first Rochester employer, Thurlow Weed, was then serving in the New York State Assembly. Weed's personal fortunes had also changed considerably since the

Morgan abduction. Weed sold his shares of the *Monroe Telegraph*, and by late 1830, he was the publisher of the *Albany Evening Journal*. In addition to the powerful platform of the paper, the *Journal* was also the official state printer, ensuring that Weed's offices were busy and profitable. If Henry had wanted to pursue a political career, it was easily within his reach.

Stanton recalled Finney as being "tall and grave" with "sparkling" blue eyes and at "the fullness of his powers" during the revival winter. However, Finney's impact on Henry's future was greater than the message he preached. Rather than employing the traditional preaching style of the time, Finney's sermons were "like a lawyer arguing a case before a court and jury."[16] According to Stanton's recollections, Finney's liberal use of legal principles to explain Biblical tenets appealed first to the "judges, the lawyers, the physicians, the bankers, and the merchants" until "nearly everybody" had joined the movement.[17] Within a few months of Finney's arrival in Rochester, the entire Stanton family joined Rochester's First Presbyterian Church.

Finney's message reached Stanton at a level that no other clergyman's sermons had done before. Although the dates and circumstances are unclear, during the spring of 1831, Henry Stanton began "supplying deficiencies in an imperfect education" by enrolling at a new manual labor institute in Monroe County. From Stanton's writings, it appears that he continued his education while still serving as deputy clerk. However, while providing a liberal arts education, the manual labor movement was designed to train young men for the ministry, suggesting that Stanton's career had already taken a decided turn by the spring of 1831.

The manual labor seminaries allowed men of all economic backgrounds to formally train for the clergy, and by requiring labor from all students regardless of their wealth, it democratized the seminaries and fostered friendship and an egalitarian atmosphere at the institutions. As payment for tuition, room, and board, students worked at the institutions, primarily in agriculture, but also in small-scale industrial shops run by the institutions while completing their studies.

It was also during the revival winter that Henry first met Theodore Weld, and the two quickly became close friends. Only two years older than Henry, by the time they met, Weld was already well respected within reform circles in the Northeast. In 1831, the wealthy evangelical

Tappan brothers from New York City hired Weld to act as an agent to promote manual labor institutions. Weld was also very close to the Rev. Charles Finney, and he was active in the temperance movement. On December 31, 1830, Weld delivered a four-hour temperance lecture in Rochester, and because of the Stanton family's previous involvement in Rochester's temperance movement and Henry's own role in organizing the local society, it seems likely that Henry Stanton and his family were in attendance. The timing of Weld's temperance lecture coincided with Henry's decision to enroll at the new Rochester Manual Labor Institute, suggesting that the shift that had begun during Finney's revivals culminated under Weld's influence and prompted the abrupt change in Henry Stanton's life direction.

On January 25, 1831, Henry's younger sister, Frances Mehitabel Stanton, married Henry's friend and co-anti-Masonic agitator, George Anson Avery, at the First Presbyterian Church of Rochester. In addition to his reform work, Avery was a successful dry goods merchant in Rochester, and until fire destroyed his holdings, he was also the owner of a gristmill on Rochester's river run. Like the Stantons, Avery was also born in Connecticut, but he arrived in the Rochester area before 1818. He was a new member of the First Presbyterian Church, and like his new brother-in-law, Avery was also a political reformer prior to his conversion by Finney. The Stanton and Avery families, who were previously united in reform efforts and religious conversion, were now also formally united by marriage.

"MR. BLANK" AND MISS ANTHONY

As a teenager and young adult, Elizabeth Cady's life was uneventful compared to that of her future husband. Unlike Susanna Stanton's children, the wealth of the Cady family meant that Elizabeth's childhood was free from most traditional domestic duties, and the Cady children didn't have to worry about the family's economic future.

Elizabeth attended the local school, the Johnstown Academy, until she was 14, and she graduated in 1830. According to her autobiography, the young girl excelled in subjects such as Greek and mathematics— subjects usually reserved for boys. Elizabeth remembered spending the next six months riding horses, learning to play chess, and "continually squabbling with [her father's] law students over the rights of women."[18]

Six months after her graduation, on January 2, 1831, Elizabeth enrolled in the Troy Female Seminary, located about 50 miles from her home in Johnstown. The seminary's founder, Emma Hart Willard, was a pioneer in female education. A native of Connecticut, she began teaching when she was just a teenager. After her marriage, Willard appealed to the New York Legislature for funds to open a female seminary, and although a bill to fund her school for women passed in the senate, it failed in the assembly. Willard's efforts were supported by Governor DeWitt Clinton, and at the urging of prominent citizens in the village of Waterford, Willard received enough funds to establish a school there in 1819.

Two years later, her school was once again without funds. Willard relocated the school to Troy, after the city fathers pledged sufficient support to keep the school afloat. Troy taxpayers supplied $4,000 in cash, and a separate subscription effort raised enough money to construct the school building.[19]

The Troy Female Seminary was the nation's first academic high school for young women, and the curriculum was not altogether different from that of similar institutions for young men. In her first term at the school, Elizabeth studied algebra, Greek, and music, but during her time in Troy, her educational subjects broadened to include, criticism, arithmetic, chemistry, and French.[20] According to Elizabeth's recollections decades later, she did not enjoy being in an all female school. Not only did she miss the boys of her youth, but Elizabeth also believed that an all girls environment created an unnatural relationship between the sexes, and she disliked the petty fighting among some of her classmates.[21]

Either before leaving Johnstown or shortly after her arrival in Troy, Elizabeth received a commonplace book. A centuries-old tradition, and what we would today refer to as a journal, commonplace books in Elizabeth's era were filled with a mixture of meaningful quotations and poetry, and they often served double-duty as an autograph book. Like her contemporaries, Elizabeth's commonplace book contains a mixture of copied verses from classic authors and remembrance notes from her schoolmates and other young women she met before her marriage in 1840.[22]

One of the first dated entries in Elizabeth's journal was a cautionary note from the drawing teacher at the seminary, Thirza Lee. "True religion is the deep basis of excellence," Lee wrote, "sound morality its lofty superstructure." "I fear that you, my E, are sailing the superstructure without having laid the true foundation," Lee continued. The entry was dated March 1831, only two months after Elizabeth's arrival. Fourteen years Elizabeth's senior, Lee graduated from the seminary shortly before Elizabeth's arrival, and she remained in Troy as a teacher for a decade before returning to her native Connecticut to open her own female seminary.[23]

Like many others at the Troy seminary, Lee was also a member of Dr. Beman's Presbyterian Church. According to historian Kathi Kern, Beman invited Charles Finney to Troy in 1826 in order to help Beman "breathe life into the lackluster Presbyterians in Troy."[24] In her autobiography, Elizabeth recounted quite a lengthy and emotional account of Finney's preaching during her stay in Troy. His message reached her so deeply, that she recalled that the "fear of the judgment seized my soul." Her mental images of the "burning depths of the liquid fires below" and the "shouts of the devils echoing through the vaulted arches" became so disturbing, that Elizabeth claimed to have taken a six-week leave of absence from school in order to recover her mental and emotional peace during a vacation to Niagara Falls.[25]

Although Elizabeth's account makes a compelling story, unfortunately, as Kathi Kern's painstaking research shows, Finney did not conduct any services or revivals during Elizabeth's stay in Troy. In fact, much of the first year that Elizabeth was in Troy, Finney was in Rochester evangelizing her future husband. Further, if Elizabeth was as tormented by fears of perdition as she claimed, one would imagine that her commonplace book would be filled with spiritual wisdom or verses containing themes of repentance. However, other than the admonishment by Thirza Lee, the book is filled with only lighthearted poems and secular verses.

Elizabeth's description of Finney in her autobiography is similar in tone to Henry's depiction of the orator. However, rather than leading Henry to despair or irrational fears, Finney's preaching led him to Christian perfectionism. Although Elizabeth's story was invented, the more subtle message she was conveying to readers in her 1898 autobiography was far more important to Stanton. By then an agnostic, Elizabeth wanted to show her readers the psychological harm and pain that this sort of preaching had on young, impressionable minds.[26]

Previous biographers did not question the timing of Elizabeth's alleged recuperative trip to Niagara Falls. Because Stanton was vague about the timing, it was assumed by historians that the Finney revivals were held in the spring of 1831, and the trip to Niagara took place that June. However, Stanton's commonplace book and the seminary records show that this was not the case. Two of her friends wrote verses in her book that were dated in June, and another in mid-July, meaning that Stanton was in residence at Troy during June and July 1831. Elizabeth's tuition bill for 1832 indicates that she took not a six, but a two-week break in July 1832. Although it's possible that Elizabeth visited Niagara Falls during this period or at another time, the circumstances of this visit were not as she stated. As Kern explains, during the era in which Stanton was writing her autobiography, the majesty of nature at Niagara Falls was a favorite destination used by agnostics to depict their belief in the "religion of nature." By tying her cautionary account of the harm inflicted on children by emotive preaching together with her own tale of redemption through nature and rational thought, Stanton used the story as a fitting allegory of her own path to agnosticism.[27]

After graduating from the Troy Seminary in 1832, Elizabeth returned to Johnstown. By this time, her two eldest sisters were married, and although Elizabeth was of marriageable age, no evidence survives that she was eager to do so. Decades later, Margaret Stanton Lawrence wrote about one potential suitor that her mother met during this time. This unidentified young man, a student at Union College, was spending the Christmas holiday with the Cady family. "Mr. Blank," as Margaret called him, was "quite smitten" with Elizabeth, and he was fond of teasing her about her love of conversation. Calling her a "chatterbox," the young man made a playful bet that Elizabeth couldn't keep silent for ten minutes. Elizabeth agreed to the challenge, and the young man suggested they take a sleigh ride in the moonlight to test Elizabeth's resolve.

Peter Teabout readied the sleigh, and Elizabeth and the other women left the room to help her get ready. The young man was soon called, and he took the reins of the sleigh after being seated beside his companion. Throughout the ride, Mr. Blank tried to engage Elizabeth in conversation, asking her questions about what she thought of the moonlight and the brisk weather, but she did not answer. Eventually growing tired of the silent ride, the young man agreed to cancel the bet so that they could enjoy the remainder of the ride. When Elizabeth still refused to answer, in frustration, Mr. Blank headed back to the

Cady home. According to Margaret, Elizabeth "kept all her lovers at arm's length," so the young man dared not touch her hand or arm while trying to get her to speak.

When the sleigh reached the Cady's front porch, the entire family was there to greet Mr. Blank and his companion—including Elizabeth. Mr. Blank could not believe his eyes when he saw Elizabeth on the porch, and when he realized that the girls dressed up a feather dress form in Elizabeth's clothes to fool him, Mr. Blank was "so disgusted that he never fully forgave" Elizabeth. News of the practical joke spread throughout the area, and the story followed poor Mr. Blank back to Union College.[28]

By 1834, the Cady family unit was forever changed when the Cady's eldest daughter, Tryphena, and her husband, Edward Bayard, left Johnstown to move to a sleepy village in central New York. Edward Bayard set up a law practice in his new home of Seneca Falls, and Elizabeth visited her sister there often. The Bayard home, near the corner of East Bayard and White Street, was located very close to the home Elizabeth would own the following decade. Elizabeth's sister Harriet and her husband, Daniel Cady Eaton, had also left the family home in Johnstown, relocating to New York City, and leaving Elizabeth as the eldest daughter in-residence. Although Elizabeth's correspondence during this time did not survive, according to her later accounts, she spent her time visiting her sisters, her friends, and her cousin Gerrit Smith in Peterboro.

Another important meeting took place in 1834, although neither history nor the women in question took notice. On January 17, 1834, Elizabeth met a young woman named Susan Anthony from the tiny hamlet of Battenville, New York.[29]

The circumstances of their meeting are not known, however, the two young women's fathers were likely the connection. Susan's father, Daniel Anthony, was a successful merchant and mill owner at the time, and Cady, an important and widely-respected lawyer. Both men were involved in the temperance movement, and it's possible that the two met through their fathers' shared reform work. Neither woman publicly recalled meeting the other until more than seventeen years later. However, while Stanton wrote that she "liked her thoroughly" when she met Anthony again in 1851, then too Elizabeth's "mind was full" from the lecture she had just attended, and she neglected to invite Susan back to her home when they met for the second time. It is certainly possible that Stanton and Anthony later privately recalled their initial meeting in 1834. However, to have admitted publicly when their first biographies were written in the late 1860s that they had met nearly two decades before, but had not formed a lasting friendship, would have seriously undermined the unity of thought and purpose that the two women were eager to present as the women's rights movement was breaking in two.

When they met in 1834, Susan was a serious girl of fourteen, and she copied a poem into Elizabeth's commonplace book entitled, "Home." Written by English poet Jane Elizabeth Roscoe in the 1820s, "Home" was reprinted without attribution to Roscoe in the March 3, 1832 issue of the Universalist newspaper, the *Christian Messenger*. Roscoe's poem originally appeared in a British poetry collection in 1828; however, the version as printed in the *Christian Messenger* contained an added verse that was included in the transcription Anthony wrote in Stanton's commonplace book.

Susan's father was a Quaker by birth, but when he married her mother out of the faith, he was asked to apologize for his choice. By the early 1830s, Daniel Anthony's membership in the local Society of Friends meeting hinged on his important place in the Battenville community, rather than his strict adherence to the rules of the faith. His father-in-law was a Universalist, and over time, Daniel Anthony's progressive views of spirituality increasingly caused conflict with Quaker doctrines, moving Anthony toward the more welcoming Universalist faith.[30]

During the 1830s and 1840s, there were no other Anthony families living in Battenville, and Battenville is such a small hamlet, that even to the present-day, no census data is available for the hamlet alone. Battenville is located within the town of Greenwich (2010 population, under 5,000), and in 1834, there was only one other Anthony family living in Greenwich. The other Anthony family had no female children, and the only female member of this family was Almyra Anthony.

Susan signed the poem she copied into Elizabeth's commonplace book, "Susan Anthony," and while many elements of her 1834 handwriting are identical to those of her surviving 1837 diary, the missing middle initial in her signature is also consistent with the 1834 period. According to Anthony biographer Ida Husted Harper, Anthony did not begin using the "B" in her name until she was "older."[31]

Although Stanton and Anthony have been written about extensively, this significant page in Stanton's commonplace book has gone unnoticed. While no further documentation of their 1834 meeting exists, there is no other reasonable explanation for this entry in Stanton's commonplace book, other than that the two women first met in 1834. However, because they did not find enough in common to maintain an ongoing friendship, and further that they each found the other so unremarkable that they didn't remember their first meeting when they met again in 1851, would indicate that the relationship of their later lives had its foundation in the cause they were championing and not in their individual personalities. Thus, what became a transformative friendship for Stanton and Anthony individually and for the nation as a whole, began, at least publicly, as an unexceptional event.

FOUR

"FANATICS AND LUNATICS"

*"Young gentlemen, don't stand before a
looking-glass and make gestures. Pump yourselves
brimful of your subject till you can't hold another drop,
and then knock out the bung and let nature caper."*[1]

Among his tasks for the Tappan brothers, Theodore Weld was
charged with finding a location to build a national manual labor
institute. The new seminary was to serve as a model institution
for other seminaries and to help to fill the growing need for trained
"millennial ministers." Although for a time Rochester was considered
as a potential site, in 1831, Weld turned his attention further west to
the Ohio Valley. J. L. Tracy, a friend of Weld and a teacher in Kentucky,
suggested the area because of his belief that Cincinnati was "to be
the great battlefield between the powers of light and darkness."[2] The
language used by Tracy to describe Cincinnati as being ideally situated
"within sight of the enemies camp," suggests a double meaning. Tracy
saw the Ohio Valley not only as fertile ground for Christian coverts to
Finneyism, but Cincinnati's location in the free state of Ohio was also
"within sight" of the neighboring slave state of Kentucky.

British reformer Charles Stuart began urging Weld to adopt
the antislavery cause as early as March 1831—only two months after
William Lloyd Garrison began publishing the *Liberator* in Boston.
Stuart's conversion to abolition began when he studied the treatment
of slaves in the British colonies, and he wrote to Weld that he found
"such burning cause for gratitude to God" for not "breaking up the
world beneath our feet" for the "amount of their misery and of our
guilt." Along with the letter to Weld, Stuart included several antislavery

pamphlets written by British authors, and he urged his close friend to work for an end to slavery.[3]

A year later, in September 1832, Weld wrote to Stuart that while his "heart aches with hope deffered [*sic*] for the slave," he, like much of the larger reform community, believed that the American Colonization Society offered the best hope of ending slavery. "Light breaks *in from no other quarter*," Weld explained to Stuart.[4] Although Henry Stanton was deeply engaged in both political and social reform prior to 1832, no evidence suggests that his interests extended to either colonization or the budding antislavery movement in the United States.

Henry's newfound devout religious faith and commitment to Finney's doctrines were solidified into a radical new future when, in the spring of 1832, Henry went forward with his decision to become a Presbyterian minister. Resigning his position as deputy clerk, Henry left his interest in the law and politics behind to pursue his new vocation. Together with two of his younger brothers, Robert and George, Henry enrolled at the new Lane Theological Seminary in Cincinnati, Ohio.[5] Although Henry decided to leave the Rochester Manual Labor Institute before selecting another seminary, his decision to enroll at Lane was likely because of Weld's influence.

The Stanton brothers could not afford the fare for the journey to Ohio, so Henry, Robert, and George traveled to Cincinnati in an unusual way. In order to pay their passage, Henry helped to load a raft full of lumber, and then he helped to steer the raft down the twisting Allegheny River from Olean, New York, to Pittsburgh, Pennsylvania. From there, the Stantons traveled by steamboat to Cincinnati. Accompanying the Stanton brothers on the raft to Pittsburgh was Theodore Weld.

The new Lane Seminary got off to a somewhat rocky financial start. To combat the institution's tight budget, the board poured the institution's small resources into securing the renowned and controversial minister Lyman Beecher to serve as the first president. The board hoped that by having Beecher at the helm of the institution, both financial donations and an increased student body would follow. Lane was a clerical institution, and like the Rochester institute that Stanton attended the year before, the seminary was founded on the manual labor model.

Although Lane is most associated with antislavery reform, seminary students also participated in temperance societies, arranged prayer meetings, and helped to establish Sunday schools throughout the Cincinnati area. The majority of those attending the Lane Sunday schools were from "the most destitute neighborhoods," and the total enrollment in these Sunday schools reached close to 1,200 by 1834.[6]

Students wishing to study at Lane were required to demonstrate "a good acquaintance with the common branches of an English education," and they were also required to possess "testimonials of a good moral character and industrious habits."[7] Like the other manual labor institutes, students were required to perform agricultural work to offset their tuition and support. Lane students were also employed at the seminary's print shop, and because both Robert and Henry had experience from the *Monroe Telegraph*, it is likely that they performed a portion of their required three hours of daily labor in the print shop.

The Stantons' arrival in Cincinnati predated that of the seminary's new president, Lyman Beecher, and throughout their first year in attendance, the school's financial future seemed uncertain. In addition, ongoing fighting between Cincinnati's Old and New School Presbytery left the administration and the board of directors in nearly constant conflict.

In the summer of 1832 and within a few months of Henry's arrival at Lane, the debate club's topic for the evening caught his attention: "If the slaves of the South were to rise in insurrection, would it be the duty of the North to aid in putting it down?" The topic was suggested because of the violent rebellion of Virginia slave Nat Turner the year before. When Henry arrived for the evening's debate, he was surprised to see that he was the only student seated in the section reserved for those responding to the debate question in the negative. It was on this occasion that Henry Stanton delivered his first antislavery address, and in his words, the evening marked "the beginning of [his] life-work, and lent color to [his] whole future existence."[8]

A few months later, the cholera epidemic that had ravaged through western New York, reached Cincinnati. However, because of Lane's isolated location in the Walnut Hills area outside of town, the disease didn't spread to the seminary for nearly ten months. Cincinnati's first recorded death was on September 20, and before it was over, nearly thirteen months later, the disease claimed over 800 lives in Cincinnati alone. An additional 5,000 residents left the city in fear.[9]

The month before the 1832 term began, the first Lane student was diagnosed with "premonitory symptoms," prompting the student-led board of health to engage a physician and to distribute disinfectant. However, on July 19, the first Lane student succumbed to the illness, and before it was over, close to thirty students exhibited symptoms and four would died of the disease. Among the dead, Henry's younger brother George, who died on July 23 after less than a day's illness. Once George's symptoms appeared, the attending physician held out little hope that he would recover, calling George's case the most "desperate" he had ever seen.

Theodore Weld attended George Stanton throughout his illness, and he stayed with George until his death. Despite the fact that George had previously attended several revivals and was being trained for the ministry as a student at Lane Seminary, throughout his final hours, George questioned his faith. On his deathbed, Weld tried repeatedly to convince George to once again accept his faith, but to no avail. In a desperate attempt, Henry "threw himself in tears upon his neck, and, with a bursting heart, cried, "Oh George! dear George, won't you listen to your brother?" George asked Henry to leave him alone, to which Henry asked, "What shall I tell your poor mother," but he received the same response.[10]

The cholera epidemic at Lane lasted only a couple of weeks, but as one student wrote shortly after it was over, "they [the students] were so surrounded by such a power of steadfast christian [*sic*] self-possession, as [to have] effectually repressed the contagion of panic fear." As young ministers in training, their strong faith helped the students and the institution to survive the ordeal, and the cholera epidemic left in its wake a more united student body, "more mature, able, self-reliant, and evangelical," in its aftermath.[11] The unity of the student body and their evangelical commitments would soon be further tested.

Henry Stanton enrolled at Lane Seminary a year before Theodore Weld and nearly two years before a large influx of Finney-converted students arrived from central New York's Oneida Institute. Although Weld was initially offered a professorship at Lane, he declined the position and enrolled as a student in June 1833. Despite Henry's intellectual opposition to slavery as he so forcefully stated in his maiden antislavery speech the previous summer, Weld contended that at the time he enrolled at Lane "there was not a single immediate abolitionist in this seminary."[12] This was soon to change.

Charles Finney's style of ministering has frequently been compared to a legal argument, and his message was delivered in such a way as to appeal to both the intellectual reasoning and the moral convictions of those in attendance. However, there was another element to Finney's doctrine that resonated with young men living in the shadows of the Revolutionary Era's ideas surrounding virtue. For Finney, sins were caused by "self-gratification," and he taught that "those who actually prefer his own selfish interest to the glory of God" were "impenitent" sinners.[13] Thus, the secular view of "virtue" as being self-subordination for the greater good of all citizens, also became a way to enter the kingdom of heaven by putting aside one's own work for the work of God. Finney's teaching that man was "a free moral agent," together with the doctrine of doing God's work before self-gratification, supplied the young ministers-in-training at Lane with a powerful reason to remake the troubled world around them.

Throughout 1833, the Lane student body increasingly began to see that the institution of slavery prevented those held in bondage from making this voluntary change for themselves, and also that slavery prevented the slaves from fulfilling their individual responsibility to God.[14] As Theodore Weld explained, "God has committed to every moral agent the privilege, the right and the responsibility of personal ownership. This is God's plan...therefore, I am deliberately, earnestly, solemnly, with my whole heart and soul and mind and strength for the immediate, universal and total abolition of slavery."[15]

Against the wishes of the seminary's administration, on February 5, 1834, the Lane students announced that they would hold a series of debates on the subject of slavery. The meetings were scheduled over the course of eighteen evenings, and each meeting would last two and a half hours. Despite the fact that by early 1834 there were only a handful of abolitionists at the seminary, it was decided that the students would confine their debate to two questions: first, "Ought the people of the Slave holding States to abolish slavery immediately," and second, "Are the doctrines, tendencies, and measures of the American Colonization Society, and the influence of its principal supporters, such as render it worthy of the patronage of the Christian public?"[16] To the student body, it was through "investigation and discussion" that their duty should be determined, and thus it was vital to their mission as Finneyites and Christians to discuss the issue of slavery, despite the warnings by the administration that the topic was too controversial.[17]

The American Colonization Society was founded in 1816, and it attracted a wide variety of supporters. The goals of the society were unified around the idea that African Americans and whites could never live peacefully side-by-side in the United States. Some approached the issue from a purely racist position, believing that the country should be a Caucasian nation. However, the majority of members, despite their intrinsic racist leanings, feared that the legacy of slavery would continue long after the institution ended. Most colonizationists believed that it was better to send both the former slaves and the free black population living in the United States to the organization's settlement in Africa. The colonizationists established the African nation of Liberia, and over time, close to 15,000 African Americans were re-settled in Liberia.

Before the announcement of the Lane debates was posted, Henry Stanton was already a committed abolitionist. Although it is unclear precisely when he converted to the cause, by January 24, 1834, Stanton was already subscribing to the abolition newspaper, the *Emancipator*, and he had paid his yearly dues to the American Antislavery Society. Henry's nephew later referred to his uncle during this time as "a radical of the radicals." Henry's brother Robert was decidedly less radical, and Robert later helped to organize the Lane Colonization Society.[18] The timing of Henry Stanton's adoption of the abolition cause suggests that he was working closely with Weld, and that he played an important role in the decision of the student body to hold the debates. On the eve of the debates, Weld was offered an agency position with the national abolition organization, the American Antislavery Society, but he declined, believing that he could do more for the cause by staying at Lane.[19]

According to Henry Stanton, when the debates began, Lane's student body included eleven men born in slave states, seven of whom were the children of slave owners, one former slave owner, and one black student, James Bradley, who was a former slave.[20]

The debates that the students were organizing were not debates in the sense we would think of them today. The students were not attempting to convert their classmates to one side or the other, and they were not relying on moral-based arguments alone in their conversations. Instead, they collected colonizationist literature and carefully compared the claims of colonizationists to the experiences of the students who had grown up in slave states. The students were concerning themselves only with what they called, "facts, facts, facts." After nine evenings of conversation, the students voted unanimously in favor of immediate abolition. After the second session of meetings, that spanned another nine evenings, nearly the entire student body denounced colonization as being un-Christian.

Although he was already firmly behind the abolitionist cause, the Lane debates had a profound impact on Henry Stanton. He was selected to write the official account of the debates for the antislavery newspapers, and he noted in his article that the experience of the Lane debates had convinced him that "prejudice is vincible, that colonization is vulnerable, and that immediate emancipation is not only right, and practicable, but is expedient."[21]

Henry's idealistic interpretation of the ease with which the former slave holding students were converted to immediate abolition, also convinced him of the value of moral suasion, and he felt certain that Southerners could be "trained and educated" and "reached and influenced by facts and arguments, as easily as any other class of our citizens." Stanton concluded his lengthy article stating quite simply, "this evening we formed an Anti-Slavery Society."[22]

The objectives of the Lane Seminary Antislavery Society reflected the influence of the students' first hand accounts of slavery, combined with an understanding of the prejudices they witnessed against the free black population of Cincinnati. Further, their goals illustrated a radical stance on the social and political equality of the races that was not only radical in 1834, but arguably a century later:

> Immediate emancipation of the whole colored race, within the United States; the emancipation of the slave from the oppression of the master, the emancipation of the free colored man from the oppression of public sentiment, and the elevation of both to an intellectual, moral, and political equality with the whites.

The formation of the antislavery society was only the beginning of the students' reform efforts. The students increased their benevolent work in Cincinnati, and one student, Augustus Wattles, opened a school at a black church in the city. Because so many students enrolled, Wattles was forced to stagger his teaching schedule to accommodate everyone. Within a few months, Wattles received funding from New York philanthropist Arthur Tappan to employ several women to help teach, and by the summer of 1834, Wattles was running four schools with a combined enrollment of two hundred students.[23]

Throughout that spring, Henry Stanton wrote lengthy articles for antislavery newspapers, describing the activities of the Lane students, their collective experiences with slavery, and their denunciation of colonization. Because of his leadership within the Lane antislavery movement and his background in reform organizations in Rochester, Henry and fellow student James A. Thome were invited to attend the first anniversary meeting of the American Antislavery Society (AAS), held in New York City, in May 1834.

Although this was Henry's first such meeting, he was an active participant, and his speech in support of a resolution he proposed dominated the press coverage of the meeting. Stanton's resolution reiterated the commitment of the Lane Seminary Antislavery Society, and he called upon the national organization to remember its fundamental principle that "prejudice is vincible." "Mr. Chairman," Stanton asked, "is not the power of this city [New York City] decidedly in favor of colonization? And is there not likewise in this same city a cruel public sentiment against the colored people? Can you separate the one from the other?"[24] At the age of 31, Henry Stanton demonstrated a keen awareness of the deep roots of racial inequality within the United States, placing him squarely at the forefront of the abolition movement.

Stanton and Thome were also delegates at the formal business meeting of the AAS held on May 6, and this meeting was attended by nearly all of the leaders of the American antislavery movement including William Lloyd Garrison, Arthur and Lewis Tappan, Robert Purvis, Elizur Wright, Jr., William Goodell, Samuel J. May, Charles Stuart, and the Rev. Joshua Leavitt. Stanton was appointed to a committee, along with Garrison, Purvis, and others, to suggest appointments for AAS officers to serve the following year. In addition, Stanton served on a committee of four to compose a set of questions for a former emigrant to Liberia who had decided to return to the United States.

Henry Stanton and Theodore Weld were also among the members appointed as managers of the AAS for the upcoming year.[25] Thus, although a young man in age and relatively new to the cause, Henry Stanton's talents as an organizer, writer, and orator were quickly recognized by the cadre of the early leaders of the abolition movement.

It was also on this trip to New York City that Henry met many of the reformers that he and his future wife would work with in the decades to come. Stopping in Philadelphia for the night on his return to Cincinnati, Henry and James Thome were guests of black abolitionist James Forten. While staying at the Forten home, Henry spent an evening with Quaker reformers James and Lucretia Mott and abolitionists William Lloyd Garrison and the Rev. Amos A. Phelps. Mott noted in a letter written shortly after meeting Stanton that she was "highly interested in [his] relation of circumstances," adding, "the cause is certainly making rapid progress."[26]

When Henry Stanton returned to Lane, he did so as a radical abolitionist, unafraid of the potential costs of his stance on black equality and willing to face public scorn and even arrest to eradicate slavery and remove racial prejudice. According to a recollection of fellow Lane student Huntington Lyman, Stanton and Weld used Lyman's horse to bring escaped slaves from bondage in Kentucky to the free soil of Cincinnati. Lyman noted, "My horse was hard used."[27]

After returning to Lane in early July, Weld sent Henry to Lexington, Kentucky, to collect an original anti-colonization manuscript recently written by James G. Birney and to update Birney on the state of abolition. Birney, a respected Southern gentleman and former slave owner, was a particularly important convert to the antislavery cause. Birney first became acquainted with Theodore Weld when Weld toured the South before enrolling at Lane. Within a short time after meeting Weld, Birney emancipated his slaves and moved to Kentucky. It was hoped that Birney's influence might induce other wealthy slave owners in the region to follow suit.[28]

Weld wrote to Birney in advance of Henry's visit, introducing Henry as one "[possessing] most fully my confidence in every respect…no man among us has pondered the whole subject of slavery and Colonization more wisely, thoroughly, prayerfully or with deeper sympathy or operated with more energy, prudence and success."[29] Following Henry's return with Birney's manuscript, Lane students used the seminary's printing press to publish over 8,000 copies of James G. Birney's critique of colonization.

The publication of Birney's *Letter on Colonization* and the other visible antislavery activities carried out by the students at Lane quickly provoked a scathing editorial by writer James Hall in a local newspaper, the *Western Monthly Magazine*. The article questioned whether or not the students' attentions should be more on their studies and less on issues "calculated to disturb its harmony." The article further claimed that slavery was too complex of an issue "to be made the theme of sophomoric declamation by young gentlemen at school, dreaming themselves into full-grown patriots."[30] However, the Lane students were far from sophomoric daydreamers; a fact they would soon prove.

Theodore Weld responded to Hall's editorial by asking questions of his own in an article he wrote for the competing *Cincinnati Journal*. Weld's article rhetorically asked, "Should not theological students investigate and discuss the sin of slavery?...Is it not the business of theological seminaries to educate the heart as well as the head?"

The citizens of Cincinnati who had not been previously alarmed by the very public activities of the seminary students, suddenly began to complain to the Lane trustees following the publication of the two editorials.[31] The community's concern was directed against the students' treatment of Cincinnati's black population as equals. It was this "commixture of blacks and whites," they insisted, that caused "a repellency of feeling in truly Christian minds." By the end of June, Lane's board of trustees began receiving formal requests that the students' activities needed to be curtailed.[32]

What was at issue throughout the Lane debates and in the months that followed, was that the students' interpretation of scripture and their belief that education would eradicate racial prejudice, led them to hold a view of racial equality that was light-years ahead of the rest of the community. As they carried their missionary zeal from the Walnut Hills into Cincinnati's black neighborhoods, their efforts took on a purpose far beyond Biblical instruction. The students' abolition efforts expanded to become more directed toward ending poverty and illiteracy, while also raising the social status of Cincinnati's black population. What began with the establishment of Sunday schools quickly became increasingly familiar association with blacks, many of whom were likely freedom-seeking slaves. As the faculty report of 1834 noted, "the doctrine of social intercourse according to character, irrespective of color, was strenuously advocated" by the students.[33]

Lane's trustees did not initially respond to the students' open fraternization with Cincinnati's black population, and they did so only after many local citizens became increasingly uncomfortable with the students' behavior. Lane students were seen escorting black women in town, openly staying with black families in Cincinnati, and they even went so far as to bring a black woman to church and seat her next to one of the city's "prominent white ladies."[34]

Despite his best efforts, Lyman Beecher was unable to convince the student body to be more discreet in their associations. He was not initially opposed to abolition or to the students' work as teachers in black neighborhoods. However, Beecher's advice did not convince the radical students to stop their work. A small group of more moderate students heeded Beecher's warning and on July 7, just as the term was ending for the year, they formed a colonization society at Lane.[35]

Throughout the summer of 1834, many students, including Henry Stanton, stayed in residence at Lane. In early September, word leaked to the board of trustees that Weld intended to print another abolitionist missive from James G. Birney. This time, the trustees acted swiftly and decisively by announcing that the seminary would close for the rest of the summer term on September 13.

Further board meetings took still more extreme action in an attempt to halt the behavior of the new radical abolitionist student population. The trustees also amended the Lane constitution to require students to have permission in order to debate, permission to organize clubs or societies, and they announced the suspension of the Lane Antislavery Society.[36]

Believing that Weld was the mastermind behind the controversial behavior, the administration hoped to force him to leave the seminary. However, in a letter to Birney, Weld also shared the information that a friend on the board had informed him that Henry Stanton and James Thome would also be expelled.[37] Weld wryly remarked, "we shall not die of broken hearts if that takes place." In a letter written before the board's decision, Henry wrote that if the antislavery society was forcibly disbanded, the students would "take a dismission from the Seminary…and spread the whole matter before the public, & I trust tell a story that will make some ears tingle."[38]

The fall term began a month after the new restrictions on the students' activities were in place. Nearly 50 returning students and close to 20 new students were in attendance when the term began on October 15. A student delegation asked for a full explanation of the new rules and then asked if the students could discuss the changes among themselves. When the faculty refused, the students once again requested permission to speak to each other, but the faculty remained unyielding. Finally, a student suggested that all of the students should decide individually and collectively whether or not they wanted to remain at the seminary. By the time the meeting was over, nearly half of the new students refused to enter at all, and 39 of the 46 continuing students requested dismissions.[39]

After their exodus from Lane, many of the students returned to their homes, while still others such as Henry Stanton became even more devoted to the abolitionist cause. Stanton's importance and leadership in the Lane rebellion was recognized in the official statement of the group. The printed record of his speech would be the first of many published speeches in his long career as an orator.[40]

The rebellion was successful in that only a handful of the students returned to the seminary at the beginning of the next semester. One of the group was Henry's younger brother Robert. Robert Stanton, who was four years younger than Henry, took a different and more conservative path than his brother. While Henry and the other "rebels" were organizing their antislavery activities, Robert was helping to organize the reviled colonization society at Lane, and he was one of only six of the original students to return to Lane following the rebellion. After completing his education, Robert was ordained as a Presbyterian minister, and he spent many years living in the South. Before the Civil War, Robert and his family moved to Ohio, and Robert was an acquaintance of Abraham Lincoln during the war years.[41]

The Stanton brothers, Henry, Robert, and George, entered Lane together. However, only three years later when Henry left Lane, he left alone. George's death and Robert's defection to colonization had forever changed the family dynamic. Although Henry was still deeply involved in the antislavery cause, when he left Lane Seminary in the fall of 1834, he still planned to continue his training for the ministry. Like many of his fellow students, the time they spent at Lane had forged an unbreakable link between the ministry and their antislavery work, and for them, the abolition of slavery was a thoroughly moral question. The "rebels" believed that Lane president and headmaster, Lyman Beecher, had thoroughly failed in his evangelistic duties by refusing to support the students' antislavery work. For the students, antislavery was seen as the "natural result" their revival ministry training.[42]

Together with eleven of his former classmates, Henry next moved to the nearby village of Cumminsville, Ohio, where the former Lane rebels formed a new seminary. They set up the seminary in a building donated by a local businessman, James C. Ludlow, and Arthur Tappan provided financial backing.[43] While the students hoped to continue in their preparation for the ministry, only two teachers were available.

Some of the Cumminsville students were advanced enough in their studies to begin teaching to supplement the small available faculty, and by mid-December, Henry was drafted as a teacher. Henry also taught Sunday school classes, and he regularly lectured at local churches, including two black congregations.[44] Henry's organizational involvement in antislavery, however, soon called him east. The following year, he became the secretary of the American Antislavery Society, sitting on the executive board and actively recruiting the so-called "seventy" antislavery agents together with Theodore Weld, John Greenleaf Whittier, and Elizur Wright.

FIVE

IN-LAWS AND OUTLIERS

*"The ultimate measure of a man is not where
he stands in moments of comfort and convenience,
but where he stands at times of challenge and controversy."*
Dr. Martin Luther King, Jr., 1963

When he left Rochester in the spring of 1832 to pursue a career in the ministry, Henry Stanton left behind not only his political aspirations, but also his mother, sisters Susan Baldwin and Frances Avery, brothers-in-law Samuel Baldwin and George Avery, and his uncle Henry Brewster. When Susanna Stanton moved west to New York in 1824, she initially settled just outside of Rochester with her brother Henry Brewster in the small town of Riga. She also joined her eldest daughter, Susan, who left Connecticut the year before her mother to marry. Susan's husband, Samuel Cutler Baldwin, was the son of one of Riga's founders and a close friend of her uncle. Like the rest of her family, Susan Stanton Baldwin also married into a family of active reformers.[1]

Henry Stanton's other brother-in-law, George Avery, was also an early political, social, and religious reformer. Arriving in Rochester from Connecticut in 1818 at the age of 15, Avery was one of the first Sunday school teachers at Rochester's First Presbyterian Church.[2] During the next decade, Avery began studying medicine, and he spent four years in Virginia training under a surgeon. Years later, when he was an abolitionist, Avery wrote about the horrific practices of southern slave holders that he observed during his years of medical training. He recalled that it was commonplace for a slave owner to turn over their sick slaves to a physician who was responsible for medical treatment and the slaves' board and care. If the patient recovered, the physician would be paid handsomely; if not, no compensation was given. Avery also witnessed cases of medical experimentation performed by physicians on sick slaves if the doctor possessed any "interest, caprice, or professional curiosity." These crimes were not punished or questioned, according to Avery.

Avery not only saw the mistreatment of the sick, but also the overall violence of the southern society. "I knew a young man who had been out hunting," Avery wrote, "and returning with some of his friends, seeing a negro man in the road, at a little distance, deliberately drew up his rifle, and shot him dead. This was done without the slightest provocation or a word passing," he continued. The assassin was put through what Avery referred to as "a form of a trial," but although the man never seriously mounted a defense of his wanton act of murder, he was nonetheless acquitted.[3]

Avery didn't explain why he abandoned his medical training, but he left Virginia and returned to Rochester. By 1828, George Avery was working for the re-election of John Quincy Adams. While serving on the standing committee of the Monroe County "Democratick [sic] Republicans," Avery first met Henry Stanton who was also on the committee.[4] The two continued to work together throughout the 1828 campaign, and they were both delegates two years later at the Young Men's Anti-Masonic State Convention held in Utica, New York.[5]

During the revival winter of 1830-31, George Avery was baptized at the First Presbyterian Church of Rochester the same month he married Henry Stanton's sister Frances.[6] The Stanton and Avery families had much in common. In addition to Henry and George's political and reform work, two of Avery's brothers also enrolled at Lane with the Stantons. George stayed behind in Rochester to run his grocery store and mill businesses. Although he was a successful merchant by trade, throughout his lifetime, Avery did not hide his reform activities from the public eye for the sake of his businesses.

By 1833, because of the reform impulse awakened during the Finney revivals of the revival winter, Henry's mother, Susanna, became active in the primary women's benevolent organization in Rochester, the Rochester Female Charitable Society. Susanna also became a board member during her first year in the association.

The Female Charitable Society was founded in 1822 at the home of newspaper publisher Everard Peck, and when Susanna joined the organization, the group was raising money to fund a school for Rochester's poor and orphaned children. That same year, Henry's sister Frances Avery served on the group's school committee—a post she would hold until 1845.[7] Despite Susanna's modest financial circumstances, she also supported the "Valley of the Mississippi Fund" with a $3 donation in 1830. The fund was established in May 1830 by Arthur Tappan to build Sunday schools throughout Ohio, Michigan, Louisiana, and Mississippi. Susanna's continued support of religious programs and missionary efforts illustrates her continuing commitment to religion and the important role it played in her life.

In the months immediately following Henry Stanton's attendance at the meeting of the American Antislavery Society in May 1834, his exact whereabouts are unknown. According to Theodore Weld, Stanton and James Thome returned to the seminary on July 7, indicating that Henry spent two months elsewhere.[8] Although the historical record is silent, the sudden involvement of Henry's Rochester family in antislavery efforts provides a clue as to his whereabouts. While the Stanton family were already members and organizers of benevolent groups, beginning in July 1834, Henry's Rochester family all converted to the abolitionist cause, suggesting that Henry stopped in Rochester and abolitionized his family before returning to Lane.

On July 4, 1834, a convention was held in the Rochester Methodist Episcopal Church to organize a county antislavery society. The male-only meeting began with the holiday's customary reading of the Declaration of Independence, followed by a reading of the Declaration of Sentiments of the American Antislavery Society. A resolution calling slavery "a national sin" was then debated, and the motion calling for the immediate abolition of slavery was passed unanimously. George Avery was appointed a vice president of the society representing Rochester's Third Ward.[9]

Although Susanna Stanton was already active in charitable reform, at the age of 53, Susanna also became an abolitionist. Immediate abolitionists were still a very small minority of the population; nevertheless, by the summer of 1834, Susanna took the same radical position on the slavery issue as her son Henry and in direct opposition to her younger son's involvement with colonization. In August of that year, Susanna made a donation to the American Antislavery Society (AAS) in her own name, as did her daughter Frances and son-in-law, George Avery.[10] By that time, and likely because of his friendship with

Henry, Susanna was already well acquainted with Theodore Weld, and Weld gave Susanna a copy of a letter he had written earlier that year to British reformer W. W. Bird.[11]

Susanna's commitment to the abolitionist cause did not end with her donation to the AAS. The following year, she joined other leading female reformers in the city to form the Ladies Antislavery Society of Rochester.[12] The new society was an auxiliary to the national society, and their constitution stated that the group's fundamental principle was that "slave-holding is a sin, and that immediate emancipation without the condition of expatriation is the duty of the master and the right of the slave."[13] At the inaugural meeting, Susanna Stanton was selected as one of three "Directresses" and she served with other local reformers including Susan (Mrs. Samuel D.) Porter.[14]

In early 1836, George and Frances Avery and Susanna Stanton left the First Presbyterian Church to form a new congregation, the Bethel Free Church, with 36 other like-minded reformers including abolitionists Samuel and Susan Porter.[15] Due to what they called "the present circumstances of Rochester," the founders believed a breakaway church was "a necessity." However, it was the group's strong ties to antislavery and temperance reform that was at the heart of the split from the mainstream First Presbyterian Church. The group declared their new congregation would be "Open for discussion on all subjects of morals, etc., such as Temperance, Slavery, etc."[16]

Seventeen of the original 39 members of the Bethel Free Church were women, and many were married to male members of the new congregation. In 1842, the name of the church was changed to the Washington Street Church, and a year later, the congregation withdrew from the Presbytery in order to become an entirely independent congregation. This change was short-lived, as the congregation renewed ties with the Presbyterians a year later. This pattern of congregations breaking from Presbyterian, Methodist, and Baptist mainstream churches persisted throughout the 1840s as the antislavery issue continued to divide churchgoers in the state.

The Bethel Free Church was also organized on missionary principles, and the congregation initially focused their attention on those closest to their meeting place. Following the Sunday prayer meeting, church members walked to the nearby Erie Canal to distribute Bibles, religious tracts, and other reform literature to the transient boatmen manning the canal barges. The Bethel Free Church also offered a Sabbath school, and George Avery was both a teacher and the assistant superintendent from the school's opening through 1845. The Bethel Free Sabbath School offered pupils more than just instruction on the scriptures. Former Liberty Party presidential nominee, James G. Birney, was a guest speaker in 1841, and the following year, Charles Finney spent nearly two months at the church. The Bethel Free Church was an early example of a reform-minded congregation. In addition to Birney and Finney, abolitionist minister Charles M. Torrey was also a visiting lecturer.[17]

Possibly as early as 1831, Susanna Stanton lived with her daughter Frances and son-in-law George Avery in Rochester's Third Ward. Because the United States Federal Census does not include the names of all household members until 1850—at which time Susanna lived with the Avery family—it is not known where Susanna resided for many of the years between 1830 and 1850. Because of her involvement in Rochester reform societies until 1838, her residence in the area is established. However, she is not listed in the 1840 census as a head of household, and she does not appear to be living with the Averys that census year.

In May 1836, Susanna requested a dismission from the First Presbyterian Church in Rochester "to any Cong. Church in Connecticut." However, her request to leave the First Presbyterian Church happened at the same time the Averys left to form the Bethel Free Church, so perhaps Susanna didn't leave the area immediately. Susanna also paid her yearly dues and participated in the Female Charitable Society through 1837, and she was living with the Averys when African American newspaper editor Charles Bennett Ray visited Rochester in November 1838. If she did return to Connecticut, it seems likely that she did so to care for her aging father, Simon Brewster, who died on August 16, 1841, at the age of 91. Susanna first reappears as a head of household in the Rochester City Directory in 1845, from records collected in 1844, and she maintained a separate household until 1848, when she moved back in with the Averys.

In many respects, George Avery's antislavery activities mirrored those of his brother-in-law Henry Stanton. Avery was also converted by Finney, became an evangelical abolitionist, and although Avery pursued moral reform to end slavery at the onset and continued to advocate the strategy in his work in the Bethel Free Church, by 1839, Avery, like his brother-in-law, enlarged his reform tactics to include political abolition. By July 1839, Avery was one of a handful of signers calling for the establishment of a dedicated antislavery political party.

The Avery-Stanton household continued to work for the antislavery cause throughout the remainder of the 1830s. After helping to form the Monroe County Antislavery Society, George Avery continued to serve as the group's secretary, and he attended the May 1836 annual meeting of the American Antislavery Society where he was selected as a vice president of the proceedings.[18] Avery also traveled to Utica in October 1835, to lend his efforts to the formation of the New York State Antislavery Society.[19] However, in addition to the family's participation in organizational abolition efforts, Avery's store at 12 Buffalo Street (now Main Street), also provided shelter for freedom-seeking slaves as part of Rochester's Underground Railroad.[20]

In 1838, Charles Barrett Ray, co-owner and editor of the *Colored American*, stopped in Rochester for five days on his way to New York City. A free black man, Ray's visit to Rochester likely came after a trip to visit former slaves who had been re-settled in Canada. Ray preached the Sunday services at one of Rochester's black churches, and he also offered a service at the Bethel Free Church. While Ray was in Rochester, he stayed at the Avery home, and he wrote about the time he spent with the Avery and Stanton families in the year before Henry and Elizabeth Cady's engagement:

> My home while in this place, was with my highly esteemed friend, Geo. A. Avery, towards whom I cannot entertain too high respect. His house is as the Temple of God, where He is worshiped in the spirit— where the melody of the heart in hymns of praise is tuned, and the voice of prayer, in its pathetic and sincerest strain, mingle around his throne. The hours I spent here I regard as among the most agreeable and gratifying of my life.—Here all are for God and humanity from the grandmother to the servant.[21]

The "grandmother" Ray referred to was Henry Stanton's mother, Susanna. Despite the very active abolition movement in Rochester, the community as a whole did not support social equality for blacks. By opening his home to an African American in 1838, Avery braved the disapproval of the Rochester community.

Henry Stanton's uncle Henry Brewster was also converted to abolitionism at nearly the same time as the other members of the family. It is not known precisely when Brewster first became involved in reform politics; however, when New York abolitionists met in Utica in October 1835 to form a state society, Henry Brewster was prominent enough in the movement to be selected to chair the proceedings. On its first day, the meeting was disrupted by a violent mob of local citizens, and the abolitionists were forced to abandon their first meeting location. They reconvened in nearby Peterboro— the home of Elizabeth Cady's first cousin, the reformer Gerrit Smith. It was there that Henry Brewster was elected a vice president of the newly formed New York State Antislavery Society, and he served on the executive committee with Smith, who had only recently converted from colonization to immediate abolition.

Henry Brewster, like many other members of Henry Stanton's family, did not confine his reform efforts to abolition. He was also active in church, temperance, and Sabbatarian reform movements throughout his life. Brewster's early reform network included others who would later play an important role in the 1848 Seneca Falls and Rochester women's rights conventions. For example, in 1841, Brewster and Thomas McClintock, husband of Mary Ann and father of Elizabeth McClintock, called a meeting in central New York to discuss the "True Christian Sabbath." More than seven years before the Seneca Falls Convention, Brewster and McClintock invited all "lovers of truth, irrespective of party, sect or sex...[to meet] for the purpose of discussing" the sabbath.[22] These previously unexplored kinship ties between Henry Stanton's family and the larger network of reformers in western and central New York illustrate an important component of the environment into which Elizabeth Cady was introduced when she married Henry in 1840.

Word of the Lane rebellion quickly spread throughout the reform community, and other revival-inspired seminaries in Ohio and New York were eager to enroll the former Lane students. Throughout the remainder of 1834, Henry Stanton and a handful of other Lane rebels continued in their efforts to establish a seminary at Cumminsville, located only six miles from Cincinnati. Former Lane faculty member John Morgan and a former Lane lecturer from Cincinnati, Gamaliel

Bailey, joined them in Cumminsville. However, because of the continued shortage of instructors, the students were still forced to rely on each other to continue in their religious studies. With the help of Morgan and Bailey, they were also able to continue operating their schools in Cincinnati's African American neighborhoods.[23]

The students lived and worked in a large house owned by James Ludlow, the brother-in-law of a young Cincinnati attorney, Salmon P. Chase. Chase was so moved by the antislavery efforts of the Lane students, that he convinced Ludlow to support the seminary at Cumminsville by providing the property for their use. Other support came from New York philanthropist Arthur Tappan, who in addition to financially backing the new seminary, also offered to endow a professorship with a $5,000 annual salary in order to entice a prominent minister to the new institution.

However, before the students had time to accept Tappan's offer, a minister from another fledgling seminary, located in the northern part of Ohio, prompted a complete change of plans. Representing the new Oberlin Theological Seminary, John Shippard implored the former Lane rebels to enroll at Oberlin. The theological students at Cumminsville, including Henry Stanton, agreed to abandon their new seminary to attend Oberlin, but only on the condition that they be allowed to hire the administration and faculty, as well as to establish the rules governing the student body at the institution. Further, they insisted that Oberlin appoint Asa Mahan, a former Lane trustee who left with the rebels, as president and that Theodore Weld and John Morgan be hired as faculty. As if this list of demands were not enough, their last stipulation nearly ended the negotiations: the students also insisted that black students were to be freely enrolled at Oberlin.[24]

Weld declined the professorship, and he suggested Charles Finney for the position; but Finney also refused. Shippard and Mahan then went to New York City to meet with Arthur Tappan. They hoped to secure both Tappan's financial backing and also the weight of his influence to pressure Finney into accepting the professorship at Oberlin. Tappan agreed with Shippard and Mahan, and he thought the new seminary offered the opportunity to provide an education for the former Lane students and free blacks, while also creating the opportunity to nurture a new generation of abolitionists.

Tappan secured sufficient financial backing from his wealthy friends, pledged a great deal of his own funds, and then he set to work trying to change Finney's mind. Henry Stanton also wrote an impassioned letter to Finney urging him to accept the position in the "impenitent West." Stanton insisted that without a strong foundation in "pure religion" brought about by powerful religious revivals and conducted by the new crop of ministers under Finney's tutelage, the region and ultimately the country would be "rushing to death, unresisted and almost unwarned."[25] Finney finally relented, and he arrived at Oberlin at the beginning of the spring semester in 1835.[26]

Although Henry helped to establish Oberlin, he did not enroll in the spring semester. In fact, although he still considered himself to be a resident of Ohio throughout most of 1835 and 1836, he spent very little time there. Shortly after Finney arrived in Oberlin, Henry attended a gathering organized by Theodore Weld in Putnam, Ohio, to form a state antislavery society. Following his departure from Lane, Weld was employed as an agent for the American Antislavery Society. In the days prior to the meeting at Putnam, Weld delivered nearly 40 antislavery addresses, and he also established societies in villages and towns throughout Ohio.

Despite the sometimes violent reception Weld faced in the Ohio countryside, he eventually selected Putnam, a town close to the Indiana border in the northern part of the state, in which to organize a state antislavery society. Writing to Lewis Tappan a year later, Weld recalled some of the violence he faced in Ohio during this time. In the days leading up to the state society's organizational meeting, free blacks in Putnam and Zanesville were also violently attacked. Weld wrote, "Large numbers of poor Colored people were turned out of employ, men were prosecuted under the vandal laws of Ohio for employing them, and the four hundred Colored people in Zanesville and Putnam were greatly oppressed in continued apprehension and panic…One Colored person attended one of the [antislavery] lectures and was knocked down on the bridge going home."

It was in this hostile and violent environment that the Ohio Antislavery Society was formed in April 1835. The local African American population was so intimidated by the events in the weeks prior to the meeting, that they dared not attend the convention.[27] Representing Hamilton (Cincinnati) County, Henry Stanton was chosen as a secretary of the meeting.[28] The meeting attracted 150 delegates, and although rocks were thrown at the building, other than broken windows and shattered nerves, no further violence marred the proceedings. The delegates left Putnam after defining their principles in much the same language as the Lane rebels had done the year before. Henry was one of seven delegates sent to New York City to attend the American Antislavery Society's annual meeting in May, after which, he planned to join the twenty other former Lane students at Oberlin.[29]

Although he still planned to be a minister, Henry Stanton had not initially considered public speaking to be his vocation. His decision to enroll at Lane for ministerial training was prompted by his profound religiosity inspired by Charles Finney's revivals in Rochester. Nevertheless, since his first speech at Lane in 1832, Stanton had been honing his speaking skills, and he had already become an expert in the persuasive, emotional rhetorical style required of an antislavery orator.

His considerable talents were already evident by the time Henry reached New York City in 1835 to attend the American Antislavery Society's annual meeting. Despite his youth and relative inexperience as compared to antislavery luminaries such as Garrison and the Tappan brothers, Henry was chosen as a secretary at the annual meeting, and he was also sent to represent the AAS at the New England Antislavery Society's meeting later that month. An attendee of the first session of the New England convention noted, "H. B. Stanton, formerly of Lane Seminary, Ohio, presented a resolution…concerning the criminality of slave holding by professing Christians. Mr. S, though young, displayed shining talents and a powerful mind." Another writer commented that Henry's address "did honor to the speaker as an orator, and was honorable to him as a man."[30]

Stanton's successes as an orator and organizer, together with his commitment to the antislavery cause, were recognized by the national organization's executive board, and they offered him an agency position shortly after the annual conventions ended. Henry's devotion to abolition gave him a practical way to incorporate his religious faith into ending the suffering of slaves and the opportunity to once again participate in organizational reform—something that he had enjoyed and excelled in before entering the seminary. Henry accepted the offer, and he became the tenth agent of the AAS.[31]

The agency system was at the heart of the recruitment strategy of the American Antislavery Society. Agents were provided with a small stipend, usually about eight dollars a week, and they lived their lives much like itinerant ministers. They were often assigned a geographic territory and would travel from town to village giving lectures and establishing town-level antislavery societies that were auxiliaries to the state and national societies. Agents were responsible for raising funds to support the activities of the AAS, and they also sold and distributed antislavery pamphlets and books along the way. Agents usually remained in a town or village no more than a day or two, and they were expected to secure lodgings and meals with local abolitionist sympathizers as they traveled.

The position also required the agents to spend up to five or six hours a day delivering speeches and answering questions in makeshift venues. In crowded or large gatherings, antislavery agents had to speak as loudly as possible in order to be heard, straining their vocal chords to the point that some agents required long periods of convalescence to continue. In addition to the physical demands of the position, agents were frequently the targets of violence, both threatened and real, by those opposing their cause.[32]

Shortly after accepting the position with the AAS, Henry was assigned to the state of Rhode Island. When he arrived, the state had no local societies, and establishing a strong antislavery network was seen as particularly important because of a pending anti-abolition bill in the state legislature. The bill aimed to stop the free discussion of antislavery petitions in the Rhode Island legislature. It was the first such bill proposed by a free state, and the abolitionists rightly worried that if the Rhode Island bill was successful, other Northern states would follow suit. The Rhode Island legislature was also considering a set of other resolutions that had already passed in some town meetings that would have curtailed the formation of antislavery societies and discouraged the free discussion of the issue of slavery.[33]

Stanton spent the last six months of 1835 organizing local societies and speaking before men, women, and "juvenile" antislavery groups in Rhode Island.[34] In a relatively short time, Henry Stanton became the face of the abolition movement in the state. In late 1835, a sixteen-year-old girl submitted a poem to the *Woonsocket Advocate* entitled, "Slavery." The moving stanzas ended with a reference to Henry: "And thou, noble man, in the cause persevere, Success may they labors attend, And Afrie's poor sons yet thy name shall revere."[35]

Rhode Island was also an important state for the abolitionists because it was already a favorite summer resort for wealthy slave holding Southerners. The AAS hoped to have a strong presence in the popular tourist resort towns of Newport and Providence before the arrival of vacationing slave holders. By December, Stanton felt that the Rhode Island abolitionists were ready to organize a state society. He believed that the state meeting would attract enough participants for the "monster" to be "staggered," and that at least one state would be redeemed. In the month leading up to the meeting's call, Stanton and Charles Burleigh worked together to insure a strong representation at the meeting from large cities, such as Providence, in order to create "a moral atmosphere so hot, that next summer [when the slave holders returned to the area on vacation] it will melt or consume them."[36]

The state organizing convention was held in Providence from February 2-4, 1836, with nearly 500 delegates in attendance from all parts of the state.[37] The meeting was closely timed to precede the pending vote of the proposed gag laws by the legislature, and Stanton believed that if the representatives were forced "to look their servants in the face when they pass laws to gag them," the measure would stand a greater chance of defeat in the legislature. Stanton's political instincts proved correct, and the gag bills were defeated by the votes of two representatives from Providence.[38]

Following the successful establishment of a strong state society in Rhode Island, Stanton traveled to New York City to meet with the executive committee and to receive his next agency assignment. While there, Henry was a guest of Lewis Tappan, and on February 23, 1836, the two men attended a temperance lecture as part of a day-long series of temperance meetings held throughout the United States.

The executive committee decided that Stanton should join Amos Phelps in Connecticut to execute the same strategy there as he had done so successfully in Rhode Island. However, for reasons that remain unclear, Henry asked permission of the board to consult with Theodore Weld concerning Biblical arguments against slavery before venturing into Connecticut. Weld, who was in Utica, New York, was unaware that Henry would soon be joining him. Writing to William Goodell, Henry's replacement in Rhode Island, Weld asked, "where is our dear Stanton," and he urged Goodell to "not force" Stanton to stay in New England.[39]

Henry was able to convince the executive committee that he needed to consult with Weld before going back into the field. However, given Henry's ministerial training and his experience with the Biblical arguments against slavery, a more likely explanation for Henry's trip to Utica was that he needed a rest from his exhausting schedule. In a letter to Phelps about his visit to Weld, Stanton explained, "By spending a month in recruiting, sharpening my armour & replenishing my stock of ammunition, I shall be able to accomplish vastly more in the succeeding 6 months than though I had continued to labor in the old harness without cessation."[40]

Henry arrived in Utica with abolitionist Charles Stuart, and the two joined Theodore Weld who was nearing the completion of a three-week lecture tour in the area. Only a year before, a violent mob in Utica had prevented the New York State Antislavery Society from meeting in their town. This year, Weld's lectures attracted huge crowds; oftentimes hundreds were turned away because they were unable to squeeze into the venues. Stanton estimated that 600 new members of the Utica Antislavery Society were recruited, and twice that amount of legal voters had signed a petition to Congress calling for the abolition of slavery in the District of Columbia.[41]

Stanton and Weld next traveled to Rochester where Weld gave a series of lectures and Henry nursed a "severe inflammation of the throat."[42] Within a few weeks, Henry was sufficiently recovered to begin lecturing in neighboring Livingston County.

After speaking in Mt. Morris and Moscow, New York, his next assignment was in the small town of Fowlersville (now Fowlerville). On April 12, 1836, Stanton delivered a two-hour antislavery lecture at a Congregational meetinghouse that was attended by "a respectable audience," but also by "some lewd fellows [who] were lurking about, partly intoxicated, swearing against abolition &c." Following the lecture, he left the village and stayed at a friend's house nearby. The following morning, the meetinghouse was burned to the ground by an arsonist.[43]

In the weeks following the destruction of the building, an investigative committee was formed, and the cause of the fire was attributed to the work of an "incendiary." Pro-slavery and anti-abolitionist sympathizers attacked the findings with newspaper editorials charging that the committee was not under oath when their testimony was given and that they must have lied. For his part, Stanton wrote to Phelps that he "esteemed [the incendiary] next to murder," and he uncharacteristically added, "I should dislike to meet the man in the night who set fire to it."[44] This was not Stanton's only brush with violence during the more than 1,000 speeches he made between 1835 and 1840. In this five-year period alone, Henry Stanton's speaking engagements were mobbed more than 150 times. Some threw stones, while others just hurled verbal tirades against the speaker. Once, Henry was hit in the head by a brick while delivering an antislavery address. It was a dangerous cause.[45]

Henry attended the May annual meeting of the American Antislavery Society as a delegate from Ohio, and he made the trip with other delegates from the Rochester area, including his brother-in-law George Avery.[46] At the annual meeting, Stanton introduced a resolution illustrating how much the influence of his ministerial training was still informing his views on the abolition of slavery. Stanton called on "individual Christians and churches of all denominations" to demand that their associations pass resolutions condemning slavery as a sin, adding, "we rely mainly for the removal of slavery upon the faithful testimony of the Christian Church against it."[47]

Clearly as of May 1836, political agitation was not one of Stanton's considerations. However, this was soon to change following the passage of a resolution in the United States House of Representatives that month requiring that all antislavery petitions be tabled without discussion. The so-called "gag rule" tied the issue of constitutional civil liberties directly to the antislavery crusade. This linking of the denial of civil liberties—in this case the right of petition—to the fight against slavery, brought many into the cause because the abolitionists were able to tie the issue to the increasing political power of the Southern states and the diminishing political power of the Northern states.[48]

At the 1835 national society's annual meeting, Stanton was once again selected as a delegate to attend the New England Antislavery Society's annual meeting the following month.[49] Although Henry's oratorical skills were already highly respected within the abolition community, his speeches at the 1836 annual meeting of the New England Antislavery Society were particularly well received. Writing for the *Lynn* [Massachusetts] *Record*, a columnist praised Henry's speeches at the meeting in even more glowing terms than usual. "Mr. Stanton is a young man, of very youthful and prepossessing appearance, of rare talents, and of surpassing eloquence," he wrote. "At times, every heart seemed melted with pity; at other times the fancy of the speaker would break forth and flash with wit, as chaste as it was cuttingly sarcastic and severe," he continued.[50]

Henry's desire to be everywhere all of the time began to wear on his health. By June, his frequent speeches and the rigors of constant traveling forced him to spend two weeks recuperating in Providence. The quiet time gave him the opportunity to consider his future. The New York State Antislavery Society offered him an agency position, but the national society was also trying to recruit Stanton to fill the vacancy on the executive board as the organization's financial agent. In addition, Henry also received frequent requests to lecture in other states. That month, Lucretia Mott invited Henry to stay at her home so that he could lecture before the Philadelphia Female Antislavery Society. However, Henry believed that before he could make a decision about future speaking engagements, he had to decide which position he was going to accept.[51]

When the executive committee of the national society reconvened in New York City on July 6, Theodore Weld was in attendance. Writing in his diary, Lewis Tappan noted that he hadn't seen Weld in nearly three years, and that he "rejoiced to once more converse with him." The morning after the meeting, Weld and Stanton joined Tappan for breakfast, and they spent "some hours" chiefly discussing Henry's possible appointment as financial agent of the AAS.[52] The committee approved Stanton's appointment, and by the end of that month, Henry was officially a member of the executive committee.[53]

In his new position, Henry's main task was to solicit and collect funds for the AAS. The organization had matured to the point that the collection of funds, on a regular and pledged basis, was seen as "a matter of necessity." Noting the amount of publications, newspapers, salaries, and traveling expenses of agents, an editorial in the *Emancipator* commented, "a few individuals pay liberally, while the mass of abolitionists, individually, pay but little."[54]

One of Henry Stanton's first meetings in his new position was held in Boston's Congress Hall where he spoke before a largely female audience. Although abolitionist Deborah Weston thought he used the word "ladies" too much in his speech, Stanton's speech made his position on women's participation within the antislavery movement very clear: "woman was in her appropriate sphere when laboring, talking, writing and praying in behalf of oppressed women."[55]

Henry's appeal to the women of Boston was "immediately responded to." More than 50 women in attendance pledged funds and half of that amount pledged lifetime membership in the society.[56] All told, when he presented his first report to the executive committee, Stanton's collections during his first month as financial agent totaled nearly $1,200.[57] By the end of August 1836, Henry Stanton had delivered 27 lectures, and he collected close to $3,000.[58]

Anti-abolitionists also noticed Stanton's success at fundraising and igniting abolitionist sentiment during his speeches. An editorial from a Washington, DC, paper expressed concern that while the abolitionists seemed to "exhibit great tact," their appeals to young people in the North were "dangerous" because the children, both male and female, might "be imbued with the views and principals of the abolitionists, and abolition, like a whirlwind, will sweep over the land. It will be too late to take precautions against it."[59]

The constant traveling, lecturing, and brushes with violent pro-slavery mobs eventually took a toll on the usually healthy, amiable, and resilient young man. Seeing him after one of his lectures, abolitionist Deborah Weston wrote to her sister that although Henry had to lecture again later that evening, "he is looking very poorly & sick & will have to give up for a long time, very soon. Mrs. Charles has to 'beat him up an egg' every now and then to keep him going."[60]

As financial agent, Henry began spending increasing amounts of time in the Boston area, and he became quite the local celebrity. Young, charismatic, and a bachelor, Stanton was often mentioned by the abolitionist Weston sisters in personal terms. Although the Weston sisters shared confidences and personal information in their letters, most of the time, they took their reform efforts very seriously, and seldom gossiped. However, Henry Stanton was an exception to this rule. In their letters to each other, the sisters often mentioned how Henry looked and what he said during his visits to their homes. Anne Weston raised funds from a ladies society to purchase a new pair of moccasins for Henry. According to Anne, when presented with the new shoes, Henry promised "both myself & the moccasins, shall be worn out in the cause of impartial righteousness."[61]

Deborah Weston, writing to her sister Anne, related an incident demonstrating how Henry's busy schedule had also taken a toll on his otherwise sunny disposition. Weston also witnessed the first known incidence of what would become a recurrent sentiment throughout Henry's lifetime—his disdain for money:

> I called at Maria's & found Henry Stanton...Those people who have Henry Stanton must be careful what they have in their room, for he searched every

part of Maria's faithfully, making remarks as he went
along…Just before he left began he to declare how
little he cared for money. "I don't care that for it" said
he throwing a pen which he was twirling in his hand
with considerable violence on to the table. It flew
over the table however & lighted close by Maria who
fishing it up threw it back to him saying "And I don't
care for that either." He was a good deal put down &
did not know what to say. I record it as being the first
time I ever saw him show the least embarrassment.[62]

In response to the growth of the abolition movement, the
Executive Committee of the AAS recognized the need for an increased
full-time presence in the New York headquarters. Theodore Weld was
brought in from the field to assist with the tremendous volume of
secretarial and record-keeping duties being handled by Elizur Wright.
Wright, an early convert to the cause, was wearing many hats for the
AAS. He was also the editor of the group's official newspaper, the
Emancipator. As part of the office's restructuring, Wright handed over
the editorship of the paper to Joshua Leavitt, former editor of the
Evangelist.[63] However, even after the addition of Weld and Leavitt to
the team, the staff could not keep up with the increased responsibilities.
The executive committee decided to bring Henry into the New York
office as corresponding secretary. Later that year, James G. Birney and
John Greenleaf Whittier rounded out the New York office staff that
Wright later called, "a dangerous clump of fanatics."[64]

In early 1837, the AAS formulated a strategy designed to overturn
the Congressional gag rule. The plan targeted state legislatures in an
attempt to convince the bodies to exert pressure on their own members
of Congress in order to overturn the resolution. Massachusetts
was selected as the first target, and Henry Stanton was assigned to
deliver the first major address. Stanton's speech to the Massachusetts
Legislature spanned two full days in late February. The speech focused
on two goals: first, to protest the gag rule and second, to present the
antislavery arguments against the slave trade and the reasons for
prohibiting slavery in the nation's capital. While the speech would not
reach the halls of Congress directly, the abolitionists knew that their
arguments against the gag rule would reach sympathetic members of
Congress, while also increasing local support for their cause.

Stanton's arguments before the legislature were designed and presented to sway his audience in both legalistic and emotional terms, echoing the influence of Finney on Stanton's oratorical style. The address provided a lengthy historical discussion concerning the establishment of the District of Columbia, and he sought to prove that Congress did have the authority to ban the "humiliating" practice of chattel slavery in the nation's capital. Stanton argued that because slavery was a creature of law, so too was antislavery.

Ending slavery in the nation's capital was seen as both a strategic and philosophical goal to Stanton and the abolitionist coalition. It was believed that if slavery and the slave trade could be ended there, the progression southward of the abolition cause could not be far behind. The largely evangelical bent of abolitionism in the 1830s was united with the beginnings of political pragmatism in the philosophical arguments outlined by Stanton before the Massachusetts Legislature:

> [The existence of slavery in the District] brings into contempt our nation's boasted love of equal rights, justly exposes us to the charge of hypocrisy, paralyzes the power of our free principles, and cripples our moral efforts for the overthrow of oppression throughout the world…The citizens of this nation have deep responsibilities, as Christians, as citizens of the world.[65]

These were powerful arguments in the wake of the democratic impulse that characterized the Age of Jackson, and as Stanton argued, the "cool blooded oppression" mocked the nation's democratic principles and showed the country to be "despotic," rather than a free society.[66]

Stanton's speech before the Massachusetts Legislature was very well received, and word of his success quickly spread within reform circles. After hearing Henry speak the first day, William Lloyd Garrison told Angelina Grimké that Stanton "completely astonished the audience." The following morning, "hundreds if not thousands" were turned away for the second day of Henry's speech due to a lack of space in the cavernous Representative's Hall.[67]

Following Henry's speech, the legislature overwhelmingly passed a resolution chastising the Congressional gag rule and affirming Congress' right to abolish slavery within the District of Columbia.

Henry's speech was quickly printed in pamphlet form, and it was soon after revised to include expanded historical details. The expanded edition went through at least seven printings and over 300,000 copies were eventually distributed.[68]

Six weeks later, after attending the May annual meeting of the AAS, Henry arrived in New York City following a grueling month of travel throughout New England. During the month of April, he delivered close to thirty lectures, often staying in one location no longer than an afternoon.[69]

Although the abolitionists still relied primarily on moral suasion to add to their ranks, some were considering political strategies as evidenced by the following resolution submitted at the American Antislavery Society's 1837 annual meeting by William Lloyd Garrison:

> As the sense of this society, that whilst abolitionists ought neither or organize [*sic*] a distinct political party, nor as abolitionists to attach themselves to any existing party, the people of all parties are solemnly bound, by the principles of our civil and religious institutions, to refuse to support any man for office who will not sustain the freedom of speech, freedom of the press, the right of petition, and the abolition of slavery and the slave trade in the District of Columbia and the territories, and who will not oppose the introduction of any new slave state into the Union.[70]

In addition to Garrison's role in drafting the resolution suggesting political action, he also proposed that abolitionists "entreat" their local representatives to vote "by the highest religious and political considerations" against the admission of Texas as a slave state.

The gag rule stimulated the linking of the political process and abolition. In their efforts to end the gag rule, many abolitionists began to see the potential benefits of political agitation as a tactic in their fight against slavery. However, other events in 1837 would also make it impossible for the abolitionists to move forward with the unity of purpose they enjoyed during the movement's first six years.

SIX

HOW QUESTIONS ABOUT
WOMEN BECAME THE
"WOMAN QUESTION"

*"The history of the introduction of the
'woman question' into our [antislavery]
meetings, may be told in a few sentences."*[1]

Although the issue will soon contribute to the wresting of the American Antislavery Society in two, at the May 1837 annual meeting, there were no women recorded in attendance, no protests regarding women's participation, and, therefore, no mention of enrolling women as full delegates. In fact, only two months earlier, the country's first national female antislavery meeting was held in New York City. The meeting was not called because of any prohibition against women's participation within the AAS, and it was organized as an independent gathering of female abolitionists.

In a published address, abolitionist Angelina Grimké called on the women of the North to organize antislavery societies, and she also urged Northern women to include African American women in their reform societies as equal members, and she did so without questioning the status of women within the larger antislavery movement.[2] Angelina and her sister Sarah were raised in South Carolina, and their father was a slave owner. As an adult, Sarah moved to Philadelphia and became a Quaker. Angelina followed, and the two sisters became ardent abolitionists and women's rights advocates.

In 1836, Angelina Grimké was commissioned by the AAS as an agent, and she attended the convention of Theodore Weld's agents known as the "Seventy." When her name was initially placed before the agency commission, the committee was unsure about the "employment of female itinerants in the cause of abolition," and the matter was then bumped up to the executive committee for a decision. After some debate, the committee approved Grimké's appointment noting simply, "it is expedient to appoint females."[3]

Not only was this a radical decision by the executive committee because Grimké was a woman, but also because of the physical hardships of the position and the ever-present threat of physical violence against antislavery agents. The appointment of Angelina Grimké as an agent demonstrates that the executive committee believed that she would be able to handle potential problems, and it also affirmed the board's confidence in her abilities to handle the rigors of travel and the life of an itinerant speaker irrespective of her gender.[4]

Together with her sister Sarah, Angelina began a difficult speaking tour in New York City that was met with some opposition from within abolitionist circles. By the spring of 1837, the sisters had been "tutored" by Weld in public speaking, and they planned a series of lectures to be held in New England.[5] Although they had not initially considered that they might be addressing "promiscuous audiences," meaning audiences comprised of both men and women, word of their powerful lectures attracted both men and women to their speaking engagements.[6] Angelina seemed to adjust rather quickly to speaking before mixed audiences, writing at the end of her first week, "Nearly thirty men present, pretty easy to speak." The numbers soon increased, and by the end of July, her mixed audiences numbered over 1,000.[7]

The controversy over Angelina's lectures began in Amesbury, Massachusetts. During one of Angelina's speeches, two men challenged her claims about slavery and suggested that the three of them debate the topic at a future date. On July 17, according to historian Carol Berkin, the result was first public debate between a man and a woman in the United States.[8] This debate and the growing sensationalism around Angelina's lectures, convinced the association of Congregational Ministers in Massachusetts to circulate a letter asking meeting houses to close their doors to speakers and issues of a controversial nature.

The effects of the "pastoral letter" were far reaching for women's rights. Issued coincident with a public letter storm between Angelina Grimké and the conservative Catherine Beecher, the strong support the Grimké sisters received from the abolition community helped them to enlist support for their right to speak before mixed audiences, but it also brought the issue of women's roles in reform to the forefront.

Although many New England abolitionists supported Angelina in continuing her speaking tour, some cautioned the sisters to stop lecturing in order to avoid the controversy altogether. Theodore Weld, who was already romantically enamored with Angelina, found himself in an uncomfortable position. Wanting to be seen as supportive of a woman's right to speak, his letters hint that he also hoped that Angelina would suspend her lecturing to mixed audiences in order to quell any controversy within the larger antislavery movement. Weld wrote to the Grimké sisters on August 15, 1837, stating that "woman in EVERY particular shares equally with man rights and responsibilities," but he added, "I do most deeply regret that you have begun a series of articles in the Papers on the rights of women."[9] John Greenleaf Whittier, wrote to the sisters the day before, and he expressed a similar sentiment.[10]

However, at the same time that both Whittier and Weld found themselves on the fence about the sisters' advocacy of women's rights, Henry Stanton's reaction was unequivocal. In an August 10 letter, Angelina wrote that Henry was "sound on the subject of women's rights." After conversing with Angelina and Sarah, Angelina wrote to a friend that Henry "wants very much so to arrange some meeting, so that we and he may speak at it together. This would be an irretrievable commitment, but I doubt whether the time has fully come for such an anomaly in Massachusetts."[11]

Henry also encouraged the Grimké sisters to continue their public speaking in the face of condemnation from the conservative clergy, and he even offered to share the lecture platform with them at the height of the controversy. As Angelina explained, "He [Henry] went to the meeting with us in the evening, opened it with a precious prayer & sat with us in the pulpit."[12] Henry Stanton's unconditional support of the sisters' right to speak in public was demonstrated long before other abolitionists—including Angelina's future husband, Theodore Weld— were willing to do so, and most importantly, before the Grimké sisters themselves were convinced that their speaking before mixed audiences was the proper course of action.

Weld wrote to Angelina and Sarah in late August stating that by pushing the idea of women's rights they were "putting the cart before the horse." Weld added that he believed that "until human rights have gone ahead and broken the path," women's rights should wait. Whittier was more severe in his letter of August 14. Chiding the Grimké sisters for forgetting about the slave, Whittier charged that their efforts for women's rights were, instead, a "selfish crusade against some paltry grievance…of their own."

Despite Theodore Weld's initial reluctance to support the Grimké sisters entering the debates about women's participation in the antislavery movement and his cautioning Angelina to tone down her public debate with Catherine Beecher, Weld's lukewarm support of women's rights during this time is seldom noted by historians. Decades later, when Weld's co-agitators' positions on women's rights were criticized, Weld insisted that he, Henry Stanton, Joshua Leavitt and Elizur Wright were all of the same mind during the controversy of 1837. At a reunion of abolitionists held in Boston after the Civil War, a speaker declared that within the New York Executive Committee of the AAS, only John Greenleaf Whittier had supported the cause of women's rights. Although habitually quiet in his later years, Theodore Weld immediately rose and with "indignant eloquence," he defended Henry and the others as early proponents of women's rights.[13] However, contemporary evidence tells quite a different story—in 1837, Henry Stanton was the only member of the executive committee who publicly supported the Grimké sisters during the controversy, and it was Henry Stanton alone who did not suggest that women wait until all other human rights had been granted before asserting their rights within the antislavery movement and within the society at large.

William Lloyd Garrison began publishing the *Liberator* on January 1, 1831, and by 1833, he was already referred to in New York newspapers as "the notorious" for his calls for immediate abolition. In May 1833, news of the parliamentary debates over emancipation in the British Isles prompted Garrison to make his first visit overseas. Garrison hoped to secure both the financial and moral endorsement of the British antislavery community to aid the cause of American immediatism.[14] Garrison also planned to study British tactics, and during his five-month stay, he met with antislavery luminaries such as George Thompson, William Wilberforce, and Thomas Clarkson. In London, Garrison attended antislavery meetings and gave speeches denouncing colonization, eventually delivering addresses to large audiences in London's Exeter Hall.[15] By the time of Garrison's overseas trip in 1833, the first abolition group formed in the United States, the New England Antislavery Society, began organizing in opposition to the American Colonization Society. The New England Society employed three agents and rapidly gained auxiliaries.[16] Still, no national American immediate abolition society existed.

Garrison was a polarizing figure from the very beginning of his conversion to abolition. Tensions quickly arose between the activists outside of Massachusetts and Garrison. Western abolitionists, including those as far away as Ohio, while deeply moved by Garrison's writings, were often leery of the effects of the firestorm created by the sensationalized literary style of Garrison's newspaper, the *Liberator*.[17]

By 1830, the wealthy New York City merchants Arthur and Lewis Tappan added opposition against slavery to their roster of benevolent works. However, after the bloody Nat Turner rebellion in August 1831, the *Liberator* began to be seen increasingly as an incendiary force, rather than as a statement of the reformers' evangelical linkage between antislavery and the repudiation of sin.[18] Even at this early time of their collaboration, the Tappan brothers were concerned that abolition's association with Garrisonian radicalism might wreck havoc on their larger benevolent agenda.

Abolitionists decided to meet in May 1834 to form an organization during the week that other benevolent groups held their annual meetings. However, at Garrison's insistence, the meeting took place months earlier. On December 4, 1833, sixty-three delegates from ten states met behind a guarded door in Philadelphia to form the American Antislavery Society. Those present included John Greenleaf Whittier, James and Lucretia Mott, and a young Massachusetts clergyman, Amos Phelps.[19]

Garrison headed the committee that prepared the new society's constitution and Declaration of Sentiments, which stated in part:

> We also maintain, that there are at the present time, the highest obligations seating upon the PEOPLE of the free-States, to remove slavery by moral and *political* action, as prescribed in the Constitution of the U.S.[20]

As the group finalized the society's founding documents, Lucretia Mott offered stylistic suggestions that were readily adopted. A young abolitionist later remarked that this was the first time he had heard a woman speak in a public meeting, and although Mott attended with three other women as a "listener and spectator," she later wrote that it did not occur to any of the women at the time "that there would be a propriety in our signing the document."[21] By the end of the 1830s, Mott and the majority of women within the antislavery ranks would no longer view themselves as "listeners and spectators," but rather, as full and equal participants with men in the antislavery cause.

Although serious tensions within the AAS would not surface for two more years, the origin of the break within the American abolitionist ranks can be dated to July 1837 and Garrison's conversion by John Humphrey Noyes to the doctrine of perfectionism or non-resistance. Noyes, a conservative minister who would later found the utopian Oneida community in 1848, counseled Garrison that mankind should "abandon human government and nominate Jesus Christ for the Presidency, not only of the United States, but of the world."[22] Garrison was also profoundly influenced and encouraged in Noyes' millennialism by fellow immediatist, Henry C. Wright. The result of his conversion was a lengthy article in the pages of the *Liberator*, declaring Garrison's allegiance to non-resistance. "We are not political partisans...we are guided by no human authority," he wrote, "the governments of this world...are all Anti-Christ."[23]

Many of Garrison's friends and co-agitators in the antislavery movement were shocked and surprised at his complete condemnation of political participation and political action. At the national organization's annual meeting held only two months before Garrison's conversion to non-resistance, he had served on the "committee on political action," and he also supported the Declaration of Sentiment's resolution calling for the use of political means to end slavery. It follows from Garrison's "no human government" principle that ritual and hierarchy within the church were also unchristian, a position that angered Phelps, Torrey, and the other clergy within the Massachusetts Antislavery Society and within the movement as a whole.

Within months of Garrison's conversion to non-resistance, many began to express concern that his dogmatic and very visible promotion of non-resistance would harm the antislavery cause. To complicate matters, Garrison's conversion occurred at nearly the same time as the public outcry over the Grimké sisters' lectures had reached a fevered pitch, making it far more difficult to understand the individual effects of these two controversies as standalone events. However, it is possible to establish which abolitionists supported the Grimké sisters' right to speak while condemning the changes in Garrison, by examining the correspondence from the summer and fall months of 1837.

Many of the abolitionists who did not convert to non-resistance, such as Henry Stanton, supported the continuation of the Grimké sisters' lecture tour. However, many of these same men expressed sincere concern for the abolitionist cause because of Garrison's actions. John Greenleaf Whittier explained the crux of the problem of Garrisonian non-resistance being co-mingled with the antislavery cause:

> Our good friend, H. C. Wright [another proponent of non-resistance and an intimate of Garrison] with the best intentions in the world, is doing great injury by a different course. He is making the anti-slavery party responsible in a great degree for his...startling opinions. I do not censure him for them, although I cannot subscribe to them in all their length and breadth. But let him keep them distinct from the cause of emancipation. This is his duty. Those who subscribe money to the Anti-Slavery Society do it in the belief that it will be spent in the propagation, not of Quakerism or Presbyterianism, but of the doctrines of Immediate Emancipation...[to combine these doctrines] is a fraud upon the patrons of the cause.[24]

Whittier took a similar position on the changes in Garrison's *Liberator*, writing that the paper's prospectus promised readers an antislavery newspaper, and subscribers paid for the paper on those grounds. Whittier charged that by filling the pages of the paper with "no governmentism," Garrison "defrauds his subscribers."[25]

Throughout the remainder of 1837 and into the following year, as serious calls for political agitation became a groundswell, Garrison's refusal to separate his own personal beliefs from the cause of antislavery set the stage for a very public breach within the movement. By the time that the Massachusetts Antislavery Society (MAS) met in January 1839, it was all out warfare.

Henry Stanton, Elizur Wright, Joshua Leavitt, and James Birney feared that the AAS would become either a Garrisonian non-

resistance society or one burdened with additional reforms such as
Sabbatarianism or women's rights. The coalition of anti-Garrisonians
was made up of those who were united in favor of political action, but
they also held diverse views on the role of the churches and the equal
participation of women in the abolition movement.

The MAS meeting opened on January 23, 1839, and it was likely
the most contentious the group had seen. To begin with, both Garrison
and his opponents were expecting a showdown over political action
and the right of women to vote at the meeting. At the last meeting of
the New England Antislavery Society, held the previous May, several
prominent clergymen, including Amos Phelps and Charles Torrey,
resigned amidst great debate over women's participation within that
society. [26]

When the MAS meeting opened, a motion was introduced
allowing "all persons present…whether men or women" to participate.
According to the printed report of the meeting, the motion was
adopted "without opposition." However, Amos Phelps, Charles Torrey,
and five other members of the clergy launched an official protest
charging that the New England Society had "connec[ed]…a subject
foreign to it" and that such connections were "injurious as a precedent
for connecting with it [the NEAS] other irrelevant topics."

While the annual report of the MAS called the women's
participation at the meeting "somewhat novel," the board of managers
disagreed that women's participation was injurious to the cause. Phelps
resigned his position as an agent for the MAS, and the board selected
Henry Stanton to replace him. However, despite the "strong hopes" of
the board, Stanton declined the position in favor of his duties on the
national society's executive committee.[27]

The leadership of the American Antislavery Society's executive
board, men such as Stanton, Wright, and Leavitt, were also seeking to
control the resolutions at the Massachusetts society's meeting, but for
entirely different reasons than many of the clergymen such as Phelps
and Torrey. Although the official published accounts of the meeting
are rather tame, letters and reminiscences of those present convey at
least some of the drama that unfolded.

The showdown began early in the proceedings when Henry
Stanton rose to speak concerning a proposed new weekly paper for the
MAS. He was soon interrupted by a request that he yield the floor to
allow a paper to be read. Stanton agreed, not knowing that the paper

was really a motion to restrict all speakers to 15 minutes each. This motion prevented serious debate before the issue of political action had even been broached.[28]

Since Garrison's conversion in 1837, Stanton and the other more pragmatic members of the AAS were growing increasingly intolerant of Garrison's elevation of non-resistance at the expense of abolitionism. They also believed that Garrison's behavior concerning the issue of political action was inconsistent—a fact ignored by many of his followers during the schism and most historians since. As early as 1834, Garrison had urged *Liberator* readers "to vote for the immediate abolition of slavery." He had also supported congressional candidates favorable to the cause, and he had even advocated on behalf of a resolution at the 1838 New England Antislavery Society meeting that stated that it was the "duty" of abolitionists to vote.[29]

However, by early 1839, it was clear that Henry had become completely alienated from Garrison and his followers. Writing that March, Garrison claimed:

> His [Stanton's] conduct throughout has been very reprehensible, and greatly has he injured himself in the eyes of the best friends of our cause. His political hobby has well-nigh ruined him, and put an end to all harmonious action in Massachusetts. My soul is filled with grief on his account. Dearly have I loved him in time past, and great have been my expectations in regard to his future career. But I fear he had made up his mind to be a man of "one idea"—for he seems to be determined to look in one direction, and with a short-sided vision.[30]

The "one idea" that Garrison was referring to was the abolition of slavery and Henry's advocacy of using political means to achieve the organization's goals. Garrison, however, was increasingly determined to achieve a multiplicity of reforms, one of which was the abolition of politics.[31]

Much of the debate concerning political action of abolitionists centered around a motion that was very similar to one supported by Garrison the year before. The motion declared that it was "the duty of abolitionists to go to the polls & there remember the slave." At the

1838 meeting of the New England Antislavery Society, a group of resolutions were nearly unanimously passed including one that stated, "*Resolved*, That in the opinion of this Convention, it is the solemn and imperative DUTY of every abolitionist in the land, to employ his political influence…it is an IMPORTANT DUTY, demanded of us by the slave, TO GO TO THE POLLS IN ALL CASES, AND VOTE."[32]

In addition, much of the discourse concerning political agitation during 1839 and 1840 was centered on the contention that voting was a "duty," rather than an option, for abolitionists. Political proponents were eager to show the gathering that Garrison, and those who did not support the resolution, were not doing all they could for the slave. During the debate, Garrison asked the crowd, "Am I recreant to the cause? Who believes it?" "No! No!" was the response. Finally, a frustrated Henry Stanton sought clarification: "Mr. Garrison, do you or do you not believe it a sin to go to the polls?" "Sin for me" was Garrison's response.[33]

The motion resolving voting to be a "duty" was soundly defeated and its supporters "well nigh mobbed down by the non-resistants."[34] Garrison then proposed a much milder substitute resolution, which was adopted by a large majority:

> *Resolved*, That those abolitionists, who feel themselves called upon, by a sense of duty, to go to the polls, and yet purposely absent themselves from the polls whenever an opportunity is presented to vote for a friend of the slave—or who, when there, follow their party predilections to the abandonment of their abolition principles—are recreant to their high professions, and unworthy of the name they assume.[35]

Writing to Birney and Wright at the end of the convention, Stanton called the proceedings a "genuine non-resistant revolution," adding that the MAS had hauled down its flag and run up the crazy banner of the "non-government heresy."[36] Stanton's choice of evocative language offers a window into just how emotional and serious the divisions were between Garrison and the politically-minded reformers.

Although Stanton, Leavitt, and Wright supported Garrison's position on women's participation generally and the Grimké sisters' public speaking efforts more particularly, they could not countenance Garrison's non-resistance advocacy. Believing political action their only remaining recourse so long as their petitions to Congress were impotent, the executive committee was alarmed by Garrison's disavowal of not only an important tactic in their efforts, but they also saw non-resistance as incompatible with the constitution of the AAS.[37]

Additionally, the anti-Garrisonians believed that non-resistance was harming the cause of antislavery. Critics both North and South already accused abolitionists of fanaticism, and because of Garrison's high visibility as the editor of the *Liberator*, it was feared that the paper's prominence within the movement might also taint the entire cause.[38] Although Stanton had come to the floor at the MAS meeting with a folder containing back issues of the *Liberator* advocating both the questioning of political candidates and Garrison's endorsement of voting, Garrison would not acknowledge the inconsistency.[39]

Garrison's new stance of "no human government" was so abhorrent and seemed so dangerous to those outside of the non-resistance circle, that it forced those in favor of political agitation to form a coalition in opposition to Garrison with other disgruntled members such as Phelps and Torrey who were also against women's participation. "The split is wide, and can never be closed up," Henry Stanton wrote James Birney following the Massachusetts Antislavery Society's convention, "Our cause in this State is ruined unless we can seperate [*sic*] the A. S. Society from everything which does not belong to it…But, I wish our friends distinctly to understand, that Garrisonism and Abolitionism in this State, are contending for the mastery."[40]

Another concern of both the executive committee and many of the Massachusetts abolitionists was Garrison's *Liberator*. Although the *Liberator* was not an official newspaper of any antislavery society, it had been perceived as a semi-official weekly for some time. As Garrison became more committed to non-resistance, more and more of the *Liberator* was devoted to his new cause. By the end of 1838, subscriptions to the paper had declined, prompting Garrison to author editorial columns reassuring free black subscribers that "their cause was not to be abandoned."[41] However, many subscribers charged that the paper was peppered with articles that were "irrelevant" and "mischievous" to the cause of antislavery.[42] In January 1839, prior to the annual meeting of the MAS, members of the national organization's executive committee joined together with anti-Garrisonian abolitionists from Massachusetts and agreed to publish a new paper as the official paper of the MAS, and Stanton began recruiting Elizur Wright as its editor.[43]

Securing Wright was an important step in insuring the success of the new paper, and although Wright negotiated a salary above Garrison and Whittier's, Stanton was confident that the prestige and legitimacy of the new Massachusetts Abolition Society, still in the planning stages, would be greatly enhanced with Wright as editor.[44] The Massachusetts Abolition Society was formed as a competing organization to the Massachusetts Antislavery Society to support political action in the Bay State. By the end of January, the still unnamed new paper, "devoted to Political Action," boasted 2,200 subscribers. Wright agreed to edit the paper, but his appointment was to remain secret until after the May annual meeting of the AAS. In the meantime, Wright was to supply columns that would supplement those of Henry Stanton and the editorial board.[45]

When the first issue of the *Massachusetts Abolitionist* was published on February 7, its masthead left little doubt as to the editorial direction the paper would take—"Supremacy of the Laws," stood in stark contrast to the no-government philosophy of Garrison's *Liberator*.[46] The editorial board was careful to refrain from articles attacking Garrison and non-resistance in order to avoid having to publish Garrisonian replies. "Ours is not a free discussionist, but an Abolitionist journal," noted Stanton.[47]

During the final months of 1838 or early in 1839, a young freedom-seeking slave heard one of Henry's speeches in New Bedford, Massachusetts. Frederick Douglass, who was staying with Nathan Johnson and his family in New Bedford after fleeing slavery in Maryland, remembered Henry's "wonderful oratorical powers" decades later. It was one of the first antislavery speeches Douglass heard, and it left an "ineffaceable impression" on his mind. Douglass wrote that Henry was "unquestionably the best orator in the anti-slavery movement" at the time, and while Douglass heard him lecture many times over the years, this first lecture "touched him the most deeply."[48]

By the time of the annual meeting of the AAS in May 1839, the division between the political coalition and Garrison had developed into a contest over the future of the American Antislavery Society. The meeting was held in New York City, and one of the first questions put to a vote concerned the roll of delegates. Originally proposed as a listing of "men, duly appointed," a substitution was quickly put forth inserting the word "persons" in place of "men." The substitute motion carried, but the following morning, the resolution was brought up again for reconsideration. Lewis Tappan asked that the "yeas" and "nays" be tallied, prompting a revision to the previously passed resolution. In the end, the simple statement that all persons "male and female" were to be enrolled members was passed 180 to 140.[49] Political abolitionists such as Gerrit Smith, Alvan Stewart, and Joshua Leavitt voted in favor of the motion, while James Birney, Lewis Tappan and two women from Massachusetts voted against it.[50] Neither Henry Stanton nor Elizur Wright's votes were recorded.

Immediately following the completion of the official roll of delegates, Lewis Tappan, Charles Torrey, and Amos Phelps launched a protest. The men proposed a resolution stating that although women were on the roll, it was not to be understood that they were entitled to "sit, speak, vote, hold office, and exercise the same rights of membership as persons of the other sex."[51] The motion did not pass, thereby allowing women equal voting rights at the meeting.[52]

Following other organizational matters, the issue of political agitation came up for debate. Several resolutions were introduced, nearly all centering on the language of "duty" versus "conscience" of abolitionists. When the modified resolution was put to the vote, it was narrowly adopted 84 to 77.[53] Not surprisingly, the Garrisonians voted against the measure, while Leavitt, Birney, and Alvan Stewart supported it. However, the meeting's resolutions concerning political action were somewhat ambiguous. Although the motion passed stating that it was the "duty" of abolitionists to vote, a related resolution chastising non-voters for not doing all they could for the slave, did not.

Shortly after the votes were counted, James Birney introduced a motion, signed by 123 members, protesting women's voting rights within the American Antislavery Society. Citing a variety of arguments against women's participation, the document charged that the practice violated the constitution of the AAS. The protest referred to the issue as "the abstract question of the rights of women and the propriety of their action in large deliberative bodies." The protest also claimed that women's participation brought "unnecessary reproach and embarrassment" to the cause of the enslaved.[54]

Both Birney and Lewis Tappan signed the protest, while Stanton, Smith, Leavitt, Whittier, Wright, and Stewart did not. Although the resolution compelling abolitionists to vote had narrowly failed, due in large part to the addition of the women's votes, only those who formed the conservative wing of the political abolitionists, endorsed Birney's protest.[55]

The *Emancipator* later presented the arguments advanced on both sides of the "woman question," noting that the convention spent three sessions debating women's participation, an issue "quite foreign to Anti-Slavery."[56] This sentiment was echoed by John Greenleaf Whittier: "we are not able to see that the American Anti-Slavery society has, constitutionally, any thing more to do with the 'appropriate spheres' of women, than it has with the 'concentric spheres' of Capt. Symmes' theory." Captain Symmes' theory held that the earth was hollow and provided one could find the "hole," thought to be in Antarctica, the earth's interior could be inhabited. To Whittier, the theory was just as unrelated to the abolition cause as women's rights.[57] Whittier also wrote that women's participation was often referred to as a "Quaker Measure," but he insisted that at the Quaker meetings, "in all business matters, the men and women hold separate meetings."[58] Although the so-called "woman question" was broached at the New England and Massachusetts state societies, the 1839 annual meeting of the AAS was the first national gathering at which the issue was debated.[59]

It is important to realize what the votes of women delegates represented, both philosophically and practically. Conservative clerical abolitionists such as Amos Phelps and Charles Torrey were opposed to women's participation because they believed it to be "unnatural." However, the majority of the political abolitionists believed that they were fighting for the continued survival of the abolition movement.

In their writings, the political abolitionists expressed genuine concern that Garrison was attaching other reform efforts to abolition, thereby diluting their efforts on behalf of the slave. They believed, and rightly so, that the abolition movement was controversial enough without the addition of other causes that might prevent the movement from attracting more support. As Stanton explained in early April, "the combat deepens here, & the breach widens. Garrison will destroy the A. S. Society rather than fail in making it subservient to his ends. Mark me in this, & see if I am not a true prophet."[60] Thus for abolitionists such as Henry Stanton, Garrison's non-resistance and his failure to adopt resolutions supporting political action were at the root of the divide.

By the end of May, Phelps and Torrey formed a new society in Massachusetts. Originally called the Massachusetts State Antislavery Society, the name was later changed to the Massachusetts Abolition Society. The group resolved to seek "equal religious, civil and political rights" for blacks, and the new society began enrolling auxiliary societies almost immediately.[61] Although the MAS had been the official state auxiliary of the AAS, because political abolitionists controlled the national society's executive board, the new Massachusetts society was also recognized. This provided the new group with the legitimacy of the AAS, while muddying the issue between Bay State abolitionists.[62]

Following the May annual meeting of the AAS, and coincident with the forming of the Massachusetts Abolition Society, another national convention was called and slated to begin on July 31 in Albany, New York. The call stated explicitly that the sole object of the convention was to discuss measures "which relate to the proper exercise of the right of suffrage by citizens of the free states. All questions and matters foreign to this object will be cautiously avoided in deliberations of the occasion."[63]

At the Albany convention, the political abolitionists held a decided majority of members, and the carefully worded call that "freemen" attend, helped to forestall much of the debate over women's participation. In addition, because the meeting was held away from the eastern seaboard, many non-resistants did not attend. Almost immediately after the meeting began, Garrison launched a protest and questioned the meaning of the word "freemen," but he was overruled at every juncture on the grounds that the call had been made to discuss political questions and questions such as that were out of order.[64]

Without the women's votes tipping the balance toward Garrisonian non-resistance, the political resolutions were readily adopted. In stark contrast to the meetings held earlier that year, the Albany convention was able to agree upon a large set of resolutions, ultimately finding consensus that the time had come for abolitionists to stop neglecting their cause at the ballot box. "A five-sixths abolitionist was a pro-slavery man," concluded a delegate following the debates. The Albany convention, however, did not yet resolve whether or not a dedicated political party was desirable.[65]

Garrison was the final speaker at the Albany convention. Trying to downplay the success of the political abolitionists, he claimed that he had been silent because he didn't find it "consistent or proper for non-resistants to discuss their views in an abolitionist convention, and therefore it was that he had remained silent, as had others who agreed with him in sentiment—when the question of coercing the consciences of those who could not vote—had been mooted."[66]

However, Garrison was also silent because for the first time, a meeting was overtly hostile to him and the non-resistants. The frustration of seeing their voting resolutions being defeated, not because of policy, but because of non-resistance, had brought the political abolitionists to the boiling point. In a biography of their father, written nearly fifty years after the Albany convention, Garrison's sons recalled, "[Clergyman] Orange Scott made furious thrusts, 'accompanied by a peculiarly appropriate expression of face,' at Mr. Garrison, who bore it like a Christian." At the time, Scott was arguing that he "doubted God would pardon a man's soul for omitting to vote for the slave."[67] By the summer of 1839, political participation by abolitionists had become a very personal fight.

SEVEN

THE WHIRLWIND & THE SUN FLOWER

"The reporter, however, made no attempt to report this part
of his [Stanton's] speech, for the same reason, that he
would not attempt to report a whirlwind or a thunder-storm." [1]

"The heart that loves truly, love, never forgets,
But as truly loves on to the close,
As the sun-flower turns to her god as he sets,
The same look that she turned when he rose." [2]

Elizabeth Cady met Henry Stanton in early October 1839, while they were both guests of her first cousin Gerrit Smith.[3] According to Elizabeth, Henry was giving a series of antislavery lectures in the area, and Smith's Peterboro home became his headquarters.[4] Guests at the Smith's, including Elizabeth, would head off in the mornings in two carriages to attend Henry's meetings. At the antislavery meetings, Elizabeth wrote that she was "spellbound" by Henry's oratory as he moved the audience "first to laughter and then to tears," and she later recalled her enjoyment of their long conversations at the end of the day.[5]

Unfortunately, like so many of Elizabeth's memories as recounted in her autobiography, the antislavery meetings she recalled were probably a later fabrication. Because Elizabeth's serious interest in reform came only after marrying Henry, by placing their first meeting at an abolition lecture, she also established her own, albeit weak, antislavery credentials prior to her marriage. Henry's speaking engagements were well documented in the press at this time, and there is no evidence of any antislavery meetings held in the Peterboro vicinity during the month of October. It is far more likely that Henry was visiting Peterboro to strategize with Gerrit Smith about the crumbling of the American Antislavery Society and to solidify Smith's support within the political abolitionist coalition.

Despite the likely fabrication about her falling in love with Henry while watching him deliver antislavery speeches, Elizabeth was very fond of debate and specifically antislavery debate long before meeting Henry. After a visit to Peterboro in 1836, Elizabeth wrote to her uncle Peter Smith about her trip: "Mr. Bayard and cousin Gerrit argued all the time upon the subject of abolition. I enjoyed it very much as they both argue well and without the least impatience either in word or manner. Every member of their household is an abolitionist even to the coachman." Before meeting Henry, however, Elizabeth did not express an opinion on the subject of abolition, only that she enjoyed the repartee.[6]

Elizabeth also later wrote that when the couple first met in Peterboro, she believed that Henry was engaged to Jane Stewart, the beautiful daughter of abolitionist Alvan Stewart, from Utica, New York. Because Elizabeth thought that Henry was no longer a potential suitor, she explained that the two were "much more free and easy in our manners than we would otherwise have been." Decades later, Fanny Seward, daughter of William Henry Seward, noted a similar phenomenon. Although often quiet and shy, Fanny met a dashing young lieutenant at a party, and she found herself "quite talkative" because it was "so easy to converse with an engaged gentleman."[7]

Individually, both Henry and Elizabeth were friends of the Stewarts, and coincidently, both had arrived at the Smith home in Peterboro from Utica and with different members of the Stewart family. Elizabeth arrived in Peterboro with Alvan Stewart, Jr., after staying with the Stewarts during her visit there. Henry also came from Utica in the company of Jane Stewart, lending support to the rumor that the two were engaged. Henry was also in Utica during September to attend the New York State Antislavery Society's meeting, held from September 18-20, 1839, before returning east. Despite their proximity to each other in September, both Henry and Elizabeth consistently maintained that they met in Peterboro the following month.

Elizabeth and Jane were correspondents prior to her visit to Utica in September, indicating that perhaps, Elizabeth was privy to at least some hint of romance between Jane and Henry. Originally, the two women planned to arrive in Peterboro during the first week of August, but they were both delayed by family obligations. That summer, the Cady household in Johnstown was full of visitors. Tryphena was visiting from Seneca Falls, and Harriet and Daniel Eaton and their two children were also in residence. By late July, in what was a scorching hot summer, the Eatons left for Newport, leaving their two children in the care of Elizabeth and the rest of the family.[8]

After many delays, Elizabeth finally left Utica with Alvan Stewart, Jr., who was "perfectly delighted" to escort her to Peterboro. Elizabeth planned to stay at the Smiths for several weeks, and she arrived on Saturday, September 14. According to Elizabeth's correspondence, Jane Stewart was scheduled to arrive three weeks later, on October 5.[9]

Utica and Peterboro were just some of Henry's stops that month. He began the month of October some 450 miles from Peterboro where he delivered an address to the Young Men's Antislavery Society convention in Maine, then he passed through Boston on his way to the Stewart home in Utica. From Utica, Henry and Jane Stewart traveled to Peterboro.[10]

Family legend recounts that Henry and Elizabeth set off on horseback one beautiful Indian summer morning, and the two were absent for "a long time."[11] Elizabeth remembered in her autobiography:

> As we were returning home we stopped often to admire the scenery and, perchance each other. When walking slowly through a beautiful grove, he laid his hand on the horn of the saddle and, to my surprise, made one of those charming revelations of human feeling which brave knights have always found eloquent words to utter, and to which fair ladies have always listened with mingled emotions of pleasure and astonishment.[12]

However, in an undated and unpublished verse that Elizabeth composed about Henry, she indicated that she was not simply a passive recipient of Henry's declaration of love:

> *But I went on from book to book*
> *And at last a prize I took*
> *I was glad to do something you did not dare*
> *But I'd given my prize for your brown curly hair*

From Elizabeth's verse, it would seem that it was she who first declared her admiration that afternoon. While from later events it is clear that the attraction she felt was mutual, Elizabeth's belief that Henry was soon to marry Jane Stewart encouraged her to do something he "did not dare."

Other than his possible causal flirtations with the Weston sisters two years before, Henry's correspondence before meeting Elizabeth was nearly entirely focused on abolition. While it's certainly possible that letters of a more personal nature have been lost, after meeting Elizabeth, she became a prominent topic in letters to those who knew her and to those who did not. This suggests that while he may have had a passing interest in a woman before meeting Elizabeth, it was not as deeply felt.

Sketch of Henry B. Stanton in 1840 by Benjamin Haydon. Henry was featured prominently in Haydon's painting of the World's Antislavery Convention, and the artist sketched Henry while the Stantons were in London. Haydon gave this drawing to Henry, and it was one of his most treasured possessions. Note Henry's "brown curly hair."

Courtesy of Coline Jenkins
Elizabeth Cady Stanton Trust

At the time of their meeting, Elizabeth was just shy of her 24th birthday. Although her surviving correspondence in the years before meeting Henry is sparse, her commonplace book was filled with verses about love and romance. One such example, "Heart in heart—hand in hand—let us welcome the weather, and sunshine or storm we will bear it together," reflects an idealistic view of marriage that was shared by the young Elizabeth.[13]

The pair returned from their horseback ride that afternoon "radiant" and announced that they had decided to marry. Although the precise date of their engagement is unknown, they were engaged before October 20 when Henry left to address the special meeting of the American Antislavery Society in Cleveland, Ohio.[14] By October 20, Henry and Elizabeth had only known each other for fifteen days.

Considering that neither one of them had a history of falling in love quickly, their profound attraction to each other must have been a welcome surprise to them both.

Despite their hopes for the future, after Henry left for Cleveland, Elizabeth soon realized that her Johnstown family would not readily accept her engagement or her choice of a husband. Elizabeth decided to extend her stay in Peterboro for a few weeks, explaining decades later that she wanted to "prolong the dream of happiness" and to delay opposition to her plans that she "feared to meet."[15]

Although Gerrit Smith was fond of Henry and respected his leadership within the emerging political arm of the abolition movement, he too worried that Daniel Cady would never approve of his daughter's marriage to an abolitionist, nor to a man with limited resources and questionable employment prospects. Elizabeth's sisters, Tryphena and Harriet, were already married to two of Daniel Cady's law clerks, and it was expected that Elizabeth would someday do the same. Smith advised Elizabeth to notify her family of the engagement by letter, and to allow him to act as a buffer between Elizabeth and her father. However, Daniel Cady was not so easily manipulated, and he withheld the fury of his displeasure until he was able to interrogate Elizabeth in person.

Henry Stanton did not have the same luxury of time to bask in his happiness. He left Peterboro to head into the firestorm that had overtaken the American Antislavery Society. When the special meeting of the AAS in Cleveland opened, it was on Henry Stanton's motion that women (all persons) be enrolled as full participants. The resolution passed, without discussion.

This motion is important to understanding the so-called "woman question," because it allows the issue of women's participation to be considered without the many side issues that confused and muddled the debates at other meetings. This meeting was held in Cleveland, far away from where the majority of Garrisonian non-resistants lived. This meant that although there were women in attendance, they were also women who were at least open to potentially supporting the idea of political participation by abolitionists. Also, because the meeting was held so far away from the eastern seaboard, Garrison was unable to pad the delegate count with male and female non-resistants. In addition, many of the conservative clergy who were against women's participation at other meetings were also not in attendance, allowing us to see the coalition of political abolitionists more clearly. Most importantly, this motion demonstrates that the political abolitionists were not anti-women or against women's equals participation within the movement. The "woman question" was not really a question at all; rather, the issue of women's exclusion was manipulated and distorted by Garrison in order to deflect the issues that were really at stake—political participation by abolitionists and control of the national organization.

A second motion, also introduced by Henry Stanton, was then quickly adopted. This motion illustrates just how far the majority of the national society's membership had shifted, since the annual meeting held only six months before, on the issue of Garrisonian non-resistance: "Slavery is the creature of law, and can be entirely abolished only by the repeal of those laws which create and sustain it; and... these laws can be repealed only by means of political action at the ballot-box."[16]

By the October 1839 Cleveland meeting, many political abolitionists had gone beyond the idea of voting and had begun to seriously debate the idea of a third political party. Myron Holley of Rochester, New York, introduced a motion calling for independent nominations, but it was tabled at the Cleveland convention.[17] During the Cleveland meeting, however, a summary of the British abolition movement was presented, and the group noted, "political action [by the British] was by no means overlooked."[18] While many in attendance supported the idea that slavery was a creature of law, the idea of breaking with the mainstream political parties was still a position that the majority of abolitionists were unwilling to take.

After the Cleveland convention, the situation between Garrison and the political abolitionists grew increasingly ugly and vindictive. Responding to an editorial in the *Massachusetts Abolitionist* calling him a "voter," Garrison responded in the pages of the *Liberator* stating that he was not a voter, being "restrained from being one...by his views of the abstract question of the rightfulness of human governments!" Garrison then reminded the author of the editorial, Elizur Wright, that while the law allowed him to vote, the law also "might allow him to be a slaveholder."[19] The gulf between Garrisonian non-resistance and the political abolitionists continued to widen.

Henry made his first visit to Johnstown to meet Elizabeth's family in early December. Although Elizabeth was happy to see

him, the rest of the family reacted "cooly [*sic*]." Following his visit to
the Cady household, Henry spent two nights with Gerrit Smith in
Peterboro, likely for personal advice and a sympathetic ear following
his icy reception at Johnstown.[20] "The idea of marrying Elizabeth to
an abolitionist is very painful to Mr. Cady," Smith wrote to his wife
shortly after Henry departed for New York City.[21] A few days later,
Daniel Cady wrote to Smith confirming Henry's worst fears:

> I understand that he [Henry] has no trade or
> profession that he is not now and never has been
> in any regular business and if so—and he willing to
> marry—he cannot in my judgment be overstocked
> with prudence—or feel much solicitude for her whom
> he seeks to marry—...I understand Mr. Stanton now
> has some employment in an Abolition society which
> yields him a living—...Mr. Stantons [*sic*] present
> business cannot be regarded as a business for life—If
> the object of the Abolitionists be soon accomplished
> he must be thrown out of business—and if success
> does not soon crown their efforts—the rank and
> file will not much longer consent to pay salaries.[22]

On Christmas Day, Henry confided to Smith that he felt
"intense solicitude" as to the situation with Elizabeth and her family's
displeasure. Henry feared that the "adverse influences" and the "pains
taken to prejudice" Elizabeth against him by her relatives had begun
to show results. "My first visit to your house may be productive of
great happiness or great misery to me," Henry reflected to Smith. The
entire Smith family seemed to have been sympathetic to Henry and
Elizabeth's situation. Writing to her daughter, Elizabeth Smith, in a
letter that was hand-delivered by Henry, Ann Smith noted, "I am sure
you will be glad to see him [Henry]."[23]

Henry Stanton remained on cordial terms with Lucretia Mott,
despite the growing tension between Garrison and the political
agitators. By 1839, Mott was a respected reformer, and she remained
a devout follower of Garrison throughout the controversy. At the end
of December, Henry Stanton gave several speeches in Philadelphia,
and he dined with the Motts during his stay. Mott seemed unaware
of how the deeply the divides in the movement ran, only noting in

her correspondence that Stanton "bore very well an allusion to their wrong-doings in New York & Mass," and she expressed the hope that these groups would soon see "the error of their ways."[24]

On January 1, 1840, Henry penned a letter to Elizabeth reassuring her of his devoted love and promising to render that year and "all future years" as happy ones.[25] It was also in this letter that Henry quoted from Thomas Moore's poem about eternal love and the steady worship of the sunflower to "her god." Elizabeth would long remember these lines of verse, sent to her when the couple was newly in love. A decade later, when writing for the temperance newspaper the *Lily*, Elizabeth selected the pen-name, Sun Flower.

Three days later, Henry wrote again, and although the letter was addressed to Elizabeth, it appears to be a thinly veiled attempt to allay the concerns expressed by Daniel Cady in his letter to Gerrit Smith two weeks before. Henry wrote that he had existed solely on his own resources since the age of thirteen, "[having] never received a dollar's gratuitous aid from anyone...because I knew it would relax my perseverance and detract from my self-reliance." Expressing a similar sentiment to that which he did in Maria Chapman's parlor in 1836, Henry also made it clear that he "never made the getting of money for its own sake an object."[26] Although Henry was attempting to convince the wealthy Daniel Cady that he could provide for Elizabeth, he also made it clear that he had no intention of abandoning the cause of abolition for a more financially lucrative career.

On April 1, 1840, the New York State Antislavery Society called a special meeting to expressly discuss the question of independent abolitionist political nominations. To insure that political questions would be the only topic of discussion, the executive committee carefully worded the call for the convention. The call asked for "freemen" to attend the convention to discuss political action.[27] By wording the announcement in this way, the political abolitionists hoped to reduce the likelihood that Garrison could prevent the political resolutions from passing.

Because many of the resolutions on political participation in the recent past were adopted or defeated by very narrow margins, every vote was critical. Most of the female delegates who attended the earlier meetings voted with Garrison, in large part, because most of them were also non-resistants. The vast majority of political abolitionists wanted to discourage women from voting at the Albany convention because they were likely to be Garrisonians, not because they were women. As a voting bloc, women were the only potential group of Garrisonians that could have been excluded on procedural lines. The events of 1839 leave little doubt that had the women delegates been in favor of political agitation or even willing to seriously engage with the idea, the "woman question" would not have arisen at all. Further, as the Cleveland convention showed, it was not women that political abolitionists wanted to exclude, but non-resistants of both genders.[28]

Henry Stanton's position on women's participation was clear. At the end of 1839, Stanton wrote to Elizur Wright that he would not have split with the group over the "woman question" and that he "never would." "I think they [are] right," Stanton concluded, but he also added that it was Garrison who had made the issue a point of contention.[29]

Dubbed the "April Fool's Convention" by Garrison, the Albany meeting considered the previously tabled motion of Myron Holley, from the October convention in Cleveland, calling for presidential and vice presidential nominations. Attending the April convention were nearly all of the political agitators from the AAS: Wright, Leavitt, Stewart, William Goodell, and Beriah Green. John Greenleaf Whittier and Gerrit Smith did not attend, citing ill health, but they each sent letters to be read before the assembly. Also absent was Henry Stanton. On April 2, following "a kind and full discussion," Holley's motion passed, and James G. Birney was nominated for president with Thomas Earle of Pennsylvania as vice president.[30]

Stanton cautioned against independent nominations in October 1839, but by April 1840, he was firmly behind the idea. After years of trying to move the abolition movement toward embracing political agitation, Stanton missed the Albany convention and seeing the culmination of his work firsthand, due to an affair of the heart.[31]

Time had not changed the Cady family's opposition to Elizabeth's engagement. By March 4, 1840, and following months of "anxiety and bewilderment," while visiting her eldest sister, Tryphena Bayard, Elizabeth finally submitted to her father's wishes and broke her engagement to Henry.[32] Henry was in New York City at the time, and he probably received Elizabeth's decision by letter. While the letter does not survive, Henry was aware in late February that he had cause for alarm. In a letter to Gerrit Smith, written before he received Elizabeth's news, Henry wrote of his concern on the eve of Elizabeth's departure to visit the Bayards. "I dread the influence of Mr. Bayard upon her," he wrote, "She has been too much under the influence of such people."[33]

Biographers have often attributed the reason for Henry's "dread" as stemming from an alleged and improbable romance in 1838 between Elizabeth and Edward Bayard, her brother-in-law.[34] However, Henry's concern was not based on worries over a rival suitor, but because the Bayards, like the Cadys, were anti-abolitionists.[35]

Henry was not only concerned about his own happiness, but to him, the direction of Elizabeth's future was also at stake. Well aware of the influence that her father and Edward Bayard exerted over Elizabeth, and knowing that they were both against immediate abolition, Henry worried that Elizabeth might "pervert her fine powers" by "wasting them in the giddy whirl of fashionable follies," away from reform and toward the social trappings of her elder sisters.[36]

The couple's correspondence did not stop after they ended their engagement. Henry continued to support Elizabeth's intellectual and moral development, writing to Smith, "I have imparted to her good advice on such topics as I thought would do her good, & she receives it kindly…She sees her error, thanks me kindly for my admonition, & says she will improve by it."[37] Observing her keen intellect and potential as a reformer years before Elizabeth ignited the woman suffrage movement, and the only one to do so at this time, Henry explained to Smith, "It pains me to see a person of so superior a mind & enlarged heart doing nothing for a ruined world's salvation."[38]

On March 4, Elizabeth wrote to her cousin Ann, Gerrit Smith's wife, to tell her of the broken engagement. Elizabeth lamented, "[the] memories…[that] bind me to the dear ones who shared these joys with me, cast a spell that cannot soon be broken."[39]

The "spell" was not broken for long. Although no correspondence from Elizabeth survives between this letter and June 25—after the Stantons were already married—Henry's correspondence indicates that the engagement was renewed within a month.[40] By April 1, Henry and Elizabeth were planning their marriage and honeymoon, and it was these plans that caused Henry to miss the very important Albany convention. This was the first and only important antislavery meeting Stanton missed since becoming an abolitionist at Lane Seminary.

In a confidential letter to Gerrit Smith, Henry explained his absence from the Albany convention writing cryptically, "I remained at home to arrange certain matters which had unexpectedly overtaken me, & which could not be postponed."[41] Stanton went on to explain that he wished to visit the Smiths on May 2, noting that he, together with a "dear friend," may come "in chains." Displaying Henry's sense of humor and using abolitionist rhetoric he continued, "as much as you abhor thralldom, we shall totally dissent from any proposition of emancipation, immediate or gradual."[42]

Henry also sent an urgent request to Theodore Weld for his back salary during the first days of April. Henry's request was so pressing, that when he received Henry's letter, Weld wrote that he could not sleep before taking action. Although it was nearly 11:00 pm, Weld sent Henry's request directly to Lewis Tappan to secure the funds that were owed to Henry.[43] While Weld was not at liberty to disclose to Tappan the reason behind Stanton's need of his back pay, he was explicit about when Henry needed the funds, stating that it "cannot wait after the first of May," and he assured Tappan that Henry was undergoing "the most perplexing and painful [extremity] of his life."[44]

While Elizabeth may have worn down her father's opposition, surviving correspondence strongly suggests that the couple had planned to wed with or without Daniel Cady's permission, and that they might even have planned to elope. On April 7, Henry confided to friend and fellow abolitionist Amos Phelps the reason why he needed to collect his back salary:

> I suppose I shall be married in about a month & that the lady will go with me to England. Altho the affair has been some months negociating [sic] yet is it only a week past that has settled it that I must take a traveling companion with me. I cannot now tell you the lady's name, nor much about her only that she is every way worthy of me, yea, far too worthy— is from a high family which is wealthy. But, parents, brothers, & sisters &c, &c have violently opposed the match, chiefly because I am an abolitionist. Her father disinherits her, & cuts her off penniless…you may judge of her character when I tell you she has cut loose from one of the most aristocratic families in the State, given up her fortune & wedded her soul to the A. S. [antislavery] cause at the call of duty. She is a lady of high mental accomplishments, pious, a

strong abolitionist. Well, the responsibility is upon me, was thrown on me unexpectedly—for, we had made arrangements not to be married till my return.[45]

According to Henry, the urgency of their wedding date was because Elizabeth did not want to be "left behind in the hands of her opposing friends," and she thought it best to be in Europe "until the storm blew over" during her time abroad.[46] Elizabeth later nostalgically remembered that they "did not wish the ocean to roll between [them]."[47]

The wedding date was set for Thursday, April 30. Henry was making the trip to Johnstown from New York City, traveling up the Hudson River. However, Henry was delayed a few miles south of Albany at the sandbar known as "Marcy's Overslaugh." The sandbar was located on the farm owned by New York Governor William Marcy, and that section of the Hudson River was notorious for difficult travel.[48] Henry and Elizabeth would have to wait another day.

Despite the warnings of the back luck to follow should they marry on a Friday, Elizabeth, who wore a "simple white evening dress," married Henry on Friday, May 1, 1840. As a first step in their new life together, the couple omitted the word "obey" from the traditional marriage vows. Although Elizabeth's biographers often use this change from the usual marriage ceremony to illustrate Elizabeth's forward thinking, the change was made at Henry's suggestion.

In 1838, Henry, his sister Frances, and his brother-in-law George Avery, attended the wedding of their close friends Theodore Weld and Angelina Grimké. The Welds omitted the promise to "obey" as part of their very non-traditional ceremony. The Weld's wedding was unusual even among reformers, as both Theodore and Angelina felt that they could not "bind themselves to any preconceived form of words." Because of this, the couple decided to forgo traditional vows and speak only the words that the "Lord gave them at the moment." Weld referred to the "unrighteous power vested in a husband by the laws of the United States over the person and property of his wife," while Angelina promised to honor and love "with a pure heart fervently."[49] As far as we know, the remainder of the Stantons' vows followed the traditional ceremony, but with a significant difference—from the very start, the Stantons began their lives together as equals.

According to her own recollections, prior to her marriage to Henry, Elizabeth often sought the approval of others by becoming as physically strong as a male child or by attempting to prove her equal intelligence and usefulness. Her decision to marry Henry, over the objections of her father, signaled an important shift away from this pattern and an increased reliance on her own assessments of Henry as a man she could both respect and trust. As biographer Alma Lutz explained, "her decision to marry Henry in spite of the opposition of her family had been a turning point in her mental life. From then on she had confidence in her ability to think things out for herself."[50]

While Lutz credited the marriage as instilling greater confidence in Elizabeth, the Stantons' daughter Harriot attached even greater significance to Henry's influence and the important role the marriage played in changing the course of her mother's life:

> In casting up values and compensations, we must not forget she escaped the conservative atmosphere, the aristocratic surroundings in marrying Henry B. Stanton. Her own family never liked her going to Peterboro, they distrusted the "extreme" views of their nephew, Gerrit Smith. With my father she was free to build up with the Smiths the friendships that meant so much to her...As the wife of an abolitionist she came into intimate contact with Whittier, Garrison, Phillips, Lucretia Mott, etc. Her marriage got her out of an element not best for her growth, and into an element congenial with every element of her being.[51]

From the time the two met, Henry and the relationship they created were instrumental in shaping Elizabeth's self-identity and an important, positive influence on both her intellectual and practical development as a reformer. Elizabeth Cady was now an emancipated woman.

EIGHT

A WHOLE NEW WORLD

*"I always regretted that the women themselves
had not taken part in the debate before the convention
was fully organized and the question of delegates settled."* [1]

T he annual meeting of the American Antislavery Society was
scheduled to begin on May 12, 1840. However, well before
May, many of the political abolitionists had already abandoned
the AAS and were busy organizing the newly formed Liberty Party.
In addition, the ceding abolitionists were also establishing a new
national organization, the American and Foreign Antislavery Society.
Although they made many bold moves that spring, many of the political
abolitionists, including Henry Stanton, were reluctant to abandon the
old organization entirely. In late February, Henry warned Gerrit Smith
that the Garrisonians were planning a "violent effort to overthrow
and displace the Executive Committee." Stanton feared that at the
May annual meeting, "an attempt will be made to make the Anti-
Slavery organization subservient to non-resistance." [2] The tensions
that first surfaced in the early 1830s between the western abolitionists
who controlled the national society's executive committee and the
Garrisonians in Boston were continuing to divide the reformers.

Despite Garrison's vitriol against Henry Stanton, not all
Garrisonians shared in his view. At the end of April, a Garrisonian
from Pennsylvania expressed anger at the defections of Elizur Wright,
Joshua Leavitt, and Gerrit Smith, but not against Henry. "When
brother Stanton was here, we were much pleased with him. His address
on political action was excellent," he explained. Henry's behavior was

not only "respectful" and "Christian-like" to those who held opposing views, but his tone was not divisive as far as the organization was concerned.[3]

The Stantons and the Liberty Party's presidential candidate, James G. Birney, sailed for the World's Antislavery Convention in London the day before the annual meeting of the American Antislavery Society began.[4] When the AAS meeting opened, it was obviously a very different gathering from any of those held in the previous decade.

The 1840 national society's annual meeting is often described by historians as the last stand of those opposing women's participation as equal members in the AAS. However, it is clear from the changes during the previous year that by 1840, the American Antislavery Society was, as the political abolitionists argued, a Garrisonian non-resistance society, and the organization was no longer representative of the broad spectrum of abolitionists.

In a letter written to Lucretia Mott just prior to the May meeting, Garrison still claimed not to understand the problem: "A most afflicting change has come over the views and feelings of E. Wright, Jr., Leavitt, Goodell, Phelps, &c., especially in regard to myself personally, whom they seem now to hate and despise more than they once apparently loved and honored." This letter and much of Garrison's behavior during this time underscores the important role that personality played within the abolition movement. To his supporters, Garrison often portrayed himself as entirely innocent of the maneuvering and posturing that he had orchestrated over the previous eighteen months. Lucretia Mott was perhaps the most level-headed and guileless reformer of her time. Garrison's tone in this letter was one of respect, but he was also attempting to further convince her that his role in the situation was that of a victim of the political abolitionists, who used to "love[d] and honor[ed]" him, in order to garner Mott's sympathy and to maintain her steadfast support.[5]

Among the first order of business at the annual meeting was the appointment of a new business committee. Abby Kelley, a female abolitionist from Massachusetts, was appointed along with the conservatives Amos Phelps and Lewis Tappan. Phelps and Tappan immediately lodged a protest against Kelley's appointment.[6] A vote was then taken, and Kelley's appointment was sustained 557 to 451. Phelps and Tappan immediately asked to be excused from their appointment on the committee.[7] The national organization had officially splintered.

Writing to his wife a few days later, Garrison was not constrained by the need to appear shocked and saddened by the breakup of the American Antislavery Society. Within the confines of his home circle, he was happy to take credit for his role in engineering the departure of the political abolitionists, and he was decidedly pleased with the outcome of the meeting. Garrison proudly reported to his wife, "We have made clean work of everything."[8]

Within the annual report for the year ending 1840, the "separatists" explained the true causes of the abolition schism and the hypocrisy of Garrison's claims that the "woman question" was anything more than a means to his end goal of capturing control of the organization:

> The same persons belonging to the Anti-Slavery ranks, who are contending for *what they call women's rights*, the civil and political equality of women with men, deny the obligation of forming, supporting or yielding obedience to civil government, and refuse to affirm the duty of political action; and they *contrived* to *bring* to the late Annual Meeting [1839] a sufficient number of men and women to compose a majority of all the members present, to sustain their views and measures. Of the whole number present this year, four hundred and sixty-four were from the single State of Massachusetts, styling themselves "non-Resistants."[9]

Although the formal rupture of the AAS can be dated from the 1840 annual meeting, and it was incidentally prompted by the appointment of Abby Kelley to the business committee, the "woman question" was neither the overarching point of contention nor the main disagreement between the political abolitionists and the Garrisonians.

As early as February 1841, the executive committee of the American and Foreign Antislavery Society (AFAS) clarified their position on the founding of the organization and the break within the AAS. "The separation from the American A. S. Society took place in May, 1840," they wrote, "The *Woman* question, as it is called, was not the cause—it was only the occasion of it."[10]

It was Garrison's linking of women's rights with non-resistance that pushed those who had previously supported women's equal participation, abolitionists such as Stanton, Leavitt, Whittier, and

Wright, away from the issue altogether for several years. The effects of this linkage were far reaching. The reformers with an awareness of the importance of political agitation and a reform strategy based on political participation were the group most able and most likely to support women's rights agitation at the legislative level, but they were repelled by the issue's close connection to Garrisonian non-resistance.

Following the 1840 meeting, the "schismatics" worked to establish their new antislavery organization, the American and Foreign Antislavery Society. James G. Birney and Henry Stanton, already en route to London, were appointed secretaries *in absentia*, while John Greenleaf Whittier, Gerrit Smith, and Theodore Weld were appointed to the executive committee. After his marriage to Angelina Grimké in 1838, Weld scaled back his lecturing and participation in the abolition movement. Because of this, he missed much of the vitriol and bad feelings of those on both sides of the split. However, he still regularly corresponded with his friends and associates, and he was well aware of how much had changed.[11] The name chosen by the new organization was modeled on that of the new British antislavery organization, the British and Foreign Antislavery Society, which was founded the previous year.[12] Securing formal recognition and potential financial help of the transatlantic abolition community was of vital importance to the new American group.

Henry Stanton and his new bride sailed for Britain aboard the *Montreal* on May 11, 1840, with James G. Birney. The two men were already well connected within British abolition circles, and due to the fracturing of the AAS, Stanton and Birney represented the new American and Foreign Antislavery Society while abroad.[13]

Although Elizabeth was exposed to reforms and reformers while visiting Gerrit Smith, her marriage also introduced Elizabeth to many new situations and new people. By all accounts, James Birney was a very serious man. On board the ship, he thought that Elizabeth "needed considerable toning down" before they reached London. Birney took offense to a variety of Elizabeth's antics: from being hoisted up the mast in a chair, to wadding up a dinner roll and hitting the captain on the nose, Elizabeth's "frolicsome humor" was not appreciated by Birney. Elizabeth also dared to call her husband by his first name in public, and she pinned notes to the back of Henry's coat and joined with others in laughing at him. While Birney was perhaps too solemn, Elizabeth was traveling with a presidential nominee and her husband to attend a very important convention. Her behavior on board the *Montreal* shows that Elizabeth still had one foot in her youth when she embarked on her honeymoon.[14]

While Birney thought Elizabeth too bold and unladylike, Henry delighted in her tricks. They were newlyweds, very much in love, and both traveling across the Atlantic for the first time. Daniel Cady's disapproval was miles away, and as a couple, they had already survived a major challenge by outsiders to their relationship. Two months later, when Elizabeth decided to stay in London while Henry toured the northern part of the county, she wrote that they "got up quite a scene at our first parting." "I never loved my country, my home, my friends, as I do now," she continued, "the heart from love to one grows bountiful to all."[15]

GARRISON'S FOLLY

> *"It was the ironical fate of the Convention*
> *to stand rather as a landmark in the history of the*
> *woman question, than in that of abolition."*[16]

The idea for a world's convention of abolitionists likely originated with Joshua Leavitt, political abolitionist and editor of the *Emancipator*.[17] The first call for the meeting was issued by the British and Foreign Antislavery Society (BFAS) in July 1839, and the BFAS "earnestly invited the friends of every nation and of every clime" to attend.[18]

In August, the BFAS sent lengthy questionnaires throughout Europe and also to the sympathetic states within the United States asking about the specific nature and characteristics of slavery in each region. In the United States, the questionnaire was sent to the executive committee of the AAS and to individual state societies. In order to prepare for the meeting, the BFAS was hoping to have a more detailed look at both the conditions of slavery and the issues facing antislavery agitators.

Ties between American and British antislavery advocates were well established by 1839, and the groups forwarded important antislavery pamphlets across the Atlantic, corresponded frequently, and some abolitionists even attended meetings on both continents.

British abolitionist Joseph Sturge toured the British Isles in 1837, and his account was widely read by American abolitionists. Other abolitionists such as Harriet Martineau, Charles Stuart, and John Scoble spent extended periods of time in the United States.

Some of these ties also led to close personal friendships. Theodore Weld named his first son after his friend, British abolitionist Charles Stuart. When the Welds were expecting their second child, Stuart wrote Theodore hoping that the second child, if a son, would be named "Theodore." Stuart wrote, "I beg you, I require you, by our love to call your younger boy Theodore. I want our names to go together." The Welds complied, naming their second son Theodore Grimké Weld.[19]

Although an ocean separated the abolitionists, the London convention's main organizer, Joseph Sturge, was very familiar with the problematic issues and divides that were already brewing within the American movement during 1839, and he hoped that they would not cross the ocean and disturb the London convention.

Word reached London in the contentious winter of 1839-1840 that some American societies planned to send female delegates to the convention. Hoping to avoid the potential disruption of the London meeting, the BFAS send a second call dated February 15. This second invitation pointedly asked the American societies to forward the names of the "Gentlemen" who would be attending. Sturge attempted to gently communicate that the London committee never considered that women would arrive as delegates, and they hoped to forestall any debates about women's participation at the meeting well in advance of the convention's opening session. However, because many of the controversies within the American antislavery organizations were waged over control of the AAS and its future course of action, and both the new organization and the Garrisonians sought to win the financial and moral endorsement of the British abolitionists, Sturge overestimated the effect the call would have on American abolitionists.[20]

Garrison not only expected a confrontation in England, he welcomed it. During his passage to London, Garrison met fellow delegate George Bourne. Bourne, who was against women's equal participation, reminded Garrison that "no woman will be allowed a seat in the Convention. Such a thing…was never heard or thought of in any part of Europe."[21] Still, Garrison took comfort in knowing that he would not easily be "intimidated or put down," and he later wrote to his wife that it was probable that he would be "foiled in his purpose."[22]

At best, Garrison was grossly uniformed about the requests from the British, and at worst, it is disturbing to realize that Garrison might not have been entirely honest with the women delegates about what they could expect when they arrived at the convention. "Presbyterians, Baptists, Quakers—Jews, Gentiles, Ishmaelites—Women, Non-Resistants, Warriors, and all—let them come," Garrison wrote in the *Liberator*. "All but those who refuse to associate for the slave's redemption with others who do not agree with them as to the divinity of human politics, and the scriptural obligation to prevent woman from opening her mouth in an anti-slavery gathering," he added.[23] According to Garrison, the political abolitionists "refused to associate" with him and the other non-resistants. However, the reality was far more complicated, and Garrison's hands were far from clean.

Garrison publicly continued to explain the abolition rupture in terms of the "woman question," rather than addressing the more salient issue of political participation. In this way, Garrison hoped to attract sympathizers from the ranks of foreign abolitionists, but this position also allowed him to continue as the self-appointed martyr of the movement and as the leader of what he believed were the more morally pure, non-politically tarnished reformers. While claiming that the other side refused to compromise, it was Garrison who would not budge from his position, even if it meant the end of the AAS.

Historical interpretation of the London convention, especially as it concerns women's rights, has relied on a combination of Garrison's martyrdom before and during the event and the section chronicling the women's experiences during the convention as written in the *History of Woman Suffrage*. Written decades after the convention, this section of the book was almost surely written by Elizabeth Cady Stanton, as she was the only one of the authors in attendance.

By the 1880s, when this section was written, Elizabeth was fully aware of the nuisances of the disputes within the American organizations before the 1840 split. However, her retelling of the events emphasized the victimhood of the women delegates and portrayed the exclusion of the American women as an unwelcome surprise following their lengthy journey across the ocean:

> The call for that Convention invited delegates from all Anti-Slavery organizations. Accordingly, several American societies saw fit to send women, as delegates,

to represent them in that august assembly. But after going three thousand miles to attend a World's convention, it was discovered that women formed no part of the constituent elements of the moral world.[24]

But was this the case? Were the women fooled or deceived into sailing across the Atlantic, only to find when they arrived that they would not be accepted as delegates?

To begin with, the London committee peppered the antislavery community in the United States with the printed second meeting call months in advance of the women's departure. Further, Garrison, Stanton, and Lewis Tappan among others had been in correspondence with the London committee in the period between February and May. The second meeting call, asking for "gentlemen only," had a broad enough circulation to have been used by Henry Stanton as letter-writing paper to at least two individuals, and Stanton was only one of many receiving copies.

Writing in support of the women delegates in November 1840, Sarah Grimké criticized the decision of the London committee, but she did not complain that the American women had been kept in the dark about the decision. "One thing is very clear I think, viz. that the Convention had no right to reject the female delegates…lest it could be proved that they were not persons," she wrote, "the 2nd call issued by the Committee to the contrary notwithstanding."[25] Although she had not participated at the center of the movement for close to two years, Sarah Grimké was also aware of the February call for "gentlemen" only.

In addition to the widely circulated February 15 notice, the antislavery newspapers insured that the abolition community was aware that only "gentlemen" were requested to attend. Even Garrison's *Liberator* ran a transcript of the February letter in the March 20 issue, two months in advance of the women leaving the United States.

On May 1, an additional letter from Joseph Sturge was also published in the *Emancipator* and soon thereafter in the *Liberator* specifically addressing the issue. Sturge wrote that although his views on women's rights were carried "as far as most on this side of the Atlantic," he believed that it would be the "kindest" thing and "the best for our cause" if the American women did not attend.[26] Sturge also wrote directly to the organizations that had selected female delegates, in an attempt to further clarify the British position.

Bowing to the increasing pressure from the British and after receiving Scoble's letter, the executive committee of the Garrisonian-controlled Pennsylvania Antislavery Society, Eastern Branch, revoked the credentials of the four female delegates originally selected to represent the organization in London.[27] The fact that the credentials of the women from Pennsylvania were revoked before they left for London was omitted from every published account of the convention in Garrisonian-controlled newspapers because it ran counter to the victimization narrative Garrison was trying to exploit. A few months after the convention, articles in the *National Anti-Slavery Standard* and the *Liberator* noted—without explanation—that the women delegates with credentials were from the Massachusetts and the national organizations only. There was no mention of women from Pennsylvania.[28]

Clearly, the more conservative British abolitionists were on the wrong side of the issue. However, it is equally clear that the American women left the United States with at least some knowledge that the British did not welcome them and that it was improbable that they would be seated as delegates. They sailed nonetheless—including four women from Pennsylvania who left without credentials from their antislavery society.

On June 6, Lucretia Mott met with Joseph Sturge in London, and it was only after this meeting that she wrote of her knowledge of the impending conflict. At the meeting, Sturge appealed to Mott and the American women to comply with the London committee's request not to present their credentials. Sturge was once again hoping to avoid problems during the convention by this last ditch effort to convince the women not to attempt to be seated as delegates.

As Garrison stated quite plainly, he was expecting a confrontation in London. Whether or not it was his intention to use the confrontation for his own tactical purposes or if he believed the British would change their minds once the women arrived, the generally accepted historical treatment of the issue, from the perspective of the women delegates, is incorrect.

Lucretia Mott's correspondence on the eve of her departure for the London convention includes letters written to prominent Garrisonian women, but she did not indicate that she was aware of any impending confrontation over her attendance or participation in the proceedings in London. In her letters, Mott discussed the abolition split, however, she did not indicate that she was privy to the London committee's call for "gentlemen" only.[29] Mott's diary, written during her trip to London, is also silent on the potential problems the women delegates might face until the entries written after her June 6 meeting with Sturge.[30] If Mott knew about the controversy, she did not reveal it to her correspondents or even to her private diary.

While it's impossible to know for certain, the evidence suggests that at least as far as the female delegates were concerned, Garrison intentionally minimized the possibility of a controversy in London before the women sailed, or he convinced them that they should sail nonetheless. In all likelihood, Mott would have mentioned it in her correspondence if she believed that she would not be seated as a delegate or if she was aware that Garrison was taking advantage of the situation. While the *Liberator* published the February 15 second meeting call and the further correspondence by Sturge, privately, it would seem that Garrison must have reassured the female delegates that they would not be making the trip in vain. However, while this might account for Mott's silence, it does not explain the Pennsylvania women's decision to sail without credentials. Whether or not Mott was concerned about the potential for exclusion from the convention, she and the other women from the United States sailed across the Atlantic believing they were in the right, and they were likely unaware that they were caught within the crossfire of Garrison's ambitions. If the women were victimized after they left the United States, it was at Garrison's doing and not because of a sudden change by the London committee.

The day before the World's Convention was set to open, Garrisonian Wendell Phillips attended a meeting of the British and Foreign Antislavery Society.[31] He brought with him a letter, signed by Pennsylvania delegate Sarah Pugh, one of the women whose credentials had been revoked. Pugh's letter, protesting the imminent exclusion of the women delegates, was read into the minutes of the meeting. However, the executive committee remained unmoved, and they passed a resolution that the women delegates should be sent visitor's tickets.[32]

When the convention opened the following morning and immediately after the convention's officers were appointed, Wendell Phillips rose with a resolution proposing a committee of five be organized to prepare a list of "all persons" holding credentials from an authorized antislavery society. Phillips' resolution called for this list to then be included on the roster of delegates.[33] Phillips was followed by Harvard Professor William Adam, another member of the Massachusetts delegation who was also present at the BFAS meeting the day before. Significantly, although Adam was a Garrisonian and rose to support Phillips' resolution, he stopped short of seconding the motion.[34]

Historian Donald Kennon argues that Adam's failure to second Phillips' motion indicated that the Garrisonians were "simply trying to exploit the statement of their principles for tactical purposes."[35] Coupled with the fact that Phillips was fully aware of the London committee's decision from the previous day's meeting, and with the knowledge that British social customs were far more conservative than those of the United States, it seems clear that Phillips' resolution had little to do with the advocacy of women's rights and more to do with furthering Garrison's strategy. However, the actions of these self-styled proponents of women's rights further humiliated the women delegates sequestered in the hall's gallery and unable to speak on their own behalf.

Despite the noble rhetoric, by bringing the issue to the floor, the Garrisonians hoped to gain the sympathy of British delegates who might be unhappy with the London executive committee's tight control of the convention. By doing so, they hoped to wrest some of the moral and financial backing of the British abolition community away from the rival American and Foreign Antislavery Society. Just as they had manipulated the issue of women's rights to obscure the struggle between non-resistance and political participation, Garrison and his surrogates again used the issue to further their own agenda, with little concern as to the fate of the women caught in the crossfire. While the Garrisonian non-resistants opposed political participation by abolitionists at the polls, they certainly did not shy away from overt political maneuvers when it came to organizational issues.

As the debates progressed, the arguments shifted toward a discussion concerning whether or not the meeting was, in fact, a "world" convention or if the word "world" was merely a rhetorical descriptive. The Garrisonians conceded that the women could be excluded had they attended an "English meeting," but they questioned whether or not a "*World's* Convention [could rightly be] measured by an English yardstick."[36] As the BFAS explained to Wendell Phillips during his meeting with them the day before, the British considered the convention a general business meeting of their own organization, and the "world" moniker was a "mere poetical license." The Garrisonians knew the answer to the question the day before, but they pressed the issue regardless.[37]

However, while the debate over the women delegates consumed the entire first day of the convention's proceedings, the motion to enroll the women did not pass. The American women delegates spent the convention in the gallery of the hall, unable to speak or vote during the sessions. Garrison arrived in London after the convention was already underway, and rather than taking his seat as a delegate and arguing his cause on the floor, he sat with the women in the gallery. With them, among other wives of delegates, was Elizabeth Cady Stanton.

Ironically, during the debates in London, Wendell Phillips asserted that "the woman question" did not cause the split within the American ranks, but rather, it was the question of political agitation that provided the impetus for the schism. By the time of the printing of the official proceedings of the London convention, Phillips amended his statement, explaining that both issues caused the split.[38]

Henry Stanton's vote on the motion is unclear. While supportive of women's participation in the United States, Stanton was aware that British custom was far more conservative on the issue of women's rights. As the American and Foreign Antislavery Society also looked to be the group officially endorsed by the British society, Stanton too was placed in an uncomfortable position. Although Elizabeth maintained in all of her written works on the subject that Henry gave a "very eloquent speech" in favor of Phillips' motion, there is no mention of such a speech in the printed proceedings.[39]

Despite the fact that they were on opposite sides of the split within the ranks of the abolition movement, Phillips and Garrison both claimed that Henry voted in favor of admitting the women delegates, while Lucretia Mott's diary did not mention Stanton's vote.[40] However, in a letter to Lewis Tappan, James Birney plainly stated, "Mr. Stanton told me, he did not vote in favor of the admission of the women."[41] Although Stanton was clearly aligned with the new organization, the Garrisonian controlled *National Anti-Slavery Standard* published a lengthy editorial reminding readers that Stanton had "always voted [in favor of women's participation] so in the societies here."[42]

Perhaps the later confusion over Stanton's vote originated in the final motion of the convention. Wendell Phillips rose once again to propose that the earlier protest concerning the women delegates be added to the official convention proceedings.[43] The motion was debated for a short time, and a motion to table the resolution was put forth by Nathaniel Colver, a conservative member of the Massachusetts clergy. Lucretia Mott wrote in her diary entry that "H. B. Stanton opposed Colver—plead for the right."[44]

Henry Stanton's speech on this occasion is also not included in the official proceedings. While he had consistently supported women's equal participation within the movement in the United States, he too was in a delicate political position in London. While voting to allow the women delegates would have put Stanton in the precarious position of knowingly opposing the explicit wishes of the British and Foreign Antislavery Society, speaking on behalf of allowing the protest to be recorded in the official minutes was not as a sharp of a break of sympathy with the BFAS.

AFTERMATH

> *"As Mrs. Mott and I walked home, arm in arm,*
> *commenting on the incidents of the day,*
> *we resolved to hold a convention as soon as*
> *we returned home, and form a society to*
> *advocate the rights of women."*
> Elizabeth Cady Stanton[45]

Before leaving for London, the newlyweds stopped in New Jersey to visit Henry's longtime friends and co-agitators, Sarah Grimké and Theodore and Angelina Weld.[46] The sisters greatly impressed Elizabeth, and she them, and Elizabeth continued to mention the Grimké sisters' philosophies on the "woman question" throughout her European travels.[47] Elizabeth's understanding of the issue, as the Grimké sisters explained, was not different from that which she heard from her husband. Henry lectured with the Grimkés throughout the controversies of 1837, and he encouraged and supported Angelina's equal status as an agent for the AAS. Nonetheless, meeting these trailblazing female reformers helped to anchor the otherwise abstract philosophical question as originally explained to her by Henry.

In her first letter to these eminent women, Elizabeth did not express any outrage at the treatment of the women delegates in London. Elizabeth benignly noted that the question "caused some little discord" at the convention, but she dispassionately added that a similar "difference of opinion" existed in America among abolitionists.[48] Although Elizabeth's later reminiscences praised Garrison for his efforts on behalf of women's rights, her contemporary correspondence does not agree with her later re-examination of the issue. In the same letter to the Grimkés, Stanton described her impression of Garrison after hearing him speak for the first time in London: "last evening," she wrote, "he opened his mouth, & forth came, in my opinion, much folly."[49]

When Elizabeth and Henry Stanton returned to the United States after a seven-month European tour that included Britain, Wales, Scotland, Ireland, and France, Elizabeth had met many important leaders within the international community of reformers. Reflecting her immersion in reform circles during the first months of her marriage to Henry, when the couple returned to the United States, Elizabeth began signing her correspondence "Elizabeth Cady Stanton," rather than the more traditional "Elizabeth C. Stanton" that she used while abroad.

There can be little doubt that the experience of the World's Antislavery Convention profoundly influenced the development of Elizabeth Cady Stanton's feminist consciousness. Further, it is largely though her retelling of the women's exclusion from participation at the London convention that the incident has become an important part of the historical narrative of the women's rights movement. However, the contests over women's equal participation in the antislavery movement did not begin in London, but rather, in America in the year prior to the 1840 convention. Similarly, the "woman question" became important primarily because of its tactical connection to the issue of political agitation.

During the 1830s, women had been present at antislavery meetings in the United States at local, state, and national levels. When the question of their equal participation arose, oftentimes, as in London, the women were forced to listen silently while men debated the issue; muted in their own defense. At some of these meetings, women freely and fully participated in the proceedings, while at others, they were only "visitors."

Elizabeth Cady Stanton was not a part of the American debates over women's participation in 1839. As Stanton assumed the leadership of the American women's rights movement after 1848, her narrative of the movement's origins also became the foundational text of the movement, and her own awakening became inexorably tied to the movement's genesis. This is further complicated by the fact that these first histories and biographies were written during the time that the women's rights movement was splitting in two. The competing groups, Stanton and Susan B. Anthony on one side and the Boston area reformers on the other, were each vying to claim their side of the split as the true foundational "origin" group of the women's rights movement.

In her own writings, Elizabeth Cady Stanton later claimed that the events in London were such an outrage that while still in London, she discussed the idea of organizing a women's rights convention with Lucretia Mott. However, Mott's diary does not offer any support of Stanton's claim. Fifteen years later, Stanton could not even remember why Garrison refused to take his seat at the World's Antislavery Convention. This illustrates that Stanton's own experiences in London did not equate Garrison with championing women's rights or that the convention was an important milestone in the fight for women's rights. Mott, like Stanton, was not very accurate about remembering precise dates, and she also held a very different memory of the initial discussion between the two women about calling a women's rights convention. In 1855, Mott shared her recollections of the conversation with Elizabeth: "Remember the first Convention originated with thee. When we were walking the streets of Boston together in 1841, to find Elizh. Moore's daughter, 'thou' asked if we could not have a Convention for Woman's Rights."[50]

While it is doubtful that Elizabeth Cady Stanton conceived of a women's rights convention in London, the experiences and ideas expressed by many of the women she met during her time in Europe provided an important component of her education as a feminist and as a reformer. Although she arrived in London with an abstract awareness from Henry about the rupture within the antislavery movement and of the events of the previous year, until the London convention, Elizabeth Stanton had never witnessed these injustices against women for herself. Although she would grow to find a deep sympathy with the rhetoric of the Garrisonians, at least as it pertained to women's rights, Elizabeth Cady Stanton was never ideologically aligned with Garrisonian non-resistance, and throughout her lifetime, she placed political rights and participation at the forefront of her reform agenda.

NINE

THE EMANCIPATION
OF ELIZABETH CADY

"Though I had been absent but ten months,
it seemed like years, and I was surprised to
find how few changes had occurred since I left." [1]

T he Stantons arrived in Boston on December 21, 1840, after a
rough and stormy seventeen-day voyage from Liverpool. [2] By
the first week of January 1841, they reached Johnstown but the
couple was "quite undecided as to [their] future occupations & place
of residence." [3]

Much of that winter was spent visiting friends and family,
including a week-long visit to Rochester to meet Henry's family,
probably for the first time as a couple. It is not known whether or not
Susanna and the Avery family attended the couple's wedding the year
before. However, because the marriage ceremony was hastily arranged
due to the Cady family's objections, it is most likely that Henry's
Rochester family did not attend. Henry's family warmly accepted
Elizabeth into the family circle, and she later wrote to a friend that
she "like[d] my friends there & I thought they liked me." [4] In Henry's
family, Elizabeth and her budding reformism found a welcome home.
Unlike her own "queenly" mother, Susanna Stanton shared her new
daughter-in-law's commitment to antislavery. Elizabeth's mother-
in-law was an active reformer in her own right, and Susanna also
provided Elizabeth with a radically different model of motherhood
from anything she experienced as a child or as a young woman.

Henry's sister Frances Avery was already a mother when she met
Elizabeth, and Frances offered her new sister-in-law an example of

a woman combining the traditional role of wife and mother with an active career in reform. The year before Henry and Elizabeth's marriage, Frances gave birth to a baby girl on Elizabeth's birthday. As a tribute to the close and warm relationship between Frances and Elizabeth, the Averys named their next daughter after their new sister-in-law. Elizabeth Cady Avery was born in 1841. The coincidences do not end there. The Averys also had a son, George Avery, born on Henry's birthday, June 27, 1847. By the time Elizabeth met the Averys, Frances Avery had given birth to four children and lost two of them as toddlers.[5]

Throughout the early years of her married life, Elizabeth met many male and female reformers, but Henry's family offered something more. Not only was the entire family involved in the founding and running of antislavery and women's organizations, as part of Elizabeth's new family, the connection between them was far more intimate and free than those of the wider league of reformers Elizabeth met through her marriage. With the Stanton and Avery families, Elizabeth could share her fears, question her new ideas, and plan her future reform efforts in a way she could not with others. Although Frances Avery was far more devoutly religious than Elizabeth, she understood family obligations and the joys and sorrows of motherhood, and through their friendship, Elizabeth was supported both as a woman and as a reformer.

In contrast to Henry's family, Gerrit Smith was the only extended Cady family member involved in reform. His wife, Ann Fitzhugh Smith, although sharing her husband's commitment to antislavery, was never an active reformer. Despite Elizabeth's love and respect for her first cousin, Gerrit Smith was not her contemporary, and he could not share in the issues confronting a new wife and mother in the way Frances Avery would. Elizabeth was also very close to the Smith's daughter, Elizabeth, but in 1840, Elizabeth Smith was single and not yet a reformer in her own right. Like Henry's family, the other reformers Elizabeth met through her marriage were equally impressed with her, "she is no common woman—she is a rare one—and Henry need be proud of her," wrote one new friend shortly after the couple returned from Europe.[6]

Even though the Stantons were unsure of their future plans, Elizabeth remembered this time as a happy one. Now married and within the bosom of her family in Johnstown, Elizabeth was able to occupy her mind with new ideas and her hands with new chores. It was during this time that she learned to mend shirts and knit socks, and she wrote gleefully to a friend that she had not "felt any of the loneliness" of married life of which her friend complained.[7] To compound her happiness, the Cady family were now "much pleased" with Henry, despite their initial opposition to the marriage.[8] After a few months of deliberation and with Elizabeth's blessing, Henry began studying law with Daniel Cady. Henry's early life in Rochester had given him an interest in the law, and at her father's suggestion, Henry began his formal legal studies.[9]

However, despite his father-in-law's dislike of abolitionists, Henry continued to be very involved in abolitionist political agitation through the newly formed Liberty Party during the time that the couple lived in Johnstown. In 1840, the third party supporters scrambled to run a slate of candidates in national and local elections. Throughout 1841, Henry managed the Liberty Party's efforts for Fulton County while continuing to study law, and by mid-summer, he was making between two to five speeches per week.[10]

In early March 1841, both Henry and James Birney submitted their resignations as corresponding secretaries of the American and Foreign Antislavery Society. The organization was initially founded as an alternative to Garrison's no-government takeover of the American Antislavery Society. However, in just two years, the group had grown increasingly conservative on issues such as women's rights due to the influence of the clergy within the organization. Although one newspaper noted that Henry's health was the cause of his resignation, Henry's support of women's rights, his liberal stance on social issues, and his full schedule of antislavery and temperance lectures were also contributing factors.[11]

Midway through her first pregnancy and only eighteen months after her marriage to Henry, Elizabeth delivered her first speech in the fall of 1841 before a gathering of 100 women in Seneca Falls. Importantly, her speech concerned temperance, the same issue that had been the focus of Henry's speeches in the previous months. This would be the first of many instances in which Henry's reform efforts directly shaped Elizabeth's development as an agitator.[12] Following her speech, Elizabeth wrote that she was "so eloquent in my appeals as to affect not only my audience but myself to tears."[13] Henry began his social reform career in the temperance movement likely because of his first-hand experience with his own violent and absent father. Now that Elizabeth was also privy to the more personal reasons for Henry's staunch advocacy of temperance, it is not surprising that this was the topic she first felt moved enough to speak about publicly. Although Elizabeth was first exposed to the temperance movement by her father, it was not until she married Henry and learned about the devastating effects of alcohol first-hand that she became a temperance reformer in her own right.

While the Stantons shared a devotion to reform causes, even in the early days of their marriage the couple fostered an unusually high degree of independence of thought within the marriage—one that was uncommon even within reform circles. Writing to friend Elizabeth Neall in late 1841, Elizabeth explained: "You do not know the extent to which I carry my rights. I do in truth think & act for myself deeming that I alone am responsible for the sayings & doings of E. C. S."[14] The independence Elizabeth asserted in this letter and in others like it, has routinely been interpreted as a sign of rebellion against the presumed iron-hand of Henry Stanton. The reality could not be further from the truth. Even at this early stage of their life together, the marriage encouraged Elizabeth's development as a reformer by providing her with a means of expression, both publicly and privately, together with a degree of intellectual freedom rarely seen in antebellum America.

Henry was rewarded for his antislavery work in the Johnstown area with an appointment to the Liberty Party's New York State central committee the following year.[15] In February 1842, Henry left for Boston to attend the Massachusetts Liberty Party convention.[16] Before an audience of 2,000 in Boston's Faneuil Hall, he delivered a speech that the *Emancipator and Free American* called "one of the most powerful and eloquent addresses ever delivered in the Hall."[17]

The Stantons welcomed their much-adored "first production," Daniel Cady Stanton, on March 2, 1842, while the couple was still living with Elizabeth's family in Johnstown. Both parents were overjoyed with their new son, making their frequent separations over the next few months all the more difficult.

By June, Henry was in Boston preparing for his examination to the state bar. While they were apart, Henry wrote gushingly to Elizabeth of his longing to be with her to "enjoy [her] smiles & kisses" and expressing concern for Elizabeth and the baby, already nicknamed Neil or Neilly. Henry's letters to Elizabeth show him to be a devoted husband, lover, and father, but he also wrote to Elizabeth in equal measure about the political issues and reformers that he encountered while away from home.[18]

As part of all previous historical portraits of the Cady-Stanton marriage, Henry Stanton is depicted as an absent and negligent husband and father. Elizabeth's most recent biographer claimed: "Henry was hardly around; he never did make it home for any of his children's births. Indeed it is hard to conjure up much of a mental image of what Henry ("the peppy") did at home, except make babies, but this he did with regularity." Similarly, another author wrote, "symptomatic of Henry Stanton's disengagement from the domestic sphere were his absences from home during the births of all of his children." Still another biographer plainly stated, "Henry was not present for the births of any of his children."[19]

Aside from citing each other, not a single Stanton biographer offered any explanation or proof of where Henry was during the births of his seven children. However, they all used this unsubstantiated claim to characterize Henry and the marriage as being a solitary burden that Elizabeth was somehow forced to bear. This same idea is then used to explain the reasons that Elizabeth became a women's rights reformer. Her private hell became her public cause.[20]

Nevertheless, despite the accepted narrative, was Henry really absent during all seven of his children's births? Elizabeth's surviving correspondence offers very little evidence one way or the other about Henry's whereabouts during her "confinements." Compounding the problem, Elizabeth's correspondence was culled during her own lifetime and then again by her children in the 1920s. What does survive in her correspondence are letters demonstrating her remarkable abilities to carry on her domestic duties until minutes before giving birth and her speedy recovery from childbirth. Elizabeth does not mention Henry in any of the existent letters to her family or friends announcing the children's births, and in only one letter, does she mention the presence of anyone at all.[21]

Working both chronologically closer to the events and with access to the recollections of the Stantons' daughter Harriot Stanton Blatch, biographer Alma Lutz stated that Henry was not home for the births of Henry Jr. in 1843, Theodore in 1851, and Margaret in 1852.[22] Lutz did not indicate where Henry was during the births of the other four children. However, without any supporting evidence, Elizabeth's later biographers adjusted the number from three to seven, claiming that Henry was absent at all of his children's births. From all available information, Henry Stanton was home during the births of children Daniel, Gerrit, Harriot, and Robert. In the case of Gerrit, Henry wrote a letter from home the day Gerrit was born announcing his new son's birth, and in the case of the others, there is no mention of his being anywhere else.

On the surface, Henry's whereabouts during the births of his children might seem like a minor point. However, this type of misinformation has resulted in an entirely inaccurate portrait of Elizabeth Stanton, her development as a reformer, and of the marriage itself. Because of these incorrect assumptions about Henry as a husband and father, the marriage is viewed as troubled, and Elizabeth's leadership at the Seneca Falls Convention is interpreted as her first public reaction against her oppressive and unfulfilling personal life.

If the Stanton marriage was oppressive, solitary, or detached, there would have been no reason for Elizabeth to stay in such a marriage. Unlike so many women of her era, Elizabeth had not only an awareness of women's subjugation within society, she also had both the financial means and the emotional strength to leave a husband who mistreated, oppressed, or abandoned her physically or emotionally. This is especially true when one considers that her mother-in-law, who truly was in an abusive and lonely marriage, divorced her husband without losing her children. By dismissing Henry's important role as a husband, father, and mentor, the impulse behind Elizabeth's reformism is also obscured and mischaracterized.

As Henry's legal studies drew to a close, he shifted all of his energy into securing a paid position in order to support his new family. On October 4, 1842, Henry was admitted to the Massachusetts Bar, and he soon rented an upper floor office in the same building as the firm of Fletcher & Sewall.

Fletcher & Sewall was one of the preeminent legal firms in Boston. Senior partner, the Hon. Richard Fletcher, returned to Boston in 1839 following a term in the 25th Congress, and Samuel E. Sewall was an old friend of Henry's and one of the founders of the New England Antislavery Society.[23] Henry hoped that because his office was so close, he could pick up some of Fletcher & Sewall's overflow cases. His new office was stocked with his brother-in-law's legal library. By this time, Edward Bayard had given up his legal practice to become a homeopath.

Within a few months, Henry formed a law partnership with John A. Bolles, and the new firm was busy and prosperous enough to hire another antislavery friend, Joel Prentiss Bishop, to work as the firm's law clerk. The following year, Bolles became the Massachusetts Secretary of State, and he later served as the Naval Solicitor Judge Advocate of the Court of the Department of the Navy during the Civil War. Because of Bolles' new position, the partnership of Stanton and Bolles lasted only until 1845.

Henry's clerk, Joel Prentiss Bishop, passed the bar in 1844, and he too had an illustrious legal career after his clerkship with the firm. Bishop became one of the nation's foremost legal scholars and the author of several legal texts garnering international attention. Bishop was also a former student at the Oneida Institute, and he served as an agent for the New York State Antislavery Society during the 1830s.[24]

In addition to building up his legal practice, Henry continued his work for the Liberty Party. His speeches during this time highlighted the "aggressions of the slave power," and he praised the independent political party as the best means of ending slavery. Henry's legal associates at this time were all members of the Whig Party, but Henry's addresses continued to stress the importance of abolitionists maintaining their independence from the major political parties.[25] By the end of 1843, Stanton had orchestrated an entire re-organization of the Liberty Party in Massachusetts, including a redistribution of local autonomy at the county and district levels.[26]

While Henry's efforts were focused on attracting new voters to the Liberty Party, Garrisonian Abby Kelley was on a speaking tour of western and central New York. Kelley's tour was arranged to try to re-consolidate support for the Garrisonian wing of the movement. Particularly in New York, the Garrisonians lost considerable support once the dust settled in 1840. Many outside of Massachusetts were re-energized by the Liberty Party and left the AAS due to Garrison's advocacy of "no human government." Garrisonian non-resistance declared war on organizations, whether religious or secular, and his extreme positions alienated many former members of the old organization. Kelley's lectures "mad[e] war on slavery, the church, civil government, and the Liberty Party," noted one observer.[27]

Kelley's speeches also attracted pro-slavery supporters who were hoping for the demise of the third party and the abolition movement, but her attacks on the Liberty Party were not always well received. At a convention in Cazenovia, New York, Kelley received such a "rebuke" for her attacks that she toned down some of her rhetoric against the party in later speeches.[28]

Coincident with Abby Kelley's speaking tour, Lydia Marie Child was attacking the Liberty Party in the Garrisonian-controlled newspapers. In an article entitled "Moral Influence," Child cautioned abolitionists that if they joined the Liberty ranks, they would destroy their moral influence. While on the surface this seems to be the standard non-resistance argument of 1839, by 1842, this rhetoric was packed full of vindictiveness with roots dating back to the 1839-40 schism. By taking aim at the Liberty Party, rather than simply arguing against voting, those abolitionists who remained with the Garrisonians but still regularly voted were more likely to continue to vote, but to vote for the Whig Party.

In an open letter to Child in the pages of the *Emancipator*, political abolitionist J. C. Jackson explained that Child's warnings about moral corruption were not equally applied to abolitionists voting for Whig and Democratic candidates. Child's editorials, Jackson wrote, were not targeted against voting, but were aimed specifically to take votes away from Liberty and to steer abolitionists toward "pro-slavery Whigism." According to Jackson, the "true" abolitionists in New York fell into three groups: Liberty Party men, non-voters, and females. Jackson added that there were very few non-voters, and that the first and third groups "comprise the vast amount of healthful moral influence." Child and those who "talk like her," he wrote, were in no position to discuss moral influence at all.[29]

During the controversy of 1842, and despite her reconsidered appreciation of Garrison, Elizabeth was still firmly behind the Liberty Party's efforts. Writing to Elizabeth Pease early in the year, Stanton explained that the third party was "the most efficient way of calling forth & directing action," and adding, "Many of the Garrison party are in favour of political action, but not of the third party. [Liberty] gives a reality to antislavery principles which 'no voting' and scatteration cannot boast."[30] By early 1842, it was clear that the disputes between the Garrisonians and the political abolitionists had already profoundly influenced Elizabeth's own understanding of the importance of political participation and reform. Explaining her own position on the political question, Elizabeth wrote:

> So long as we are to be governed by human laws, I should be unwilling to have the making & administering of those laws left entirely to the selfish & unprincipled part of the community, which would be the case should all our honest men, refuse to mingle in political affairs.[31]

Although Elizabeth Cady Stanton respected and sympathized with Garrison and his followers with respect to women's rights, from the beginning of her exposure to the inner sanctum of reform, she recognized and appreciated the importance of participation within the political process, by use of the vote, to effect change.

Elizabeth and baby Neil divided their time between Boston, Johnstown, and Albany throughout much of 1842 and 1843. In addition to the family home in Johnstown, Daniel Cady also owned a townhome at 15 Montgomery Street in Albany, not too far from his offices and close to the State Capitol and court buildings.[32] The many separations the Stantons endured during the first two years of their marriage were more difficult for Henry than Elizabeth. While living in Johnstown and later in Albany, Elizabeth was surrounded by her family and free from most domestic duties. Her father had a large household staff, giving Elizabeth enough free time to learn to enjoy more traditional female pursuits such as knitting and tending to her young son.[33] However, despite his full days and exhausting schedule, Henry longed to be with his wife and son, "I am lonesome, cheerless, & homeless without you," he wrote to Elizabeth while they were apart.[34]

Elizabeth's two eldest sisters had each married men who were former law students of their father. Tryphena, nine years older than Elizabeth, was married in 1826 to Edward Bayard, a classmate of Eleazar Cady at Union College. Bayard was a much beloved member of the family, and the marriage brought happiness to a household that was so devastated by Eleazar's death that summer. Harriet Cady, five years Elizabeth's senior, married her first cousin Daniel Cady Eaton on December 27, 1830 in Johnstown, and Elizabeth's childhood mentor Rev. Simon Hosack conducted the ceremony.

By 1842, Elizabeth's two younger sisters followed the family tradition by selecting a husband from among their father's law students. The youngest Cady daughter, Catherine, married Samuel Wilkeson, originally from Buffalo and a graduate of Union College, on June 14, 1841. Margaret, the last Cady daughter to marry, wed Duncan McMartin in September 1842.[35] Of the five Cady daughters, Elizabeth was the only one to marry below her economic class and from outside of the narrowly approved group of young men Daniel Cady believed were suitable husbands for his daughters.

During the winter 1842-1843, Daniel Cady was in Albany to help his two newest sons-in-law set up their legal practices.[36] Wilkeson partnered with Samuel Van Vechten, the son of one of Daniel Cady's former associates, at the Cady law office on State Street. McMartin also likely worked for Van Vechten and Wilkeson, but he only stayed in Albany for a year before returning to Johnstown. Within a few years, McMartin once again resumed his practice in Albany, but by that time, Wilkeson had given up the law to establish a newspaper in Buffalo, the Buffalo *Democracy*.[37]

Elizabeth claimed in her letters that her family warmed up to Henry once the couple returned from Europe. While Henry initially began studying law under Daniel Cady, for reasons that are not known, he chose to finish his studies in Boston. The weight of Daniel Cady's considerable influence in Albany and Johnstown would have insured the financial success and prestige of any young lawyer under his wing. However, Henry wanted something more. The move to Boston also suggests that while Daniel Cady might have been friendlier to Henry than he was prior to the marriage, the rift between the two men was far from healed. In addition to his paid legal work, Henry intended to use his legal skills toward reform efforts, and his father-in-law also continued to frown on Henry's abolition work. Politically, Cady was a Whig, and increasingly throughout the 1840s, as an organization, the Whig Party became the nemesis of the Liberty Party. While it would have been far easier and more financially rewarding for Henry to follow in the footsteps of Bayard, Eaton, Wilkeson, and McMartin, he was not willing to give up his own life's work in payment for financial success.

Although Henry broke away from the fold of the Cady family shortly after marrying Elizabeth, he didn't stop trying to prove himself to Daniel Cady or stop trying to earn Cady's respect. When Henry was elected to the New York State Senate in 1849, Cady was displeased. In addition to Cady's opposition to abolitionism, it is also likely that Cady blamed Henry for Elizabeth's controversial and public reform work, especially after the Seneca Falls Convention. As late as 1855, when Cady retired from the New York Supreme Court, Henry wrote an extended tribute about his father-in-law's legal career for the newspapers. Although by that time Samuel Wilkeson was a newspaperman by trade, Henry's praise of Cady's accomplishments was widely reprinted. Despite Henry's best efforts to earn the respect of his father-in-law, when Cady died in 1859, Duncan McMartin was named as the estate's attorney, serving as co-executor of Cady's estate. Cady's choice of McMartin is also illustrative of his lack of respect for Henry's legal talents. By the time of Cady's death, Edward Bayard was no longer a practicing attorney, Daniel Cady Eaton was dead, thus making Henry the family's senior lawyer in 1859. However, a month before his death, Cady passed over his third daughter's husband, selecting McMartin instead. Although McMartin was living in Johnstown in 1859, co-executrix, Tryphena Bayard, was not. In the absence of any positive or complimentary letters from Cady to Henry Stanton, Cady's selection of McMartin would seem to have involved more than logistics.[38]

In addition to the emotional weight of Henry and Elizabeth's separations during the winter and spring of 1842-1843, they also faced financial difficulties and illnesses. During the winter months, baby Neil was very sick, requiring extensive treatments from a physician. In mid-March, Henry fell down a long flight of stairs in Boston, breaking his wrist in five or six places and confining him to bed for four weeks. In Rochester, George Avery endorsed notes from debtors who defaulted, necessitating Henry's help in covering more than $300 worth of bad debts.[39]

According to Henry, the couple was facing a difficult financial stretch of two or three years until his legal practice was profitable. "My wife," he wrote to a friend, "feels very bad, and is sometimes quite gloomy with the apprehension that we shall not get through the coming year." However, Henry's "organ of hope" was larger than hers, and by collecting debts owed to him and hard work, he believed he could carry himself and his family through the time "without feeling the pinching of want." Although Daniel Cady was financially able to help, he did not "give his sons-in-law a dollar...except to keep them from starving, thinking it better (and wisely) to aid them indirectly by throwing business in their way." In fairness to Cady, he was also very generous in providing the Stantons with a roof over their heads, both in Boston and later in Seneca Falls. Happily, prosperity came sooner than Henry had earlier hoped, and by the summer of 1845, Henry's law practice was doing well enough to support both his family in Boston and his mother in Rochester.[40]

Once Henry's law practice was firmly established, Elizabeth and Neil joined him in Boston on a more permanent basis. Initially the Stantons rented rooms from a distant Livingston cousin in Chelsea. But shortly after the birth of the couple's second son, Henry, in March 1844, Daniel Cady gave his daughter and her husband a house nearby, and the Stantons set up housekeeping in their own home in Chelsea that June.[41]

For her part, Elizabeth was very taken with Boston, writing to a friend, "I am enjoying myself more than I ever did in any city." However, it wasn't the parties and social gatherings that prompted Elizabeth to consider the city her own "moral museum," but rather, she greatly enjoyed the wide array of reform meetings and lectures that were ubiquitous in Boston during this era.[42]

Decades later, Elizabeth wrote in her autobiography that she spent a great deal of time during these years at the home of William Lloyd Garrison; however, she is not mentioned in any of Garrison's extensive collected letters from 1841 to 1849. Although she probably attended a wide variety of lectures, including lectures by Garrison, and she met reformers from many different circles during her time in Boston, Elizabeth's own participation during the Boston years was that of a spectator and not a reformer.

Henry Stanton and the other Liberty supporters in Massachusetts saw their ranks grow considerably during the early 1840s. When the party was formed in 1840, Liberty voters in the state numbered close to 1,100. Only four years later, the Liberty gubernatorial vote was close to 10,000. In 1840, they captured only 0.8% of the total votes cast, but by 1844, that number had risen to 7.2%.[43] Because of Henry's successful efforts in Massachusetts for the Liberty Party, in 1843 he was elected chairman of the state central committee. As part of his work, Henry restructured the party's operations from the precinct level to the top of the organizational committee in order to insure a successful campaign during the presidential election cycle the following year.[44]

On the national level, however, things were not so harmonious within the Liberty Party. Many Liberty members wanted to nominate Founding Father John Jay's son, Judge William Jay, as their next presidential nominee. Jay's support in Ohio and New England was strong, but many feared that Jay's commitment to Liberty principles was tenuous. Henry supported Jay's candidacy, provided that Jay could assure the convention of his convictions to Liberty's "principle & feeling." James G. Birney also hoped to once again secure the presidential nomination, but not at the expense of party unity. Although Stanton considered himself "a Birney man," he was anxious to maintain harmony at the convention and throughout the election cycle. Liberty Party leaders hoped that their recent successes at the state and local levels throughout the North would translate into greater support on the national stage the following November.[45]

When the party met, Birney successfully received his second presidential nomination, but the selection of his running mate, Thomas Morris, suggests both a maturing of the party and the beginning of the party's relaxing of principle in the hope of securing greater political successes. Morris, a former senator from Ohio, was a committed abolitionist, but he did not support black male suffrage, and this was the point of contention among the Liberty ranks. When his name came up for nomination at the convention, however, Morris' views on the issue were largely ignored in favor of his national reputation and the hope that he would add voters to the Liberty ranks.

Henry Stanton, together with Salmon P. Chase of Ohio and Alvan Stewart of New York, wrote the Liberty Party's platform. The final document included a call for Liberty supporters to champion the removal of all inequalities of rights on the basis of race, but the document stopped short of advocating universal black male suffrage.[46] Political pragmatism was now an acknowledged reality of the Liberty Party.

In the election of 1844, and despite the encouraging results of the Massachusetts Liberty Party's campaign efforts, the Whigs were victorious in the Old Bay State. Stanton expected party support to increase by 50% in the closing months, and while they fell short of that number, Liberty votes showed a respectable increase of 25%.[47]

Rather than attributing the success of the Whig candidates to the efforts of the Whig organization, Stanton claimed that their victory was aided by Garrison's efforts that played "desperately into the hands" of the Whig Party. By campaigning against Liberty, as the Garrisonian speakers had done for the previous three years, Stanton believed that many abolitionists had shifted away from antislavery politics and cast their votes with the Whigs.[48] In the closing weeks of the election cycle, Stanton gave lectures nearly every evening, and he often added daytime speeches to his schedule to try to counter the damage done to the Liberty Party by the Garrisonians.

As a show of support by local Liberty leaders and voters, and despite his "positively declin[ing] to accept," Henry was nominated for congress in the Essex South district, and he received close to 1,500 votes.[49] Although Henry had enjoyed more cordial relations with his father-in-law following the couple's return from Europe, Daniel Cady had not changed his mind about abolition by the mid-1840s. In a letter to Gerrit Smith, Henry wrote that Cady was most likely "greatly distressed" at the possibility of Henry's congressional run, and he asked Smith to reassure Cady that he had not sought the nomination.[50]

As an attorney, Henry Stanton's cases often dealt with causes overlapping his efforts as a reformer. One such landmark case, *William Wilbar v. B. D. Williams and others* for an action of libel, involved the legal right of a temperance newspaper, the *Dew Drop,* to publicly condemn a local saloonkeeper. Henry's arguments in defense of the writers and publisher of the *Dew Drop* were extensively reprinted by temperance groups because of the power of his arguments for free speech and against the "man-killing business" of rum selling. Reporters noted that Stanton "repeatedly drew tears from many persons in the Court House" as he related the "terrible effects" of alcohol upon the population.[51]

During one of Henry's temperance lectures, he was faced with an unusual situation. He was speaking on a platform covered by a thick oilcloth. The cloth was so sturdy that instead of bending over the edge of the stage, it protruded on its own by a few inches. "In the midst of one of his most eloquent passages," Elizabeth wrote, "he was comparing the inebriate's downward course to the Falls of Niagara, and the struggle with drink to the hopeless efforts of a man in the rapids. Just as he reached, in his description, the fatal plunge over the precipice, he advanced to the edge of the platform, the oilcloth gave way under his feet, and in an instant he went down headlong into the audience, carrying with him desk, glass, pitcher and water." Henry quickly recovered and got back on the stage, and according to

Elizabeth, "he immediately remarked with great coolness: 'I carried my illustration further than I had intended to. Yet even so it is that the drunkard falls, glass in hand, carrying destruction with him. But not so readily does he rise again from the terrible depths into which he has precipitated himself.' The whole house cheered again and again," Elizabeth reported.[52]

Henry also defended a doctor charged with "unlawful intimacy" with "a pretty looking young woman named Mary Olive Drew." The *Boston Daily Post* reported that the woman's father, Cricket Smith, a local procurer of prostitutes who had caused the "ruin and fall of this intelligent looking girl," was behind the charges. The doctor, G. E. Morrill of the local Thomsonian Infirmary, prescribed animal magnetism to the young woman, a subject that Elizabeth had studied only a few years before, and the doctor's treatment "led to the intimacy charged." The disposition of the case is unknown.[53]

The Stantons welcomed the birth of their third son on September 18, 1845. The exuberant father wrote to Gerrit Smith later that evening, proudly exclaiming that the baby was "fat, stout & weighing about 9 pounds!" In addition to announcing the baby's birth and to let Smith know that Elizabeth "had less pain" and "was now comfortable," the brief letter also advised Smith that Elizabeth decided to name the baby after her illustrious cousin.[54] Within a few months, Henry reported to Smith that the baby's weight had already doubled, and the proud father jokingly wrote that if Smith's namesake "will not make a great man, we shall change his name."[55]

Although the personal relationships between Garrisonian and political abolitionists had been strained and bloodied since 1839, an incident in Boston in 1846 stunned both groups and served as a reminder of the cause that drew them to the antislavery ranks fifteen years earlier. That September, a freedom-seeking slave was marched through the streets of Boston on his way back into bondage in Louisiana, and the incident once again reunited, albeit briefly, both camps of the abolition movement.

His name was not recorded, but the young man managed to stowaway with a small supply of food on board a ship headed to Boston, and he was discovered shortly after the ship dropped anchor in the port. The ship's owners, fearing both the antislavery crowds and the local laws prohibiting the return of fugitive slaves, tried to conceal the man on board while in port. The former slave managed to escape, but he was once again captured in front of onlookers in the streets of Boston. Before the citizens and the magistrates were able to act, the ship and the man disappeared, presumably bringing the man back into slavery in Louisiana.[56]

Within a few days, a meeting was called in Boston's Faneuil Hall. The first speaker was the venerable John Quincy Adams who gave a brief opening address. That evening, a "Committee of Vigilance" was formed to prevent any similar incidents from happening in the future, and the committee was funded by the collection of $1,000.[57] The Committee of Vigilance was made up of men from both sides of the abolition chasm, including Henry Stanton, Wendell Phillips, and Samuel May. Although the group seemed to disappear following their first meeting on September 30, 1846, the coming together of abolitionists from all parts of the spectrum was a hopeful sign of things to come in the movement, and it showed that perhaps the scars of the early part of the decade were, at last, beginning to heal.[58]

𝒢𝒞 TEN 𝒟𝒮

PERFECTIONISM
AND PRAGMATISM

*"I have been tracing in the clearest language
I can command the line of argument that my learned
opponent will no doubt pursue, and I shall now
proceed to show how utterly futile and untenable it is."*[1]

T hroughout the 1840s, William Lloyd Garrison's influence
in the overall antislavery movement was in a steady decline.
Beginning in the immediate aftermath of the abolition split in
1840, the overall income of the then Garrisonian-controlled American
Antislavery Society dropped from over $47,000 per year to just
$7,000. Subscriptions to the *Liberator* and the Garrisonian *National
Anti-Slavery Standard* also saw similar drops in subscribers. In 1837,
there were close to 1,400 subscribers to the *Liberator*. Following the
abolition schism, the paper immediately lost 500 subscribers, while
close to 300 more were dropped from the subscription rolls in 1840
for non-payment. Figures for the *National Anti-Slavery Standard*, the
official publication of the post-schism AAS, also showed a similar
pattern of falling support between 1844 and 1846, with subscriptions
dropping from 3,500 to 1,400.[2] The precipitous drop in support of
Garrison and his anti-voting policies during the 1840s, demonstrates
that in the aftermath of the breakup of the AAS, he was no longer the
leader of the abolition movement, nor did his doctrines inform the
quest for women's political rights.

By the mid-1840s, many who still belonged to the AAS were
beginning to soften in their initial rejection of the Liberty Party in the
face of the extremism of Garrison's non-resistance. What had begun
with refusing to vote had led to a host of questionable ideas, including

secession. Although not a formal policy until the 1843 Massachusetts Antislavery Society's annual meeting, Garrisonian non-resistance had crossed a line for many of his former supporters. At that meeting, Garrison and Wendell Phillips championed a pair of resolutions calling for disunion. The first resolution stated quite plainly: "No abolitionist can consistently demand less than a dissolution of the union between Northern freedom and Southern slavery," however, the motion did not pass. The second resolution, "That the compact which exists between the North and the South…should be immediately annulled," was adopted two days later.[3]

Writing to Maria Chapman in 1845, Lucretia Mott exemplified this reconsideration as she explained her dislike of the actions of many of Garrison's agents. "I cannot join with the agents who have been among us in their condemnation of those of a different opinion," she wrote, "nor am I prepared to say that the Third Party is not an instrumentality in the Anti-Slavery cause."[4] The core of Garrison's coalition was beginning to collapse under the weight of his fanaticism.

One of the issues that both the Garrisonians and the Libertyites agreed upon was their longstanding opposition to the annexation of Texas. When the Lone Star State joined the United States in December 1845, many within and outside of the political system saw it as a defeat of antislavery principles and as a failure of their political agitation efforts. However, in many respects, the discourse engendered by the party's labors against annexation would prove beneficial to political abolitionists as they sought to reinvigorate politically-based reform before, during, and after the Mexican War.

As early as 1840, the Liberty Party charged that the federal government was subservient to the "Slave Power." When Henry Stanton wrote the call for the presidential nominating convention four years later, he developed this point still further by claiming that the "Slave Power" was "controlling every department of the government— monopolizing the chief offices of the nation—shaping our Federal legislation—controlling our judiciary…[and] prescribing the character of our foreign relations." Stanton was one of the first to articulate a philosophy that would become a rallying cry for many Northerners, and a political siren that brought many Northern moderates into the antislavery ranks in the coming years.[5]

Stanton's last point referred most specifically to Texas. Stanton charged that both the Democrats and the Whigs were complacent in the "habitual scoffing at the self-evident truths of the Declaration of Independence," and he called on those from both major parties who opposed the slave power "to concentrate their influence, through the Ballot Box" by voting with the Liberty Party.[6] Although the Liberty Party conceded that the annexation of Texas "would not add a slave or a foot of slave territory in the world," the discourse during the Texas debate gave the party the opportunity to appeal to a broader coalition. The Texas annexation debates awakened many Northern voters who were sympathetic to the idea that the preservation and extension of slavery was trumping the very foundations of government at home and foreign policy abroad. Stanton and many other Liberty Party supporters campaigned vigorously against the annexation of Texas.[7]

Despite the failure of the anti-Texas crusade, the debate nevertheless also revealed to Henry Stanton the very real possibility of a large-scale defection by antislavery Whigs to an antislavery political party. However, Stanton feared that unless the so-called "Conscience Whigs" formally broke with their national party, they would find themselves "borne along by the current to support a slaveholder or a slaveholder's tool for the presidency in 1848." Stanton devoted the next three years to making sure that the momentum he witnessed during the Texas annexation debates would not be lost in 1848.[8]

In late 1845, when hostilities with Mexico seemed certain, Stanton hoped that the bloodshed might lead to emancipation. "If anything could reconcile me to a war it would be the overthrow of our giant sin," Henry explained to Gerrit Smith, adding that he believed the British would be brought into the conflict, eventually occupying Southern territory when the fighting was over. The North, Henry wrote, would then "expel the invaders" if the South agreed to end slavery.[9] However, when the fighting finally began, Stanton blamed President Polk and his "Slave Power" administration for provoking the conflict "for the benefit of their darling institution."[10]

Some within the Whig Party, most especially a very vocal group of "Conscience Whigs" from Massachusetts, were equally against the "immoral war." Early in the hostilities, an editorial in the antiwar *New York Tribune* charged that only "Whig Courage…could rescue the country from the Loco-Foco [Democratic] mismanagement" of a war the country was unprepared to fight.[11]

As one of the architects of the Liberty Party's strategy, Stanton was both encouraged and worried by the Mexican War and the antiwar sentiment expressed by many within the Whig Party. On the one hand, many Whigs might leave their party because of the war, but Stanton also feared that the seriousness of the war could force former Whigs and current Liberty voters back to the major parties during wartime.[12] Despite the strong antiwar support expressed by many in Massachusetts, the Whigs failed to endorse an antiwar, antislavery resolution at their 1846 state convention. This disappointment convinced Stanton that the Whig Party would not be the political organization to lead the next round of antislavery reform.

The Whigs further frustrated Stanton by their failure to embrace the Wilmot Proviso. Introduced in 1846 by Pennsylvania Democrat David Wilmot, the resolution called for the exclusion of slavery from any territory acquired from Mexico, without touching slavery where it already existed. To Stanton, if the Whigs failed to take what he considered the small step of halting the spread of slavery further west, abolition had little hope within the party.[13]

In 1845, former Liberty presidential candidate, James G. Birney, suggested to Lewis Tappan that while antislavery would always be the foundation of the Liberty Party, the time had come to "apply the principles of the Liberty Party" to a broader platform. Birney cautioned, "A party that does not take the whole of it—but seeks a particular object—will soon, in the strife of the other parties, become a lost party."[14] In 1845, this idea was still premature; however, by 1847, many Libertyites, including most notably Gerrit Smith, were calling for an expanded, multi-issue Liberty Party platform.[15]

Calling themselves the Liberty League, this new group within the Liberty Party held a three-day long convention in Macedon, New York, in June 1847 to formulate their broader program. The Liberty League's adopted platform took the controversial position that the Constitution of the United States held that slavery was both "illegal and unconstitutional," and they offered the South a choice: abolish slavery or "peacefully, withdraw from the Union."[16]

To explain the expansion of the platform to include other reforms, Liberty Leaguers asserted that no one cause, even antislavery, should be deemed the "greatest...moral evil," and that no one cause should be pursued as though it were the nation's only problem.[17] The platform dismissed the "boasted potency" of a party of "one idea," and they explained the existence of civil government and the authority of such a government's powers as emanating from God. Before the meeting adjourned, they nominated Gerrit Smith as their presidential candidate, well in advance of the November 1848 contest.[18]

Despite his close friendship with Smith, Henry Stanton stood squarely against the group he called the "Macedonians," and many other political abolitionists joined with Stanton in his condemnation of the splinter group.[19] However, throughout much of 1847, the former Liberty Party coalition was fracturing in many different directions. In addition to Gerrit Smith, Liberty League supporters included William Goodell, Elizur Wright, and Frederick Douglass. Others, such as Joshua Leavitt, were against enlarging the Liberty platform and were thereby against the League, but Leavitt also could not conceive of an antislavery party that would be satisfied just to stop slavery's extension, without ending it where it already existed.[20]

A month after the Liberty League was formed, Henry Stanton wrote to New Hampshire Senator John P. Hale requesting a meeting to discuss Hale's potential candidacy for an 1848 presidential antislavery coalition ticket. Hale was not, nor had he ever been a member of the Liberty Party, but to Stanton, Whittier, and others, he seemed to embody the ideal traits to attract not only previous Liberty voters, but also those antislavery voters who were still casting their votes with the two major political parties.

A Democrat, Hale was an outspoken critic of both the annexation of Texas and the Mexican War, contrary to the wishes of his state Democratic Party. Despite his bucking the party platform, he was elected to serve in the United States Senate in 1847.[21] Stanton acknowledged in his first letter to Hale that the odds of a coalition party securing the presidency in 1848 were slim; however, Stanton nevertheless believed that Hale's first candidacy would set the stage for broad support and a successful run in 1852.[22]

Hale's "interview" for a potential Liberty Party candidacy took place on July 24, 1847, and in addition to Henry Stanton, those in attendance included Joshua Leavitt, John Greenleaf Whittier, Amos Tuck, and Lewis Tappan. The day-long meeting sufficiently satisfied the committee that Hale was "with the Liberty party in principles, measures & feeling."[23] Two days later, the group officially asked Hale for his permission to present his name as a candidate for president at the national Liberty convention in October.[24]

While Henry and the others were meeting with Hale, one of Gerrit Smith's supporters was marshaling support for Smith's nomination at the upcoming convention. When he heard the news, Stanton confided to Salmon Chase that he would vote against Smith if his name came up at the convention. Throughout the years that the Stantons lived in Boston, Smith and Henry were in nearly constant communication. However, during this time, no correspondence survives between the two men, indicating that the political feuds also took a toll on their friendship. Henry's uncle Henry Brewster, another close friend of Smith's, also felt that the "Macedonians" had weakened the Liberty Party's influence by splintering the group in two.[25]

By the summer of 1847, Henry Stanton was firmly convinced that the future of political reform was pragmatic rather than idealistic, and that success rested on reaching a compromise with antislavery members of the Whig and Democratic parties and bringing them into the fold.[26] Henry was so sure that Hale was the right man at the right time to unite these groups, that in the months prior to the convention, he decided to withhold support for any candidate other than Hale until after the two major parties put forth their nominees the following year.

The national Liberty convention began on October 20, 1847, in a large tent erected near the corner of Eagle and Ellicott Streets in Buffalo, New York. Previous Liberty conventions were essentially harmonious meetings with little dissent. However, from the convention's minutes, it is clear that this meeting had more in common with the contentious AAS meetings of the late 1830s than previous Liberty gatherings. The entire first day—close to six hours of sessions—were taken up by debates concerning parliamentary voting procedures. Historian Harry Rice explains that three distinct schools of thought were contending for supremacy at the convention: one was led by Stanton, Leavitt, and Lewis Tappan seeking the immediate nomination of Hale; another, led by Salmon Chase, were not against Hale's nomination, but wanted to forestall the nomination of any candidate until the following spring; and the third group was composed of Gerrit Smith and his supporters who were hoping to steer the national platform close to that of the Liberty League.[27]

The groups with the most in common, Stanton and Chase's coalitions, were able to defeat Smith's motions of expanding the Liberty Party platform, and they were thereby successful in keeping the party committed to a one-idea platform. The question then remained as to when to proceed with the nomination of candidates. Although Stanton wanted to wait until the following year, the events at the convention convinced him that the selection of candidates would help strengthen the resolve of the group to remain a one-issue party. Stanton, Leavitt, and Tappan decided to throw their support toward immediate nominations, and the membership agreed.

On the first informal ballot, Hale received just over 100 votes to Smith's 44. Hale was then unanimously nominated by acclamation, leaving the battered Liberty Leaguers to nominate Smith as the presidential candidate for yet another new party, the National Liberty Party.[28] Henry Stanton's coalition at the convention won the battle, and Stanton believed that in Hale, antislavery voters at long last had a leader with broad enough appeal to bring together a diverse alliance of support. To Stanton, Hale was a candidate who was radical enough to "plant the standard of Liberty at Washington."[29]

Henry attended the national Liberty convention in October 1847 as a delegate from New York, not from Massachusetts. By all surviving accounts, the Stantons enjoyed living at the center of reform in Boston, but as early as 1843, Henry began to question whether or not they should stay in the city.[30]

The Stanton family's move from cosmopolitan Boston to rural central New York is usually explained as being due to Henry's presumed political ambitions or because of some unspecified defeat that he suffered. The move to New York thus becomes a contributing source of Elizabeth's discontent in the months leading up to the Seneca Falls Convention, and thereby, the move serves as another example of her alleged oppressive home life. One biographer claimed, "After another unsuccessful electoral season, he [Henry] began to search for a more hospitable district." Another writer attributed the move to Henry's "failure to achieve the financial or political success he desired." As with Henry's "absences" at the birth of his children, these claims are also not sourced, and the records that do exist contradict these accounts. Still another author claimed that part of the reason for the move was because Henry's mother died of consumption, and the Stantons were afraid of catching the disease in Boston. However, this too was a mistake. Susanna Stanton lived, consumption free, in Rochester for six years after the Stantons moved to Seneca Falls.[31]

The historical record offers an entirely different set of circumstances surrounding the Stanton family's move to Seneca Falls. Shortly after arriving in Boston in 1842, Henry began suffering "severe" and "pertinacious coughs," a condition he attributed to the "east winds."[32]

In the spring of 1844, his condition continued to deteriorate and his physicians were concerned about Henry's chronic lung inflammation, and they suggested he relocate to a healthier climate. Among other physicians, Henry consulted with his brother-in-law and homeopath Edward Bayard, and Bayard too joined with the other physicians who suggested that Henry leave the eastern seaboard as soon as possible. After discussing the matter privately at home, Henry wrote to Gerrit Smith in 1844 seeking his advice about where the couple should move. Henry outlined the qualities he was looking for in a new location in his letter to Smith: a healthy climate, a city in which to establish a legal practice, and a place possessing "a fine atmosphere on the subject of abolition."[33]

Following his bouts of lung congestion in 1844, Henry found some symptom relief by restricting his public speaking efforts. However, given his commitment to antislavery political agitation, this was not a practical or a long-term solution. Although he had expressed a desire to relocate in central New York, Stanton's sights were set on the region's larger cities of Auburn, Syracuse, or Utica, and not the smaller village of Seneca Falls.[34] However, for reasons that were not recorded, on June 22, 1847, Daniel Cady transferred ownership of an investment property consisting of a house, outbuildings, and two acres of land to his daughter Elizabeth.[35] The move to Seneca Falls did not cure Henry's lung difficulties completely, and his daughter Harriot Stanton Blatch later wrote that her father "always had a delicate throat and chest. He was a chilly mortal, always feeling drafts, always putting on extra clothing."[36]

The Stantons' new home was unoccupied for several years before they arrived, and according to Elizabeth, the property "needed many repairs." Elizabeth and the children left Boston and traveled to Johnstown with their many trunks accompanied by Elizabeth's sister Harriet Eaton. Elizabeth stayed in Johnstown for "a few days rest," and although the date cannot be stated for certain, while in Johnstown, Elizabeth spent an evening with the Rev. David Eyster and his wife, Rebecca. Rev. Eyster was the longtime pastor of St. Paul's Lutheran Church in Johnstown. In 1855, the Eysters moved to Gettysburg, Pennsylvania, and they opened the Gettysburg Female Institute. The Eysters married in 1840, the same year as the Stantons.

The day after their dinner together, Elizabeth wrote to Rebecca Eyster with some additional thoughts concerning their conversation the previous evening. Much of the letter discussed Elizabeth's belief in the propriety and necessity of women, "particularly when public mention is made of her," being addressed by their first names and not taking their husband's full name. Stanton outlined the importance of one's own name, and she drew a moving parallel between the "nameless" slaves and women. "We are in truth slaves," Elizabeth explained, "You and I are not so socially because we have husbands who look upon us as equals. But we are civilly dead."[37]

Elizabeth continued by telling Rebecca that she "had talked this matter over with my husband and he says it would be quite *outré* for us to appear in the papers with either titles or men's names." Thus on the eve of the Seneca Falls Convention or shortly thereafter, Elizabeth felt that her marriage to Henry was not one of "tyrant" and "slave" but rather, Elizabeth's husband believed her to be his equal. Further, Henry also held the progressive view that it would be strange for women's rights activists to be addressed by the customary "Mrs." or without their own first names in the newspapers.

The sections of this letter explaining Elizabeth's comments about the significance of one's first name and comparing women to slaves have been quoted by nearly all of Elizabeth's biographers and in other histories of the Seneca Falls Convention. The letter is used to support the overall claim that Elizabeth's reformism in Seneca Falls was a reaction against her unhappy and oppressive home life. However, no author included Elizabeth's very straightforward statement, in the middle of this same letter, that she lived in an egalitarian marriage.[38] Some of these works also included Elizabeth's observations that women were "civilly dead," yet Stanton's previous sentence was omitted.

The omission of this important sentence concerning the nature of the Stantons' marriage does an obvious disservice to Henry, but even more to Elizabeth. Instead of a strong woman seeking to help others, Stanton is "a woman besieged," and while incorrectly depicting the marriage as the unhappy cause of her reformism, they thereby deny that Elizabeth possessed the intellectual capacity or empathy to conceive of the need for a women's rights movement outside of her own struggles.[39] The historical Elizabeth Cady Stanton, according to the prevailing narrative, had to be neglected and mistreated personally in order to understand the subjugation of women and to be moved to action. By the time Elizabeth Cady Stanton arrived in Seneca Falls, according to the prevailing narrative, the teapot was ready to boil. The previous historical narrative was unable to imagine Stanton's feminism arising from a position of strength, and it was unwilling to credit her egalitarian marriage as contributing to this awareness.

When Elizabeth reached her new home in Seneca Falls, she was armed with funds from her father to make the house more livable, and after "a minute survey of the premises," she began hiring a variety of contractors to ready her new home.[40] The renovations took a month, and during that time, the couple's children stayed with Elizabeth's parents in Johnstown.

Henry remained in Boston for a few months, but he was in residence in Seneca Falls by October 1847. In addition to tying up his legal cases, after eight years as the editor of the *Emancipator*, Joshua Leavitt resigned his position that August. In order to fill the pages of the paper until a replacement for Leavitt could be found, Henry, Samuel E. Sewall, and Joseph C. Lovejoy (brother of Owen) supplied the necessary content. During the interim, Henry served as the paper's Washington correspondent.[41]

Having spent much of her life in a town similar in size to Seneca Falls, Elizabeth hoped that Henry would "be [as] happy & contented" in their new village as she would surely be. Already accustomed to upstate New York winters, Elizabeth found the climate "very delightful," but she worried that Henry, who was dreading the change, would "long for the strong excitement of a city life," and she hoped that he would have soon have time for rest." Anyone spending a winter in central New York might question the "delightful climate," however, 1848 would bring little rest to either Henry or Elizabeth.[42]

On February 8, Henry Stanton was admitted as an attorney and counselor of the United States Supreme Court, and throughout the early months of 1848, he spent quite a bit of time arguing cases both in Washington and in Boston.[43] While he was in Washington, Henry met former President John Quincy Adams "by the fireplace in the rear of the Speaker's chair" in the House of Representatives on "the chilly morning of February 21." Stanton noted that when they shook hands, Adams "trembled with cold." When the day's session opened, Henry was seated at the reporter's desk, and the location offered him a direct view of Adams' chair at a distance of only 15-20 feet.

The morning's business included a special resolution by a representative from Tennessee extending thanks to several generals for their service in the Mexican War. The resolution required a suspension of House rules, and it was that motion that was taken up first. According to Stanton, when a voice vote was called, "the House was in perfect turmoil." Anxious to see the former president's response, Stanton kept Adams in his gaze. Moment's later, amid all the shouting and chaos on the floor, Henry noticed Adams' face become red, and his right hand move as if he were trying to grasp something. Soon Adams' grasp became "convulsive," and Henry saw him lean toward the left as if he would soon fall from his seat. Stanton realized amid the confusion and noise in the chamber that Adams' condition had not been noticed by others. He called out to a member of the House standing nearby to alert him to the ailing Adams. By that time, Adams "had sunk quite on the arm of his chair" before being discovered by several other members.[44] Old Man Eloquent died two days later in the speaker's office, and his funeral was held the following day.

Henry left Washington en route to Seneca Falls with a stopover in Johnstown, and when he returned to New York State, he arrived to find a Democratic Party rife with the possibility of significant defection to the Liberty Party.[45] By 1848, politics in New York State had already experienced a long history of bitter partisanship and a fluidity of alliances and defections.

Through the earlier efforts of Martin Van Buren and the Albany Regency, by 1830, the Democratic Party in New York State was "united, intrenched [*sic*] in power, and seemingly invincible." The party controlled nearly every state office, and their political opponents were effectively silenced.[46] By the end of the 1830s, and after bitter contests over tax revenues and canal construction, the majority party began unraveling.[47] Party unity also suffered from the financial crises brought about by the economic Panic of 1837. The shortfall in state revenues was also exacerbated by the huge debts incurred from the state-funded expansion of the Erie Canal.

During the administration of Whig Governor William Seward in the early 1840s, state debt again skyrocketed due to Seward's increased spending on infrastructure improvements and canal expansion. The state's high debt caused its credit rating to plummet and bond prices to drop sharply.[48]

The economic turmoil also had political ramifications, and beginning in 1843, New York Democrats who supported a measure to stop state spending and restore a direct tax became known as "Barnburners," while those opposed to the "Stop and Tax" law were known as "Hunkers." Although the name was originally intended to be a slight by the group's political enemies, the Barnburner name likely came from the story of a Dutch farmer who had burned down his barn in order to rid it of rats. As historian Herbert Donovan explains: "the implication being that the Barnburners were willing to destroy the public works and corporations to stop the abuses connected with them." The Hunker name likely derived from a pejorative depiction of the group as wanting to obtain a "hunk" of the spoils of office, but it was popularly attributed, especially in light of the group's politics in the 1850s, to being the group who wanted to "hunker down," thereby avoiding change.[49]

When the national Democratic Party met for their presidential nominating convention in Baltimore in April 1844, it was expected that they would re-nominate former president Martin Van Buren. However, Van Buren's public denunciation of the annexation of Texas caused him to lose support among Southern Democrats. At the convention, Van Buren's enemies successfully restored a procedural rule, originally adopted in 1832, requiring the support of two-thirds of the delegates to secure the nomination. Because Van Buren did not have the support of the Southern Democrats, obtaining a two-thirds majority was impossible. When the voting began, Van Buren received the most votes, followed by Lewis Cass of Michigan. With each succeeding ballot, Van Buren's support continued to dwindle in favor of Cass. When it was clear to Van Buren's supporters that he would not be able to garner enough votes, Van Buren withdrew his nomination in favor of James K. Polk of Tennessee.[50]

The New York Barnburners were Van Buren's largest base of support at the 1844 convention, and they returned to New York embittered and resentful. In 1847, still carrying the memory of the "treachery" of 1844, the Barnburners hoped to avenge the defeat of Van Buren by securing control of the state party. By 1848 the political landscape had changed as well. The annexation of Texas, the Wilmot Proviso, and the Mexican War exposed the sectional divides not only within the Democratic Party, but also within the nation as a whole.

Van Buren's record as president would hardly seem to attract support from antislavery voters. His critics charged that he had done nothing throughout his term to slow the power of the slave states, and further, that his actions during the trial of the Amistad Africans, coupled with his continuance of Andrew Jackson's policies toward

Native Americans, had seemingly permanently alienated him from the abolition ranks.

His presidential record notwithstanding, in 1847, Van Buren let it be known that he supported the Wilmot Proviso.[51] While some questioned Van Buren's change of heart, his supporters explained that the former president had "ample leisure time to reflect" on the issues, and that Van Buren was also alarmed by the growth of the "Slave Power." In November 1847, hoping to put an end to any suspicions that he was posturing for support, Van Buren penned an open letter to a newspaper claiming, "I am not a candidate for the Presidency, nor for any other position, nor do I intend to be."[52] However, the New York Barnburners had other plans.

Henry Stanton attended the New York State Democratic convention, held in Syracuse on September 29, 1847, and he witnessed the proceedings from the gallery. Even before the official opening, the convention was a contentious one, as each faction within the party attempted to manipulate the selection of delegates at the district and county levels. When the group finally assembled, the Barnburners attempted to insert a resolution supporting the Wilmot Proviso into the platform, but they were defeated 73 to 63. By the time the meeting adjourned, most of the Barnburners had already left in protest, effectively tearing the New York "Democracy" in two.[53] As a delegate from western New York explained, "If it was barnburnerism to stand up for the rights of free labor to the soil, he was a barnburner."[54] Although a minority even within the state organization, to Henry Stanton, the Barnburners seemed ready to engage in fusion politics.

Stanton's final confirmation came during the spring national party nominating conventions, and his political predictions proved to be correct. The Democrats, meeting again in Baltimore, denied the credentials of the New York Barnburners, and the convention eventually selected Lewis Cass as its nominee in 1848. Not to be outmaneuvered, the Barnburner delegation held a convention the following month in Utica and nominated Martin Van Buren. The selection of Van Buren was historic. It was the first instance of an ex-President being nominated for the office. The New York Barnburners also saw Van Buren's nomination as avenging their candidate's mistreatment in 1844.[55]

The Whigs were also in disarray, and both national political parties were finding it increasingly difficult to settle on a candidate who would be acceptable to both the Northern and Southern wings of the party. According to Henry Stanton, the Whig's choice of Zachary Taylor as their nominee "would disgust tens of thousands of Whigs in this state." Stanton and many others believed that the time had finally come for a fusion ticket.[56] In June, at the Free Territory convention in Ohio, Salmon Chase introduced a resolution calling for a convention of all those opposed to the extension of slavery, irrespective of party allegiance. The "Free Soil" coalition selected Buffalo, New York, for their convention set to begin on August 9, 1848.[57]

Quite understandably, Henry Stanton was encouraged and hopeful at the turn of events. By 1848, he had devoted the better part of fifteen years to fighting slavery, and although he dared not hope that the fusion party might win the 1848 contest, he believed that the political efforts of the abolitionists had finally begun to succeed among Northerners who had been agnostic about the issue only a few years before. The road had been full of twists, rancor, disappointments, and compromise, but by the summer of 1848, Henry Stanton had every reason to believe that the county was on its way to finally delivering on the promises of the Declaration of Independence. Although Stanton would have preferred the coalition to be in favor of immediate abolition, rather than only opposing the spread of slavery westward, Stanton was also a pragmatist. By 1848, experience had shown him that the Liberty Party was stalled, and the major parties were not open to such a drastic change. In an 1847 article in the *Emancipator*, Stanton explained that if the abolition of slavery throughout the nation was the final goal, the spread of slavery must first be stopped. "Confine it to its own limits," Stanton explained, "restrict it to its own means, and it soon must perish."[58]

ELEVEN

THE MIGHTY VOTE

> *"The vote, the vote, the mighty vote,*
> *Though once we used a humbler note,*
> *And prayed our servants be just,*
> *We tell them now, they must! they must!*
> *The tyrant's grapple, by our vote,*
> *We'll loosen them from our brother's throat,*
> *With Washington we here agree*
> *The vote's the weapon of the free."*[1]

However joyous the political news might have been in 1848, personally, many members of the Stanton family had a very difficult summer. In Rochester, Frances and George Avery lost their three-year-old daughter, Anna, to croup on June 12.[2] Throughout the 1840s, the Avery family suffered both business and personal losses. In 1843, George Avery endorsed notes for creditors who failed to pay their obligations, and in 1845, he sustained heavy losses to his store and lost his mill in two separate fires. Despite their personal trials, the couple continued in their reform efforts. In 1841, George Avery was the Rochester Liberty Party mayoral candidate, and two years later, he was the Liberty nominee for Rochester assessor, running as part of a full slate of city offices, including Fifth Ward constable candidate, the boat builder and master carpenter, Sears Shepard.

Throughout the decade, George Avery also served on the executive committee of the Canada Missions—a group formed in 1841 to financially support escaped slaves who successfully reached freedom in Canada, and the Avery home was also safe spot for freedom-seeking slaves on their way across the border.[3] Serving alongside Avery on the Canada Mission's board, was his uncle-in-law Henry Brewster.[4]

In late June, barely two weeks after the loss of their daughter, Frances and her youngest child, George, visited Henry and Elizabeth. Although this is the only documented visit by Frances to the Stantons in Seneca Falls, because the Avery and Stanton families shared not only kinship but also a commitment to reform, it is very unlikely that this was the only such visit. Well before 1848, railroad travel between the two places made the trip an easy one.

The Avery family arrived to celebrate Henry's birthday on June 27, and more than likely, Henry's mother, Susanna, also made the trip from Rochester. Little George Avery shared the same birthday as his uncle, making the day a double celebration. Sadly, the occasion took a tragic turn. On his first birthday, George Avery died at the Stanton home in Seneca Falls of the same ailment that killed his sister fifteen-days earlier.[5] His funeral was held the following day in Rochester.

On the political front, many that summer were referring to the new antislavery political movement as a distinct new entity, the Free Soil Party. Particularly before the August 9 convention in Buffalo, local groups had little consistency in the choice of names they selected to define their new groups. In an announcement of a meeting held on July 27 in Canandaigua, Frederick Douglass referred to the group as "A Meeting of the Opponents of Cass and Taylor."[6] In Rochester, free soilers organized themselves as a "Jeffersonian Free Soil League."[7] Still, whatever name an individual group selected, the message was the same, and throughout the summer months of 1848, Henry Stanton fanned the free soil fires whenever and wherever possible.

Close to home, Henry Stanton and neighbor Ansel Bascom called a meeting of the "Freemen" of Seneca Falls on June 15. Bascom, a former Whig, was a Seneca Falls lawyer and a delegate to the 1846 New York Constitution Convention. Bascom and his family lived at the southeast corner of Ovid and East Bayard Streets in Seneca Falls, just down the road from the Stanton home. Elizabeth first made Bascom's acquaintance when she was readying the Seneca Falls home for her family.

Although the reformers took their work very seriously, they also enjoyed themselves. One summer, Henry Stanton and Ansel Bascom had a watermelon growing contest. Henry won the wager, and he invited Bascom to dinner. The prized watermelon was saved for dessert, and when the "much-praised and long-cared-for melon" was brought to the table, "and the host, knife in hand, was about to cut it open," the melon collapsed and fell apart. The Stantons' cook had never seen a watermelon, and thinking that the rind was the edible part, she hollowed out the melon and served only the rind. Elizabeth wrote,

Above: Elizabeth Cady Stanton with sons Henry (left)
and Daniel (right), circa 1848.
Courtesy of Coline Jenkins/Elizabeth Cady Stanton Trust

Below: The Stanton home in 2010. The tree on the left is the only
remaining "witness" tree on the property. The buckeye tree, although
still standing, was severely damaged by a storm in 2012.
(*author's collection*)

"General surprise was followed by as general a laugh, and [Henry] turning to his guest, asked: 'Bascom, why am I at this moment like that melon? We are equally crusty.'"[8]

The Seneca Falls free soilers met in the Wesleyan Chapel on Fall Street, the site of many area reform meetings since it was built in 1843. At the meeting, Ansel Bascom was chosen as the 1848 Free Soil nominee for the 31st Congressional District (Seneca Falls) pitting Bascom against his friend and former legal associate, Whig candidate Gary Sackett. The meeting also selected a slate of delegates to attend the Free Soil Convention in Buffalo.

The Seneca Falls Wesleyan Methodist Church, known more commonly as the Wesleyan Chapel, was established by a small group of Liberty Party leaders in the village, and the chapel became the center of Liberty campaigning in Seneca Falls from its founding. The Wesleyan Chapel was built during the period when antislavery sentiment was increasingly dividing church congregations over whether or not to include reform as part of their ministries.[9]

Despite the community's long history of antislavery political agitation, a convention of a different sort would immortalize the Wesleyan Chapel and the Village of Seneca Falls in the summer of 1848. It was there, on July 19 and 20, 1848, that Elizabeth Cady Stanton and a small group of Quaker women organized the first women's rights convention in the United States.

Philadelphia reformers Lucretia and James Mott, spent the better part of the early summer of 1848 in New York State. Attending a very contentious meeting of the Friends, the Motts also visited inmates at the Auburn Prison, met with leaders on the Seneca Reservation, and they often stayed with Lucretia's sister Martha Wright, in nearby Auburn.[10]

Fellow Quaker Jane Hunt invited Mott and her sister to spend the afternoon of July 9 at her home in the town of Waterloo, a neighboring village of Seneca Falls. Also invited were the Hunt's neighbor Mary Ann McClintock and Mott's friend Elizabeth Cady Stanton. What was to be a simple afternoon gathering of friends soon became something much more. According to Stanton's autobiography, written nearly 50 years after the event:

> I poured out, that day, the torrent of my long-accumulating discontent, with such vehemence and

indignation that I stirred myself, as well as the rest of the party, to do and dare anything. My discontent, according to Emerson, must have been healthy, for it moved us all to prompt action, and we decided, then and there, to call a "Woman's Rights Convention."[11]

Although this meeting has been written about extensively, Stanton's account is the most concise and likely the most accurate in explaining what happened at Jane Hunt's gathering, because it is free of the embellishments and attachments added by most of the later chroniclers of the event.

According to both Stanton and Mott, they had discussed holding such a meeting years before, but this time, they moved quickly to take advantage of Mott's visit to the area. That afternoon, the women composed a meeting notice for the newspapers, and they decided to hold the convention only ten days later. The chosen site, the Wesleyan Chapel, was a logical one. As the center of local reform agitation, it was the one facility in the twin towns of Seneca Falls and Waterloo that was open to free discussion. The meeting call was first printed in the *Seneca County Courier* on Tuesday, July 11, but the *Ovid Bee* and Frederick Douglass' *North Star* also ran the notice on July 14.[12]

Contemporary accounts of the events between July 9 and the opening of the convention on the 19th are few. However, the fact remains that no one in attendance at the Hunt home that afternoon had ever organized a reform convention. Although Lucretia Mott was already a well-respected and well-known speaker within reform circles, she did not have organizational experience, and she was not from the area. Elizabeth Cady Stanton was the only woman in attendance with a close connection to a reformer who could help—her husband, Henry.

The similarities between the published notice of the Seneca Falls Women's Rights Convention and the Free Soil meeting held the month before, reflect more than the language of the times. The Free Soil meeting call was addressed to "The Freemen of Seneca Falls," while the minutes of the Women's Rights Convention noted that "The Women of Seneca County, N.Y." called the meeting. Although the Free Soil meeting notice also carried an extensive list of endorsers—close to 200 names—as with the women's rights convention, no organizers' names were listed. In addition, the message of both calls was the same: both meetings were seeking to depict the gathering as a part of the community at large, and not simply as an aggrieved group within the village. The calls were written in a similar format, both encouraging a broad coalition of attendees, and both were seeking to discuss, rather than to dictate, the topic at hand. Of course, both meetings were also held in the same venue.[13]

Between the initial meeting on Sunday, July 9 and Friday, July 14, Elizabeth Cady Stanton wrote the first draft what would become known as the Declaration of Sentiments for presentation and discussion at the meeting.[14] Stanton's first draft did not survive, so it is impossible to know for certain how closely it resembled the final document. The historical consensus, however, acknowledges that Henry helped Elizabeth compile the list of grievances that survived the editing process.[15] As was customary at reform conventions, a list of resolutions for debate and adoption was also prepared, again most likely originating, at least in draft form, at the Stanton household.

On Sunday, July 16, Elizabeth again traveled to Waterloo, this time to the McClintock's home, to review the two documents and to make any suggested "alterations and improvements."[16] According to Stanton, "one of the circle" that afternoon "took up the Declaration of 1776...and it was at once decided to adopt the historic document, with some slight changes such as substituting 'all men' for 'King George.'"[17] The Declaration of Sentiments, like the Declaration of Independence opened with a bold statement, but with one important difference: the Seneca Falls Declaration of Sentiments asserted that "all men and women were created equal."[18]

THE NINTH RESOLUTION

Resolved, That it is the duty of the women
of this country to secure to themselves
their sacred right to the elective franchise.[19]

While it is certain that the Seneca Falls Convention would have been a historically important event with or without the Ninth Resolution demanding women's suffrage, it is equally clear that had this resolution not been conceived of and fought for by Elizabeth Cady Stanton—both before and after the convention—the movement that began in

Seneca Falls would have been an entirely different movement, if a movement at all, and it would have taken a decidedly different path. That is not to say that the convention would have been inconsequential or that a demand for woman suffrage would not have occurred at a later date; however, what made the Seneca Falls Convention so significant, aside from it being the first in the nation, was the suffrage resolution. The importance of the suffrage resolution can also be seen through the hotly contested debates within the historiography of the women's rights movement that still continues today.

Beginning with the 1884 publication of a biographical chapter about Elizabeth in the compilation, *Our Famous Women*, author Laura Curtis Bullard was the first to write about how Elizabeth's resolution demanding woman suffrage was received at home.[20] Bullard wrote that Henry and Elizabeth worked together on the development of what became the Declaration of Sentiments. According to Bullard, everything was fine until Henry realized that Elizabeth was going to include a resolution demanding woman suffrage. At that point, so the story goes, Henry charged that Elizabeth was going to turn the whole proceedings into a "farce," and he promptly left town on trumped up antislavery business.

Nearly every biographer and historian, with no additional substantiation or evidence, has accepted Bullard's narrative of the days leading up to the convention. However, no author has ever explained where Henry allegedly went or why he may have had this reaction, if, in fact, he did.[21]

Biographer Alma Lutz persisted in repeating Bullard's story, even after the Stantons' daughter Harriot Stanton Blatch questioned its truthfulness. "I did not know my father opposed the IX Resolution," Blatch pointedly wrote, "Have you authority for the statement?"[22] Because the Seneca Falls Convention was so important in shaping Elizabeth's public career as a reformer, one could easily imagine that if Bullard and Lutz's claims were true, Henry's lack of support in 1848 would have been a point of anger and resentment between her parents throughout their long marriage. However, Harriot was unaware of any such problem, and she responded to Lutz with surprise at the accusations against her father.

The traditional account also holds that Henry was not alone in his hostile reaction to the resolution. Lucretia Mott, a co-organizer of the convention, was also against Elizabeth's proposing woman suffrage at the Seneca Falls Convention. Harriot Stanton Blatch contended that Mott "jumped on Mrs. Stanton's political demand, & tried to stamp out the one original idea, the demand for the vote."[23] According to Bullard, Susan B. Anthony—still nearly three years away from her second meeting with Elizabeth— thought the resolution "ridiculous."[24]

Alma Lutz carried Bullard's fabrication even further, while contradicting her own account. Lutz claimed that Elizabeth told no one about the resolution, and yet, somehow, Henry was against it:

> With Henry's help [Elizabeth] collected a list of eighteen legal grievances from the statute books to correspond with the eighteen listed by the signers of the original Declaration of Independence... She was planning a speech which would sum up all she had been thinking about women through the years. She drafted a resolution wholly her own. No one else had anything to do with it or knew anything about it. It was to come ninth on the list.[25]

The *History of Woman Suffrage* recounts a similar sentiment to the Bullard account, yet importantly, the "farce" concerning the call for women's suffrage was not in reference to Henry's reactions prior to the convention, but rather, it was mentioned as a part of the debates occurring during the second day of the convention. "Those who took part in the debate," the author explained, "feared a demand for the right to vote would defeat others they deemed more rational, and make the whole movement ridiculous."[26]

Unfortunately, we may never know for certain whether or not the suffrage resolution was debated within the Stanton household. Elizabeth's surviving correspondence during these pivotal ten days is silent, as is Henry's. However, when considering the whole of Henry Stanton's reform career, his documented positions on women's equality and enfranchisement, and his persistent advocacy of suffrage as being the primary tool of reform in the decade before the Seneca Falls Convention, it is possible to offer a substantive challenge to the prevailing narrative.

Henry Stanton's mother and sister were both active reformers long before he met Elizabeth. Further, unlike most men of his time, Henry was raised by a mother who publicly asserted her rights, both civilly and against the clergy. Since the early years of his involvement in the antislavery movement, Henry had worked alongside female abolitionists, and he helped them to establish antislavery societies throughout the North. Henry boldly and very publicly supported the Grimké sisters' right to speak before mixed audiences, and he married without the customary promise that his wife would "obey" him. Finally, beginning in 1839, Henry Stanton had unceasingly relied on the power of suffrage and of electoral politics to end slavery. In short, there is nothing in Henry Stanton's background that would suggest he might have been opposed to woman suffrage and much to support the position that he heartily endorsed the resolution.

The prevailing narrative also claims that Henry was away from home much of the time around the convention, and it would thereby not have been unusual for him to have abruptly left town upon learning about the suffrage resolution. However, the historical record in the weeks and months surrounding the women's rights convention tells an entirely different story.

During the months of June, July, and August 1848, Henry Stanton never ventured farther away from home than Buffalo, and that was only to attend the Free Soil Convention on August 9. Every speaking engagement or meeting that he attended during these months could be reached by a short train or coach ride, and they were certainly close enough to enable him to return home every evening. For example, on July 13, Henry addressed a Free Soil meeting in Warsaw, Wyoming County. The following day, July 14, he was in Varick, Seneca County. On the 15th, he was home in Seneca Falls. He was also home on July 17, the day after the Declaration of Sentiments was finalized. His next known speaking engagement was July 27 in Canandaigua, and he was home on July 31.[27] The early weeks of August reveal a similar schedule: Henry spoke in nearby Penn Yan on August 1, Seneca Falls on the 3rd, and Auburn on the 5th. Henry was in Buffalo on August 9th for the Free Soil Convention, but he was back in Seneca Falls before the 18th.[28] Further, there is nothing in the historical record to suggest he was not at home on any of the days he was not mentioned in the press.

In addition to his known attendance at meetings, throughout July and early August, Henry was also working behind the scenes with the various groups attending the Buffalo convention, necessitating not only his continued attention, but also his availability to receive and reply to correspondence in a timely manner. For example, on July 15,

Henry wrote to Charles Sumner asking him to stop in Seneca County for a Free Soil rally on his way to Buffalo. Henry concluded his request, asking Sumner for "an immediate reply."[29] As this last-minute meeting would hinge on Sumner's participation, it seems unlikely that Henry would leave town before receiving a reply. In another letter, written on July 17 from Seneca Falls, Henry stated that he was receiving "from six to a dozen letters daily" from those inquiring about the Buffalo convention.[30] In short, it is illogical to presume that Henry Stanton would have put aside a project of this magnitude to leave town, "thunderstruck" or otherwise.

The language used by Elizabeth Cady Stanton in crafting both the Ninth Resolution and the related passages in the Declaration of Sentiments also offer an intriguing window into Elizabeth's thoughts about her own marriage in the years surrounding the Seneca Falls Convention. The Declaration of Sentiments charges: He has made her if married, in the eye of the law, civilly dead." In her letter to Rebecca Eyster, likely written the previous year, Elizabeth used very similar language: "We are in truth slaves. You and I are not so socially because we have husbands who look upon us as equals. But we are civilly dead."[31] Similarly, the Ninth Resolution's emphasis on the word "duty," harkens back to Henry's fights in 1838 and 1839 over the "duty" of abolitionists to go to the polls.

In Elizabeth's first speech regarding the issue of suffrage, delivered only two months after the Seneca Falls Convention, she rhetorically asked her audience, "Might not 'woman's rights' come to be as great as question as 'free soil?'" Clearly the Stantons both understood the necessity of voting as a means to change the world around them, and the experiences of each, served to reinforce the ideas of the other.[32]

While it seems certain that Henry Stanton did not oppose the suffrage resolution, the question remains as to whether or not he attended the Seneca Falls Convention. The names of most of those in attendance, perhaps as many as 300 over the course of the two-day convention, were not recorded, and the original document is lost. Only 100 signatures were included in the convention's surviving printed report. Henry's lecture partner that summer, Ansel Bascom, attended the convention, but he did not sign the declaration. Bascom, however, participated in the debate, and he was therefore mentioned in the minutes. Without his comments during the convention, Bascom's attendance would have gone otherwise unrecorded.

However, there is also nothing to suggest that if Henry did not attend the convention, that his absence was indicative of a lack of support of Elizabeth or her leadership in the new movement. Perhaps, as with Ansel Bascom, Henry attended the convention and supported women's rights, but he did not sign the Declaration of Sentiments. Because of the delicate political coalition the two men were building that summer, it is possible that by not signing the declaration, Henry and Bascom were both trying to avoid being publicly associated with a controversial issue in the weeks before the Free Soil Convention.

It is also not known if Henry's sister and mother attended either the Seneca Falls or Rochester conventions. The minutes of the Rochester Women's Rights Convention, held two weeks after the Seneca Falls Convention, mention only a handful of attendees by name. Over 100 women signed the declaration in Rochester, but the signatures from the meeting are lost.[33] Frances Avery and Susanna Stanton worked alongside many of the women who served on committees at the Rochester convention, and given their own reform work and interests, it seems probable that they would have attended at least the Rochester convention.

To fully understand the events of 1848, it is also important to recognize Elizabeth Cady Stanton's growth as a reformer within her own time. While it's easy to imagine, especially based on the prevailing historical narrative, that Elizabeth was a seasoned reformer in 1848, it would not be a correct depiction. In 1848, Elizabeth was learning how to be an advocate on her own, and she did not yet have the confidence in her own abilities that she would exhibit even a few years later. For example, at the Rochester convention, Elizabeth "thought it a most hazardous experiment to have a woman President" during the proceedings, but only six weeks later, she realized that she had made a mistake. "My only excuse," she wrote Amy Post, "is that woman has been so little accustomed to act in a public capacity that she does not always know what is due to those around her."[34] Henry's encouragement and support of her efforts during this time were especially important as Elizabeth learned to navigate her own way as the leader of a reform movement.

If one removes the completely unsubstantiated accusations against Henry Stanton in the generally accepted narrative, it is even possible to imagine that if he did not attend the convention, Henry arranged his schedule to be home during the convention to allow Elizabeth the freedom to attend the meetings without worrying about their three rambunctious young sons. In any event, rather than suggesting that Henry was not in favor of Elizabeth's suffrage resolution, the events of July and August 1848 reinforce the couple's shared appreciation of the power of the vote and serve to illustrate the foundational influence of Henry's years of political agitation on Elizabeth's development as a reformer.

THE BUFFALO CONVENTION

> *"In politics a man to be of any practical use to his country or the world, must work with the multitudes."*
> Frederick Douglass[35]

Although the Barnburners, "Conscience" (antislavery) Whigs and Liberty Party members seemed to be in agreement that the "Slave Power" must be checked, how this coming together would work on a practical level was far from settled when the delegates arrived in Buffalo. Prior to the Buffalo convention, Henry Stanton considered himself a Liberty man, and he supported the candidacy of John P. Hale in the 1848 contest. However, after the Barnburner convention nominated Martin Van Buren, Stanton became increasingly concerned that it would be difficult for the three groups to agree on a candidate.

Writing from Seneca Falls on July 17, Henry explained to Hale that Van Buren's nomination "will [be] pushed with zeal" by the Barnburners. Although the Whigs in New York State were defecting to the coalition party in large numbers, few believed that the former Whigs could be convinced to support Van Buren. Many Massachusetts Liberty men also expressed a growing concern that a true coalition would be impossible because they too could never accept Van Buren. Lewis Tappan and some of the more conservative New York Liberty men, distrusted both the Barnburners and the Conscience Whigs, and maintained that the Liberty Party had "nothing to gain by seeking an alliance with either" group.[36] While the time may have been right for a coalition party, it would not be an easy task.

The Barnburner candidate was not the only problem. At least a month before the opening of the Buffalo convention, newspapers began speculating whether or not John P. Hale would step aside and relinquish his Liberty Party nomination in order to allow for the selection of a fusion candidate at the convention.[37] Stanton also sensed that if Hale's candidacy was pressed at the convention, the entire coalition might fall apart. On July 17, Stanton asked Hale whether or not he would be willing to step aside to preserve unity at the Buffalo convention.[38] Hale agreed with Stanton and many others that unity was more important than maintaining his candidacy as the Liberty nominee, and Hale suggested that a committee consisting of Stanton, John Greenleaf Whittier, Amos Tuck, Samuel Lewis, and Joshua Leavitt be authorized to "decide upon his duty as to withdrawing" at the Buffalo convention.[39]

Ten days before the Buffalo convention, and because of his close contact with those in all camps of the coalition, Henry decided what his own priorities would be at the meeting. Writing to his old friend John Greenleaf Whittier, Henry very clearly explained why he planned to support Van Buren over Hale, if necessary, at the convention. Comparing the circumstances in the previous election with the current contest, Stanton explained that in 1844, "the question was territorial extension; now it is slavery extension. Then the candidate was a slaveholder; now he is not."

According to Stanton, the abolitionists of 1848 were in a different position than they were in the elections of 1840 and 1844. The 1848 contest offered the opportunity to join with those from all parties "rallying on independent ground" to challenge the "Slave Power." To Stanton, the question was entirely pragmatic: if the Liberty men were willing to give up some of their "*isms*" to settle the question of "peaceful abolition or bloody revolution" once and for all, the election of 1848 offered that chance. By voting for the nominee, whether Van Buren, Hale, or another, Stanton asserted, "I do not give up any principle I ever held; and do not feel any danger of being lost hereafter."[40]

Henry's position mirrored that of the Liberty candidate, John P. Hale. Already sensing the potential for problems in Buffalo within the Liberty Party base, Hale cautioned Lewis Tappan a month before the convention, "Does not the present aspect of things present the question of duty in a somewhat different light from that in which it was to be viewed?" "Is it not better for us to enter into and endeavor to influence and guide [the choice of the convention] than to stand aloof and oppose," Hale asked.[41]

When the Free Soil Convention opened on August 9, it was estimated that 20,000 men and women were in attendance under a large tent erected in Lafayette Park in Buffalo's downtown.[42] Much of the important work, however, was conducted in closed-door sessions held in a small church nearby. It was in these small meetings that party leaders wrangled over the platform, the selection of nominees, and where they settled many of the other issues before presenting them to the mass of attendees inside the tent. The group that met behind closed-doors consisted of an equal number of Whigs, Democrats, and Liberty Party members, and the atmosphere inside was one of "enthusiasm and excitement."[43]

Henry Stanton was called to the podium by acclamation during the first morning session, and his remarks were focused on uniting the disparate groups against the "Slave Power." Early that day, the Liberty men caucused in a closed session, and they agreed to submit Hale's resignation—provided that the platform was agreeable to Liberty principles.[44] The stage was set for a harmonious selection of candidates.

The platform of the new party was settled first. Although not as strong as previous Liberty Party platforms concerning the abolition of slavery where it already existed, antislavery was at the document's core. Those in attendance at the private meetings, particularly the Whigs and Democrats, felt that they had compromised sufficiently on the platform, and they were unwilling to accept Hale for either the presidential or vice presidential slots. While unity still prevailed in the private meetings, the Whigs and Democrats believed that allowing Liberty principles to dominate the party platform was a sufficient compromise.[45]

At the conference committee's meeting, the wheels were set in motion for Van Buren's nomination. Salmon P. Chase officially withdrew the candidacy of Ohio Whig John McLean, leaving only Hale and Van Buren left in the running. Benjamin Butler, a prominent New York Barnburner, followed Chase's motion with a speech in support of Van Buren, including a promise that if elected, Van Buren would support a bill outlawing slavery in the nation's capital. This promise soothed a major objection to Van Buren's candidacy by the Liberty men, and it allowed Stanton to present the letter given to him by Hale the previous month offering to step aside in favor of the convention's wishes. An informal ballot followed, and although many Liberty men continued to back Hale, it was clear that the New

York Barnburners' support would carry the day for Van Buren. Henry Stanton voted for Van Buren on the informal ballot believing that "no one doubted he would be the nominee," and he added, "I thought it wise that he should have a fair majority on the first trial."[46] It was then decided by the Liberty men on the committee to send Joshua Leavitt to the convention's podium to officially propose the motion advancing Van Buren as the nominee.

Leavitt's address traced the history of the Liberty Party, moving many to tears and shouts of joy. Leavitt ended his speech with his own belief that "The Liberty Party is not dead but translated…we have gained everything [by this movement], lost nothing." He then moved that Martin Van Buren be unanimously nominated. The motion carried, and Whig Charles Francis Adams was selected as the vice presidential candidate.[47]

Although the majority of Liberty men, with the exception of the remaining Liberty Leaguers, supported Van Buren in the election, not all of them were happy with the turn of events in Buffalo. Most notably, Lewis Tappan felt betrayed by both Leavitt's speech and Stanton's withdrawal of Hale's candidacy. On September 25, 1848, Tappan wrote a scathing letter to his old friend Henry Stanton, calling Henry's conduct at the meeting both dishonest and "injurious" to his reputation. No correspondence after this date between the two old friends and co-agitators survives.[48]

Despite the vigorous campaigning by Stanton and others, the free soilers were unable to deliver New York State's electoral votes for Van Buren. There was also disappointment on the national level, as the Free Soil Party did not win any electoral votes. Although they fell short of their goals, the new party received close to 15% of the total votes cast in the free states. However, the campaign of 1848 brought the issue of antislavery to a wider audience than ever before, and it exposed serious rifts within the sectional interests of the two major political parties.[49] The fight was far from over.

EPILOGUE

A TRUE CONJUGAL UNION

"My philosophy is to live one day at a time;
neither to waste my forces in apprehension
of evils to come, nor regrets for
the blunders of the past." [1]

The struggles of 1848 caused Henry Stanton to question the effectiveness of third party politics, and he employed an entirely different strategy going forward. Believing that the so-called "Free Democracy" (Barnburners) of New York State offered the best chance to swing one of the major parties toward an antislavery position, beginning in 1849, Henry allied with that party.

The new year began tragically for the Stantons. In February 1849, Elizabeth suffered a miscarriage, five months into her fourth pregnancy. The loss of the baby was "a great disappointment" compounded by the fact that the child she lost would have been the couple's first daughter. Even the family's cook was devastated by the loss, spending two hours crying in the kitchen. [2]

With the election behind him and Elizabeth visiting in Johnstown, Henry turned his attention to his legal practice. Seeking to expand his business opportunities beyond the confines of Seneca County, Henry approached Auburn attorney David Wright, and he proposed that the two men enter into a formal partnership. Wright was agreeable to the idea, and Henry then began the process of admission to the courts of Cayuga County.

Later that year, the Barnburner Democrats drafted Henry as their candidate for state senate, and this time, he accepted the nomination. On November 6, 1849, Henry Stanton was elected to the New York

State Senate from the 25th District, which included Seneca and Yates counties.[3]

A little over a month after the beginning of the second session of his term, on February 9, 1851, the couple's fourth son, Theodore, was born with a dislocated collarbone.[4] Although the baby's shoulder would heal quickly from Elizabeth's own doctoring, the other Stanton children were shaken by the ordeal, and they were concerned about the impact of the growing number of children on the small salary their father received. "Gat [Gerrit] asked me what Father would do if he had six boys," Elizabeth wrote to Henry, "They seemed quite relieved when I told them I thought you could feed and clothe little Theodore."[5]

During his senate term, Henry Stanton was not only a supporter of the women's rights efforts of his wife, but also an agitator in his own right. On February 14, 1851, Henry introduced two petitions in the senate calling for the enfranchisement of women, one from Seneca Falls and the other from the neighboring town of Waterloo.[6] Writing to Elizabeth the next day, Henry described the derision these petitions provoked in the senate, telling her that when presented, "two Senators tried to throw ridicule upon them."[7] According to Henry's letter, one of the displeased senators suggested that the petitions should be referred to the Committee on Federal Relations, while the other, wanted to assign them to an *ad hoc* select committee comprised only of Senator Stanton. However, such an arrangement was not acceptable to Henry who "pounced upon them and they backed out."[8]

The woman suffrage petitions were ultimately referred to the Committee of the Judiciary, where despite Henry's efforts, they languished, and they did not make it out of committee during the senate term. Sadly, such petitions are no longer existent. A fire in 1911 at the state capitol building in Albany destroyed nearly all archival state government documents.[9]

Although we cannot know for certain without the original documents, the suffrage petitions that Henry introduced might have originated with Elizabeth, but were circulated by other men or women in his constituency. Elizabeth sent a woman suffrage petition to Martha Wright two months earlier, asking Wright to "take charge" of the Auburn district and to collect signatures. Elizabeth explained to Martha that "the whole western part" of the state was assigned to her, but that she was incapacitated by one of her "biennial attacks." At the time, Elizabeth was in the final months of her fifth pregnancy, and she gave birth only a few days before Henry introduced the petitions in the senate. Henry's letter to Elizabeth describing the introduction of the petitions does not indicate that he introduced "her" petitions, but rather, "two petitions."[10]

Henry's willingness to advocate for woman suffrage on the floor of the senate, despite the certain ridicule of other members, illustrates Henry's support of woman suffrage beyond the confines of his own household. Even Martha Wright, one of the Seneca Falls Convention organizers, asked her sister Lucretia Mott for advice on how to avoid helping Elizabeth in the "benighted region" of Auburn where there were "not three women who would consider it safe to touch such a petition unfumigated." Henry was not only willing to introduce the petitions; he fought for them to be taken seriously.[11]

In contrast to Henry's support of woman suffrage, Martha Wright's husband, David, was staunchly opposed to the idea. In the 1840s, David Wright stood against the idea of married women owing property in their own names, arguing that "in nine cases out of ten when a man failed in business it was traced to a wife's extravagance." Wright believed that while a woman "shared in her husband's good fortune," she should also share his "reverses." As late as five years after the Seneca Falls Convention, David Wright refused to sign a woman suffrage petition, believing that only tax-paying women should be allowed to vote.[12]

Although the petitions Henry introduced did not result in a serious debate of the issue of women's suffrage in the New York State Senate, because of Henry's fight, when the only other similar petitions were presented a month later by Ashel Stone of New York's 20th District, Stone's petitions did not have to endure the hostilities that greeted Henry's proposals. Because of the precedent set by Henry, Stone's petitions were referred directly to the Judiciary Committee.[13]

Only two months later, Henry faced the biggest political crisis of his life. A bill proposed by the Whig majority in the senate forced dramatic action by Henry and the Barnburner Democrats. The measure, which had already passed in the Whig controlled assembly, called for the state of New York to spend upwards of eight million dollars for another expansion of the Erie Canal. On April 16, Henry introduced a motion to postpone the third and final reading of the canal bill, but his motion did not pass.[14] Because all appropriation bills required a three-fifths quorum for passage, on April 17, 1851, twelve elected members resigned their seats in the senate in order to prevent a quorum and stall the vote on the canal enlargement; among them was Henry Stanton.[15] New York's Whig Governor Washington Hunt called for special elections to fill the vacant seats almost immediately. The elections were set for May 27, and the governor called for a special session of the senate to begin on June 10.[16]

Henry sat for re-election in a hotly contested district. The local Whig paper, the *Seneca County Courier*, referred to Henry as a "runaway" and a "Jacobin," and the editor charged him with neglecting the interests of his constituents, while seeking "to obtain more notoriety and more pay."[17] To Henry, nothing could have been further from the truth. The Barnburner faction was formed in the early 1840s in response to the state's heavy debt load incurred by the Whigs' overenthusiastic expansion of the canal. Not only did the resignations have nothing to do with senatorial pay, the Barnburners were standing on principle, misguided or not. A local Democratic paper noted, "The utmost harmony and enthusiasm prevails among the Democracy of this district," and the Democrats staged anti-canal meetings throughout the districts on almost a daily basis. Henry was officially re-nominated by acclamation on May 8, giving him very little time to campaign.[18]

Henry's opponent, Josiah B. Williams, received help from an unexpected source—Elizabeth's first-cousin and Henry's old friend, Gerrit Smith. Daniel Cady was also against his son-in-law's re-election bid.[19] Smith supported the canal enlargement project, and he agreed to make several speeches in Henry's district for Williams. The announcements of Smith's speeches in the Whig papers did not fail to note the personal connection between Smith and Henry:

> It is significant of the importance of the approaching contest that such a man as Gerrit Smith should feel it incumbent on him as a citizen of the State, having a deep and abiding interest in the stability of our Government, to take the field in opposition to the re-election of Mr. Stanton, who is his intimate personal friend.—He is actuated by considerations far above those of a private or personal nature.[20]

Compounding Henry's embarrassment and sadness at Smith and Daniel Cady's lack of support, Elizabeth unknowingly made the situation worse. Elizabeth attended one of Smith's speeches, and she left the rally with her cousin. Although she was firmly behind her husband's re-election bid, Elizabeth underestimated the uproar that her attendance at Smith's speech would cause. The local newspapers claimed that Henry's "family and friends were against him, even his wife disapproving of his course."[21]

To make matters still worse for Henry, Elizabeth began accompanying Henry to his speaking engagements literally wearing her latest reform effort in plain sight. Elizabeth had recently donned the new "bloomer costume" which became a hot topic of press coverage on its own. Even some "good Democrats" said they could not vote for a candidate whose wife wore such attire.[22] Still, Elizabeth continued to appear with Henry at campaign speeches and events in her bloomer outfit, prompting calls of "breeches" whenever she appeared. According to Elizabeth, her bloomer outfits prompted a "chorus of street urchins" to recite this verse as she walked down the street:

> Heigh! ho! the carrion crow,
> Mrs. Stanton's all the go;
> Twenty tailors take the stitches,
> Mrs. Stanton wears the breeches.[23]

Although Henry was fighting for his political future, he did not try to stop Elizabeth from pursuing her chosen course of reform, even though her new cause gave his political enemies additional fodder from which to attack his already shaky candidacy. Elizabeth was firmly behind Henry's efforts writing, "I would sooner see every relative and friend I have on the face of the earth blown into thin air…than have had Henry mortified by a defeat in this election."[24] Henry viewed Gerrit Smith's campaign efforts for Williams as both a personal and public slight. Commenting to the newspapers, Henry called it, "the unkindest cut of all." Even the Stanton children understood the importance of the election. Six-year-old Gat Stanton, solidly behind his father, anxiously asked his mother who was bathing the newborn Theodore, "Mother, is the baby for or against father?"[25]

The election was so close that the final election results were not immediately available. Whig papers cheered Henry's defeat, but in the end, Henry won his re-election bid by only four votes, down from a comfortable majority of 800 in 1849.[26] The other "runaways" did not

Above: Engraving of Stanton in her "Bloomer costume" from Stanton and Blatch, *Elizabeth Cady Stanton...1922* (Vol. 2 - Letters)

Below: Elizabeth Cady Stanton and son Henry Brewster Stanton, Jr., in 1854 from *Eighty Years*, European Publishing Company, 1898.
Courtesy of Coline Jenkins/Elizabeth Cady Stanton Trust

fare as well. Of the six members standing for re-election from canal districts, only Henry was victorious.[27]

While Elizabeth was "rejoicing with her whole soul," Henry's former opponent was preparing to formally challenge the election results.[28] On June 28, the Committee on Privileges and Elections met to decide whether or not the Williams case had merit.[29] Williams claimed that a variety of fraudulent activities had given Henry the victory. Williams' charges ranged from "illegal voting and improperly counting double votes given for said Stanton," to "destroying legal votes for Josiah B. Williams."[30]

Williams ultimately dropped his challenge, and the investigation did not prevent Henry from taking his seat when the special session met in June. During the debates before the bill's final passage, Henry proposed a dozen amendments and changes to the bill, only one of which was accepted, in order to prevent what he saw as excessive state spending. The canal bill finally passed during the special session on June 24, 1851.[31] Although Henry enthusiastically believed that as a politician he could effect change, the financial needs of his family took precedence over his personal ambitions. Explaining his refusal to run for re-election again that November, Henry simply stated that he "could not afford to be a member."[32]

In May, shortly after Henry was re-nominated, William Lloyd Garrison and British abolitionist George Thompson arrived in Seneca Falls for a speaking engagement at the Wesleyan Chapel. Garrison's *Liberator* reported that the meeting was well attended by "a first rate audience." According to legend, both Elizabeth and Susan B. Anthony were in attendance.

Elizabeth later remembered that while walking home with Garrison and Thompson, she met Amelia Bloomer who introduced her to Anthony and her "good earnest face." Stanton claimed to like Anthony immediately, but she neglected to invite Anthony to her home for dinner with Garrison and Thompson. The reporter from the *Liberator* wrote that Garrison and Thompson stayed with the McClintocks in Waterloo while in the area, but it's also possible that they enjoyed a meal or a visit to the Stantons while in Seneca Falls.[33]

Historian Ann Gordon explains that throughout Stanton's lifetime, she either changed or added to her account of how she met Anthony in 1851. At first, Stanton claimed the two met through the temperance movement. In 1881, Stanton changed the story, adding the detail of Garrison and Thompson's visit to her recollection. Stanton's earliest biographers and Anthony biographer Ida Husted Harper, often adjusted the date to 1850 and then back to 1851. Further, as Gordon's research revealed, there is also no surviving documentary evidence about how the friendship between the two women developed. However, as late as the following January, Elizabeth still referred to Anthony as "Miss Susan B. Anthony," rather than "My Dear Friend" or even "Dear Susan." Clearly, while the friendship did mature into one of the most significant collaborative and long-lasting relationships between reformers in the nation's history, it was not formed at a first or even a second sight.[34]

By April 1852, however, Stanton and Anthony were working together in their first joint reform effort. The Women's Temperance Convention, held in Rochester, was organized in reaction to women's voices being excluded from the New York State Temperance Convention held a few months before. Stanton was elected president at the convention with Anthony serving as one of two secretaries. Among the event's vice presidents was Henry's sister, Frances Avery. While Stanton and Anthony were becoming acquainted, Anthony was already working with the Averys in Rochester. George Avery served on the committee endorsing the women's meeting that was included in the meeting's call, alongside Susan's father, Daniel Anthony.[35] Avery and Daniel Anthony continued to be active in the Rochester temperance movement, helping to found the Temperance League of Monroe County the following year.[36]

Despite their financial problems and personal tragedies, the Averys continued to organize and participate in reform movements throughout the early 1850s. Although he originally supported the Liberty Party in the 1840s, George Avery did so from a perfectionist position, much like Gerrit Smith. When Smith broke with the original coalition to form the Liberty League, Avery continued to work with Smith. Avery was also active in local efforts. Working with the New York State Antislavery Society, Avery launched a major fundraising effort to establish an antislavery reading room in Rochester.[37]

Both Frances and George Avery also supported Frederick Douglass' efforts to keep his newspapers afloat. While George collected and donated funds, Frances launched organizational efforts in Rochester. In September 1851, Frances helped to organize the Rochester Female Antislavery Sewing Circle, working alongside many of the women she had collaborated with for nearly two decades. As with her mother's service as a founder of the Rochester Female Antislavery Society, Frances Avery's important role in the group's revival has gone unnoticed.

The constitution of the Female Antislavery Society Sewing Circle stated that the group's purpose was to raise funds for a variety of antislavery efforts, including helping freedom--seeking slaves. A month after the group's founding, the preamble to the organization's constitution was changed to include a sentence welcoming antislavery advocates from both Garrisonian and Liberty Party ranks.[38]

The Female Antislavery Sewing Circle had a productive first year. The group met at least four times, and three of these meetings were held at the Avery home on Washington Street. In July 1852, the group sponsored an oration by Frederick Douglass at Rochester's Corinthian Hall. It was at this lecture that Douglass delivered one of his most moving and widely respected speeches, "What to the American Slave is your 4th of July?" The speech was printed shortly thereafter, and the group distributed copies to raise funds.[39]

Frances and George Avery continued to be active in antislavery and temperance reform until George's death at the age of 53 in May 1856. Shortly after her husband's death, Frances and her two youngest children moved to Oberlin, Ohio, where her youngest daughter, Elizabeth Cady Avery, attended school. Frances outlived her husband by 14 years, dying of heart disease at the age of 62 in Cleveland, Ohio.[40]

In the summer of 1853, Henry's last surviving brother, Robert Lodowick Stanton, together with his wife, Anna, and son, Robert, visited the Stanton families in Seneca Falls and Rochester. Robert L. Stanton was an ordained Presbyterian minister, and he was serving as a pastor and a divinity instructor at Oakland College in Mississippi.[41] Although Robert's son, also named Robert, was only six-years-old at the time of his visit to New York, the experiences he had on this trip left a lasting impression.

In Rochester, the young boy met his paternal grandmother, Susanna, for the first time. Many years later in a family history that he compiled for his children, Robert recollected that his grandmother was a "Grand dame." She was "tall, dignified and commanding; strict to severity, earnest and of indomitable will, and yet at the same time, kind, sympathetic and affectionate." Then in her 72nd year and within six months of her death, Robert recalled only one remark Susanna made during their visit. When the conversation turned to a discussion of nervous people, Susanna quipped, "thank God [I] was born before nerves were invented."[42]

During the summer of 1853, Susanna fell and severely injured her right arm and hand. Her inability to use her right hand required her to use a specially designed piece of cutlery in order to eat. A few months later, Susanna suffered a bout of lung inflammation, and she died on October 30, 1853, at the age of 72. Her funeral, held on November 1, took place at the home of her daughter Frances Avery. Although her death notice identified Susanna as the mother of H. B. and R. L. Stanton, it is not known which family members attended her funeral.[43]

Henry Stanton was a voluminous letter writer, composing and receiving over a dozen letters per week. Sadly, only about 350 of Henry's letters survive, and only a handful of letters addressed to him still exist. While Elizabeth's correspondence has fared much better overall, the editing and transcribing of her letters by the Stanton children after their mother's death created another set of problems.

Before her death, Elizabeth's condemnation of organized religion and the Bible as the root cause of women's subjugation caused her to lose many friends and supporters. The 1895 publication of the *Woman's Bible* alienated many of the era's more conservative women's rights activists, and the book directly impacted Stanton's legacy as a reformer. More than a decade later, the next generation of suffragists shied away from acknowledging Stanton's contributions because of the controversy created by the *Woman's Bible*.[44] By 1920, Elizabeth's role as the founding mother of the woman suffrage movement had been substantially minimized, and Susan B. Anthony was popularly perceived as the sole face of the nineteenth century suffrage movement. Even to the present day, many still inaccurately believe that Anthony attended or helped organize the Seneca Falls Convention.

In their eagerness to resurrect their mother from historical oblivion, in 1922, Harriot Stanton Blatch and Theodore Stanton published an edition of their mother's edited letters, together with an edited version of Elizabeth's 1898 autobiography, *Eighty Years and More*. In their quest to present their mother in the best possible light and to minimize what they believed were unimportant details, Harriot and Theodore often combined the content of several of Elizabeth's letters, even those addressed to different correspondents and written years apart, and reprinted the amalgamated version in their edited volume. Because of these editorial practices, many of Elizabeth's letters, particularly those written before the Civil War, exist only as a typed transcript, potentially combining several letters, and making it difficult to know for certain the nature of her relationships with her family.

We will probably never know for certain how much Susanna Stanton's pioneering assertion of her right to self-determination influenced Elizabeth's understanding of religious and civil rights for women. However, Susanna's "indomitable will" and the breadth of her reformism must have been inspirational to her daughter-in-law. The Stanton children were very protective of their mother's legacy, and in their editorial practices, they omitted references to many who helped Elizabeth, including her husband and his family.

It does, however, seem likely that Susanna and Elizabeth shared more than a passing acquaintance, particularly after Elizabeth moved from Boston to Seneca Falls in 1847. Rochester was a short train ride away from Seneca Falls, and it is highly doubtful that the two women—related by marriage and tied together by their reform activities and shared reform networks—would not have had a great deal to talk about and share. Susanna had asserted her rights when Elizabeth was only a child of seven, and she helped to establish reform organizations when Elizabeth was a young woman. By the time they met, Susanna had already braved the disapproval of her family and neighbors by her excommunication because she believed it was her right to seek a divorce, rather than to be forced to live as a *femme covert* to an abusive husband. While Susanna Brewster Stanton's example cannot provide an explanation for her daughter-in-law's work for women's rights or even her radical beliefs concerning divorce reform, it would be an equally grave error to conclude that Susanna's unusual life experiences were of no consequence as Elizabeth's reformism was developing and maturing.[45]

The Stanton family continued to grow during the 1850s. After four sons, the couple welcomed their first daughter, Margaret, in 1852, daughter Harriot in 1856, and their fifth son and seventh child, Robert in 1859.[46] The children enjoyed an environment rich with intellectual stimulation. In addition to their vast knowledge of politics, the children's education was also well-rounded. "The dining table was a platform for debate," Harriot later wrote, with their mother serving as the "arbitrator on moral and sociological issues," and their father acting as "referee in political and historical disputes."[47]

Elizabeth also remembered how much the children loved hearing their father arguing cases for their amusement. Theodore would sit on the piano, and Henry would argue cases before the young judge complete "with vehement gestures and pironettings," while the other Stanton boys acted as the jury. Theodore was only four or five-years-old at the time, and his sisters were too young to participate. The younger boys didn't understand most of what their father was saying, but they "remained spellbound" by Henry's passionate arguments during the performances. Theodore didn't smile or take his eyes off his father, even after the "court" was adjourned. Henry also taught his children about history through his own collection of engravings and photographs. Theodore remembered the "admirable way" his father's history lessons were taught and the "circle of children...eyes riveted on the pictures and ears open to all that was said."[48]

During the late 1850s, and once again practicing law full-time, Henry spent much of his time in Washington and Albany. However, he was still very much involved with his family and home in Seneca Falls while out of town. Writing to Elizabeth on a snowy evening in 1857, he asked her to remind their hired help to "tread the snow around the apple trees" and "to haul in the wood."[49]

As he had done throughout the couple's marriage, Henry worried about his family while he was away from home, and he missed his wife, his children, and the familiar comforts of home. In January 1857, Henry wrote four or five letters to Elizabeth over the course of a few days without receiving a reply. Growing frustrated and concerned by her lack of a response, he tried a different tactic. Rather than writing again to Elizabeth, he composed a letter to the couple's four-year-old daughter, Margaret. Henry asked Margaret, who was too young to read or write, to "take a pen & sit down & tell [him] all the news." Henry asked specific questions about each of his children, including whether or not "the young judge [Theodore]" still hid under the table when a neighbor played nearby in a hoop skirt and whether or not Margaret was attending dancing school. He asked Margaret to tell her baby sister that although he had "seen a great many babies" since leaving home, "none of them were as handsome as she."

It was, however, Henry's message to Elizabeth that illustrates the love and humor that the Stantons shared. "Tell your mother," Henry wrote to Margaret, "that I have seen a throng of handsome ladies, but I had rather see her than the whole of them; but, I intend to cut her

Henry B. Stanton circa 1885. Despite being 80 years old, a reporter from the *New York Times* described him as "a tall, thin gentleman, apparently about 60 years old." (*NYT*, 6/28/1885) Unlike his wife who was photographed often, this photo and the one that follows are from Henry Stanton's only known photography session. From *Eighty Years*, European Publishing Company, 1898. *Courtesy of Coline Jenkins/Elizabeth Cady Stanton Trust*

acquaintance unless she writes me a letter." It is likely that had more of Henry's letters survived, history would have recorded a much different marriage between the Stantons. However, the sixty or so surviving letters Henry wrote to his wife are filled with longing, questions about their home and family, and a detailed portrait of the political news of the day.[50]

The Stantons' marriage was also not devoid of romance. In 1858, after nearly two decades of marriage, Henry wrote to Elizabeth on Valentine's Day from Washington, DC, "I send you this my Valentine, in the form of the expression of my ardent attachment to you…you may look for me by Tuesday next. So, open wide your arms, for I shall rush into them with all the impulse which love and longing can inspire."[51]

The following year, Henry was pressured to buy tickets to a ball for a visiting dignitary while in Washington, and he wrote to Elizabeth that "he could not bear to go without her," so he sold the tickets to an associate. However, the tickets were non-transferable and engraved in the names of Mr. and Mrs. H. B. Stanton. "I suppose that some dashing young belle at this present moment is being pointed out as the distinguished advocate of free suffrage for woman, from New York," Henry lamented to Elizabeth.[52]

While Henry was proud of his wife's accomplishments, outside of the couple's circle of reformers, Elizabeth was criticized for her suffrage advocacy. In 1858, a man from Auburn accused Elizabeth of "neglecting her family & running about to advocate for woman's rights." Despite the later inaccurate depictions of Henry as an absent husband and father, in their own time, Elizabeth was perceived by some as being the neglectful spouse and parent.[53]

During the presidential election of 1860, both Henry and Elizabeth actively campaigned for Lincoln and the new Republican Party. On September 10, representing the women of Seneca Falls, Elizabeth presented a banner to a local chapter of a young Republican marching club called the "Wide Awakes." The Wide Awakes earned their name by carrying lanterns during ritualized nighttime processions for their candidates. Their moniker, a version of the "all seeing eye," was prominently featured on banners and broadsides, and they proclaimed that they were "awakened" by the issues of the day.[54]

At the presentation in Seneca Falls, Elizabeth gave a speech reminding the Wide Awakes that they must not be contented to merely stop the spread of slavery, but to oppose its existence entirely.[55] Two weeks later, the Wide Awakes held another local drill, this time, with Henry in attendance. Later that evening, after Henry had returned home, the entire marching group, resplendent with lanterns and music, arrived at the Stanton home. Lamps were immediately lit, and the group marched through the gate in single file until their leader yelled, "halt." Henry, "doffing his hat, & bowing most gracefully, said, 'Gentlemen Wide awakes—we welcome you to our home—You are here in honor of Mrs. Stanton, and she no doubt is ready to extend to you a hearty greeting—I have the pleasure of introducing you to Mrs. Stanton.'" The group called for "three cheers for Mrs. Stanton," three more for Mr. Stanton, and three more for "the little Stantons." After the marching corps left for the evening, the Wide Awake Glee Club arrived, and the family invited them to stay for dessert. When the household was finally silent, Henry and Elizabeth noticed that Theodore, then age nine, was missing. During the commotion, Theodore joined the first procession's march, and he later returned with a neighbor's son and mother just before eleven that night.[56]

Henry left the following day for a Republican mass meeting in Amsterdam, New York, and he continued throughout the fall months canvassing the state for Lincoln, sometimes delivering two major speeches per day.[57] On October 1, Henry wrote to Elizabeth telling her to "work some [John Greenleaf] Whittier into your speech" to the Wide Awakes, and he would see that it was published in the *New York Tribune*. Eventually, at least four newspapers printed her speech. Embedded within both the middle of the surviving handwritten manuscript, as well as prominently at the end of the speech, are several lines from Whittier's the *Crisis*.

Without the existence of this brief note, another instance of Henry's direct help to Elizabeth would have been lost to the historical record. This letter and the revisions Elizabeth made to her speech as a result of Henry's advice, have been overlooked in previous works. Although more than a decade had passed since the Seneca Falls Convention, this letter demonstrates that Henry still offered valuable advice to Elizabeth, and he also helped to promote her and her contributions on the national reform stage.

Following Lincoln's victory in 1860, Henry was rewarded with a political appointment as deputy collector of the Customs House in the Port of New York.[58] The Stanton family left Seneca Falls, and they spent most of their remaining years in the New York City area. Throughout the Civil War, Henry continued to advocate for the enlistment of black troops, and at the war's end, he supported the Reconstruction amendments granting black suffrage.

By 1870 and the passage of the Fifteenth Amendment, Henry Stanton had spent 35 years working for a cause that had finally been won. Stanton never lost his interest in politics, and throughout the remainder of his life, he continued to editorialize for candidates and issues he supported as an editor for the *New York Sun* until his death in 1887 at the age of 82.[59]

Henry B. Stanton circa 1885.
Courtesy of Coline Jenkins/Elizabeth Cady Stanton Trust

Henry Stanton spent much of his life focused on securing social and political equality for African Americans, often at the expense of his health and his finances. His pragmatic strategies enlarged support for his cause, but often alienated him from his more idealistic friends and former allies. By 1860, the political coalition that Henry helped to establish in the 1840s enjoyed broad support in the North, and resulted in the election of Abraham Lincoln. While his life as an agitator came to an end in the late 1860s, Elizabeth's career as a reformer was just beginning.

In 1879, after almost forty years of marriage, Elizabeth wrote to a friend, "A man's love brings into a woman's existence an inspiration, a completeness, a satisfaction that a mother's cannot. A true conjugal union is the highest kind of human love—divine, creative in the realm of thought as well as in the material world."[60] Elizabeth's touching and insightful views on love and marriage came not from an abstract or intellectual understanding, but from her own experiences as a wife of many decades.

Throughout the first two decades of their marriage, Henry showed Elizabeth how to practically organize and execute a reform agenda. From its first days, the marriage introduced her to the upper echelon of male and female reformers and government officials with whom she would continue to work to advance the cause of women's rights until her death in 1902.

Elizabeth's family by marriage provided her with examples and models of male and female reformism that were far more compatible with her life's work than any member of her own family, including the idealistic Gerrit Smith. Similarly, Henry's advocacy of political action over Garrisonian moral suasion, profoundly influenced Elizabeth's understanding and conviction that woman suffrage was the linchpin of female equality.

Certainly the tactical examples and social mobility provided by the marriage alone would not be sufficient to explain the vision and intellect that Elizabeth brought to the women's rights movement. However, as Henry noted shortly after they met, if Elizabeth's marital life not been supportive of her "superior mind," it is equally true that she likely would not have had the opportunity to use her considerable talents as the leader of the nineteenth century woman suffrage movement. Within her intimate life, she was not only her husband's equal, she was supported by the foundation of her marriage as she sought equality outside the confines of her own home.

In 1840, Elizabeth's life direction pivoted between the "world of fashionable follies" and marriage to a man who respected her mind as much as he loved her spirit. The marriage emancipated Elizabeth Cady from her social class and her family's conservative rules and expectations, and by escaping these rigid confines, Elizabeth was able to challenge and ultimately transcend the societal restrictions of her era and to develop as a reformer with the support and encouragement of her husband.

Although Henry Stanton oftentimes helped his wife pursue her own reform goals and shared in many of them, perhaps we can best understand Henry's thoughts on women's rights through Elizabeth's words about her own life's calling:

> Two years ago, I bound myself with some of my friends and together we resolved to devote our lives to the elevation of woman. It is the branch of moral reform most dear to me. I feel deeply for the slave, the drunkard and the outcast, but deeper still for the unhappy woman.[61]

While for Henry Stanton, the abolition of slavery was the moral reform most "dear" to him, he too "felt deeply" for the drunkard and the unhappy woman.

Elizabeth outlived her husband by seventeen years, and she spent the majority of the remainder of life as the leader of the national women's suffrage organizations. Two years before her death, on her 85th birthday, Elizabeth was suffering with a bad toothache. She confided to her diary that if she had it to do over again she would marry a dentist so as to have someone to watch over her "molars, cuspids and bicuspids." She remembered having to take herself and the children through harrowing nineteenth century dental procedures, but it was Henry, she recalled, who could not summon up the courage to have a tooth pulled unless she was there with him.[62]

The course of history and the quest for women's rights was forever changed when instead of a dentist, Elizabeth chose to marry a man who devoted his life to universal equality and emphasized the vote as the means to achieve that equality. While both Henry and Elizabeth Stanton together and alone accomplished extraordinary things during their lifetimes, in the end, neither would have been who they were without the other. Each supplied what the other lacked, and the marriage provided fertile ground and the opportunity for the development of one of the foremost intellectual minds in the history of the United States. It was, truly, an uncommon union.

NOTES

In the notes that follow, Henry B. Stanton is referred to as HBS, while Elizabeth Cady Stanton is abbreviated as ECS.

PREFACE

[1] *Philadelphia Inquirer*, November 24, 1866. Report of HBS' speech made at the Pennsylvania Antislavery Society's meeting. Henry's speech followed those of Lucretia Mott, Susan B. Anthony and Frances Gage.

[2] Stanton and Blatch, eds., *Elizabeth Cady Stanton as Revealed in Her Letters, Diary and Reminiscences*, Vol. 1:252-253. Hereafter, Stanton-Blatch.

[3] Elizabeth Cady Stanton's autobiography, *Eighty Years and More*, is often a problematic source because Stanton combined events and happenings out of chronological order in order to make her points. While there is much of value in her autobiography, it is also difficult to rely on as an evidentiary source. Although I utilize Stanton's autobiography where no other source exists, I do so as sparingly as possible and primarily to supply personal information or observations, rather than for political or historical questions. For two important essays about Stanton's autobiography, see Ellen Dubois' introduction and Ann Gordon's afterword in Elizabeth Cady Stanton, *Eighty Years and More*: T. Fisher Unwin, 1898; reprint, Introduction by Ellen Carol DuBois. Afterword by Ann D. Gordon. Boston: Northeastern University Press, 1993. Hereafter: Stanton, *80Y*. See also Kathi Kern, *Mrs. Stanton's Bible*, Ithaca: Cornell University Press, 2001, esp. Chapter 1.

[4] Some historians attribute different meaning to the words "antislavery" and "abolition." The term "antislavery" is often used by historians to refer to the movement to end slavery gradually and/or with compensation for the loss of "property." In contrast, the term "abolition" then refers to the immediate and uncompensated end to slavery. However, the abolitionists themselves used the terms interchangeably, and I follow their lead. In addition, I have standardized the names of abolition groups and societies. For example, some were referred to as an "Anti-Slavery" society while others as "Antislavery," and these spellings were inconsistent in newspapers and other published

sources. For clarity, all are "Antislavery" within this book. For works relying on Garrisonian moral suasion as the influence for the women's rights movement, see for example: Ellen Carol DuBois, *Feminism and Suffrage the Emergence of an Independent Women's Movement in America 1848-1869*, Reprint Edition, 1999 ed. Ithaca: Cornell University Press, 1978. Aileen S. Kraditor, *Means and Ends in American Abolitionism: Garrison and His Critics on Strategy and Tactics, 1834-1850*, New York: Pantheon Books, 1967. Blanche Glassman Hersh, *The Slavery of Sex: Feminist-Abolitionists in America*, Urbana, IL: University of Illinois Press, 1978. Henry Mayer, *All on Fire: William Lloyd Garrison and the Abolition of Slavery*, New York: St. Martin's Griffin, 1998. Elisabeth Griffith, *In Her Own Right: The Life of Elizabeth Cady Stanton*, New York: Oxford University Press, 1984. Lois W. Banner, *Elizabeth Cady Stanton: A Radical for Woman's Rights*, Boston: Little, Brown and Company, 1980.

[5] Elizabeth Cady Stanton used the terms "women's rights" and "woman suffrage" interchangeably after the 1848 convention. Prior to that time, which was also before the formal introduction of the suffrage resolution, the term "woman's rights" was used more as a catchall phrase that encompassed ideological, Biblical, and social arguments for female equality. The terms were also employed primarily by women in the antislavery movement, rather than in the broader society. Especially after the 1837 "pastoral letter" and during the abolition rupture, this term was used to argue for women's equal participation within antislavery circles. Unless otherwise stipulated, I follow Elizabeth Cady Stanton's lead.

[6] Douglas M. Strong, *Perfectionist Politics: Abolitionism and the Religious Tensions of American Democracy*, Syracuse: Syracuse University Press, 1999.

[7] The goal of both parties was to elect candidates—from the local to the national level—who would legislate the end of slavery (as in the case of Liberty) and to stop the extension of slavery (as in the case of Free Soil). See Reinhard O. Johnson, *The Liberty Party, 1840-1848; Antislavery Third-Party Politics in the United States*, Baton Rouge: Louisiana State University Press, 2009. Theodore Clarke Smith, *The Liberty and Free Soil Parties in the Northwest*, New York: Longmans, Green & Co., 1897; Vernon L. Volpe, *Forlorn Hope of Freedom: The Liberty Party in the Old Northwest, 1838-1848*, Kent, OH: Kent State University Press, 1990. Strong, *Perfectionist Politics: Abolitionism and the Religious Tensions of American Democracy*.

CHAPTER ONE: THE RIGHT TO DETERMINE FOR HERSELF

[1] Henry B. Stanton, *Random Recollections*, Third ed. New York: Harper & Brothers, 1887, p. 17. Hereafter, Stanton, *RR*. Third edition used unless otherwise stated.

[2] *Connecticut Gazette* [New London, CT], May 27, 1801.

[3] *Connecticut Gazette* May 20, 1812 and June 3, 1812.

[4] Stanton *RR* p. 5. Throughout Henry Stanton's lifetime, there was no clear historical consensus concerning the battle between Uncas and Miantonomoh, nor what occurred following Miantonomoh's defeat. Many accounts claimed that Miantonomoh was the unprovoked aggressor, and he had planned an attack on Uncas that was discovered, preventing a rout. In order to spare the deaths of his warriors, Uncas allegedly proposed that he fight one-on-one with Miantonomoh, and the winner would be the victor of the battle. Miantonomoh rejected this suggestion; however, Uncas had prearranged a signal to his men, who began firing upon the unprepared Narragansetts. When Miantonomoh was captured, due in part to being encumbered by heavy armor given to him by an English ally, he was taken to English magistrates in Norwich, who then released him back to Uncas for execution. According to Henry Stanton's retelling of the incident, Uncas was the aggressor; and the English delivered the innocent and noble Miantonomoh to Uncas to be slaughtered. Uncas and his descendants were considered royalty by later generations, and his family retained a burial ground in Norwich. In contrast, Miantonomoh's burial location was not marked by the State of Connecticut until the mid-nineteenth century, although the spot was sacred to the Narragansetts since Miantonomoh's death. Currently, a marker commemorating the site is more in line with Henry Stanton's depiction. See esp. William L. Stone, *Uncas and Miantonomoh, a Historical Discourse, Delivered at Norwich, (Conn.,) on the Fourth Day of July 1842, on the Occasion of the Erection of a Monument to the Memory of Uncas, the White Man's Friend, and First Chief of the Mohegans,* New York: Dayton & Newman, 1842, pp. 151-55.

[5] Frances Manwaring Caulkins, *History of New London, Connecticut,* New London, Conn.: H. D. Utley, 1895, pp. 630-36. Joseph Stanton served as a Captain in Lt. Com. William Belcher's Company during the summer of 1813. See Daniel L. Phillips, *Griswold—a History. Being a History of the Town of Griswold Connecticut from the Earliest Times to the Entrance of Our Country into the World War in 1917,* New Haven, Conn.: Tuttle, Morehouse & Taylor Company, 1929 p. 87 and 333, and Stanton, *RR,* p. 6-7. After the War of 1812, Joseph Stanton was frequently referred to as "Capt. Joseph" or "Capt. Stanton."

[6] 1813 militia pay register of Belcher's 8th Company, author's collection.

[7] Stanton, *RR,* pp. 9-10.

[8] *Roger Coit vs. Joseph Stanton,* October 7, 1813. Connecticut State Library, New London County Superior Court Files.

[9] Ibid.

[10] Stanton, *RR,* p. 9.

[11] *Norwich Courier,* June 1, 1814.

[12] Grace L. Rogers, "The Scholfield Wool-Carding Machines," *United States*

National Museum. Contributions from the Museum of History and Technology Bulletin 218. (1959). Stanton, *RR*, p. 19.

[13] *Norwich Courier,* July 19, 1815.

[14] *Norwich Courier,* January 10, 1816.

[15] *Norwich Courier,* April 17, 1816.

[16] See Bruce H. Mann, *Republic of Debtors: Bankruptcy in the Age of American Independence,* Cambridge, Mass.: Harvard University Press, 2002, pp. 78-89 for an overview of the transition.

[17] New London [Connecticut] County Superior Court Papers by Subject, 1711-1900, Inquests-Insolvents.

[18] HBS to Elizabeth Cady, January 4, 1840 in Stanton-Blatch, *Letters,* pp. II:4-5.

[19] Robert Brewster Stanton's family history is unpublished and lacking page numbers. Robert Brewster Stanton, "Notes from My Note Books," Robert Brewster Stanton Collection, New York Public Library, ca. 1909.

[20] HBS to Elizabeth Cady, January 4, 1840 in Stanton-Blatch, *Letters,* pp. II:4-5.

[21] Stanton, *RR*, p. 4.

[22] *Susan Stanton vs. Joseph Stanton,* Connecticut State Archives, New London County, Superior Court Papers.

[23] Ibid.

[24] "Griswold [Connecticut] First Congregational Church Records, 1720-1887. Volume 2, Meetings, 1812-1867," pp. 46-47.

[25] Ibid., p. 48.

[26] Ibid.

[27] Nancy F. Cott, *Public Vows: A History of Marriage and the Nation,* Cambridge, Mass.: Harvard University Press, 2000, p. 38 and 107. See also Hendrik Hartog, *Man & Wife in America: A History,* Cambridge, Mass.: Harvard University Press, 2000, esp. pp. 64-76.

[28] Cott, *Public Vows: A History of Marriage and the Nation.* For self-divorce, see p. 38ff.

[29] Ibid., p. 11.

[30] Ibid., esp. pp.11-12. See also Hartog, *Man & Wife in America: A History,* 115-22.

[31] Hartog, *Man & Wife in America: A History,* p. 125.

[32] New York *Evening Post,* July 27, 1827.

CHAPTER TWO: THE WORLD OF FASHIONABLE FOLLIES

[1] Stanton, *80Y,* p. 4.

[2] ECS's childhood and young adulthood have been previously chronicled

by her biographers, most notably Alma Lutz and Elisabeth Griffith, and also in her own autobiography, *Eighty Years & More*. Important additions to Elizabeth's biographies can be found in Kathi Kern's *Mrs. Stanton's Bible*. For a meaningful critique of Elizabeth's autobiography, see Ann D. Gordon's afterward in Stanton, *80Y*.

[3] Orrin Peer Allen, *Descendants of Nicholas Cady of Watertown, Mass., 1645–1910*, Palmer, Mass.: The Author, 1910, p. 91.

[4] Cuyler Reynolds, *Hudson–Mohawk Genealogical and Family Memoirs*, Vol. III New York: Lewis Historical Publishing Company, 1911, pp. 1154.

[5] Henry B. Stanton, "Daniel Cady," *New York Daily Times*, January 25 1855.

[6] Norman Dann, *Practical Dreamer: Gerrit Smith and the Crusade for Social Reform*, Hamilton, NY: Log Cabin Books, 2009, pp. 17- 19. See also Octavius Brooks Frothingham, *Gerrit Smith: A Biography*, New York: G. P. Putnam's Sons, 1878; reprint, New York: Negro Universities Press, 1969, pp. 6-10.

[7] For the partnership between Smith and Cady see Dann, *Practical Dreamer: Gerrit Smith and the Crusade for Social Reform*, p. 22. Frothingham, *Gerrit Smith: A Biography*, pp. 20-21. Substantiation for the income requirement is found in Daniel Cady to Gerrit Smith, March 24, 1820, Peter Smith Collection, Syracuse University. Transcription available at www.danielcady.com.

[8] *New York* [NY] *Commercial Advertiser*, June 11, 1814, p. 2.

[9] For example, see *Journal of the House of Representatives*, Vol. 10:39; 10:70; 10:163; and 10:357.

[10] James Parton, et. al., *Eminent Women of the Age: Being Narratives of the Lives and Deeds of the Most Prominent Women of the Present Generation*, Hartford, Conn.: S. M. Betts & Company, 1869, pp. 336-37. The story was repeated, nearly verbatim, fifteen years later in Elizabeth Stuart Phelps, ed. *Our Famous Women*, Hartford, Conn.: A. D. Worthington & Co., 1884, pp. 605-06. An abbreviated version was included in *80Y*, and Stanton retained the word "mechanical" in her description of her father's physical affection. Stanton, *80Y*, p. 20.

[11] Allen, *Descendants of Nicholas Cady of Watertown, Mass., 1645- 1910*, pp. 173-74.

[12] Many aspects of Stanton's recollections have been expertly examined by Kathi Kern and Ann Gordon. See especially Chapter 1 in Kern, *Mrs. Stanton's Bible*. Ann D. Gordon, afterword essay in Stanton, *80Y*.

[13] Daniel Cady to Peter Smith, December 2, 1814. Elizabeth Cady Stanton Papers, Library of Congress.

[14] Ibid.

[15] *Warpole v. Hosford*. Abbott Collection, New York State Archives, Albany, New York.

[16] HBS to sons Daniel and Henry, Jr. February 22, 1852. Elizabeth Cady

Stanton Papers, Library of Congress.

[17] Kern, *Mrs. Stanton's Bible*, pp. 24-25.

[18] Margaret Stanton Lawrence, "Elizabeth Cady Stanton, 1815-1915: A Sketch of Her Life by Her Elder Daughter Margaret Stanton Lawrence. An Afterword by Her Younger Daughter Harriot Stanton Blatch," (Poughkeepsie, NY: Vassar College, [1915]), p. 4.

[19] Stanton, *80Y*, p. 32.

[20] Alma Lutz, *Created Equal: A Biography of Elizabeth Cady Stanton 1815-1902*, New York: John Day Company, 1940, p. 4.

[21] Banner, *Elizabeth Cady Stanton: A Radical for Woman's Rights*, pp. 7-8. Griffith changed Flora Campbell's story altogether. In her version, the family farm passed to the Campbell's son "who treated his mother unkindly." Griffith, *In Her Own Right: The Life of Elizabeth Cady Stanton*, p. 11. Kathi Kern notes that in Stanton's 1894 "Reminiscences of Elizabeth Cady Stanton" (undated typescript, Political Equality Club of Minneapolis Papers, Minnesota Historical Society), Stanton used the story of Flora Campbell to not only show that she was keenly aware of women's inequality within the legal system, but Stanton added that she planned to carry out the editing of her father's legal books on a Sunday morning "when they are all at church." Kern notes that in this way, Stanton was able to show "evidence of her childhood anticlericalism." Kern, *Mrs. Stanton's Bible*, p. 236 n 63.

[22] 1830 U.S. Census: Johnstown, Montgomery County, New York, Page 188; NARA Roll: M19-95; Family History Film: 0017155. Johnstown, p. 7. The 1820 census shows the James Campbell family as including two males between the ages of 16 and 25, one was the couple's son, James Campbell, Jr., who later became a merchant in Albany. While the Campbell family is listed immediately following the Cady residence, it appears that the census records for that year were either compiled or recopied in rough alphabetical order. The Cady entry in the 1820 census also shows male one slave, age 26 to 45, likely representing Peter Teabout. 1820 U S Census: Johnstown, Montgomery, New York, Page: 358; NARA Roll: M33_63; Image: 266. Johnstown, p. 4.

[23] Records of the Johnstown Cemetery, Johnstown, NY. The Campbell family is buried in Section "O." See also, the *New York Spectator*, May 2, 1828 (James' death notice) and September 6, 1831 (Ann's death notice).

[24] Although Kathi Kern offers the first detailed look at Peter Teabout's influence on Elizabeth's childhood, and she offers the most thorough interpretation of Stanton's autobiographical account of her childhood, Kern stops short of considering Peter's potential influence on Elizabeth's interest in the law and the courts.

[25] Lawrence, "Elizabeth Cady Stanton, 1815-1915: A Sketch of Her Life by Her Elder Daughter Margaret Stanton Lawrence. An Afterword by Her Younger Daughter Harriot Stanton Blatch," pp. 4-5.

[26] Stanton, *80Y*, p. 3.

CHAPTER THREE: THE INFECTED DISTRICT

[1] Stanton, *RR*, p. 25

[2] Paul E. Johnson, *A Shopkeeper's Millennium: Society and Revivals in Rochester, New York, 1815-1837*, New York: Hill and Wang, 2004; reprint, 2004, p. 72. Henry Stanton noted a population of only 3,500 Stanton, *RR*, p. 24.

[3] Johnson, *A Shopkeeper's Millennium: Society and Revivals in Rochester, New York, 1815-1837*, p. 13.

[4] Ibid., p. 37. Johnson also found that less than one in six new residents stayed in Rochester for six years or longer.

[5] Ibid., p. 25.

[6] Stanton, *RR*, p. 30.

[7] The *Telegraph* became a daily paper by April 1827. Catskill [New York] *Republican*, May 2, 1827.

[8] Thurlow Weed, *Autobiography of Thurlow Weed*, ed. Harriet A. Weed Boston: Houghton, Mifflin and Company, 1884, pp. esp. 250-52.

[9] Stanton, *RR*, pp. 24-25 and 9.

[10] [Rochester, New York] *Album*, date unknown (after February 4, 1828).

[11] [Rochester, New York] *Album*, date unknown (ca. February 12, 1828).

[12] [Rochester, New York] *Album*, May 27, 1828. Also on the committee was Henry's brother-in-law Samuel Baldwin of Riga, New York.

[13] Johnson, *A Shopkeeper's Millennium: Society and Revivals in Rochester, New York, 1815-1837*, p. 79.

[14] Ibid., pp. 77-82.

[15] Ibid., p. 113.

[16] Stanton, *RR*, pp. 40-41.

[17] Ibid., p. 41.

[18] Stanton, *80Y*, p. 34.

[19] *Emma Willard and her pupils, or, Fifty years of Troy Female Seminary: 1822-1872*, New York: Mrs. R. Sage, 1898, pp 16-19.

[20] September 21, 1831 register, Troy Female Seminary. See also Griffith, *In Her Own Right: The Life of Elizabeth Cady Stanton*, p. 17.

[21] Ibid., p. 17.

[22] The vast majority of the entries are dated prior to 1839. A few were written in the months following the Stantons' return from Europe in 1841. Elizabeth embellished her book during her honeymoon trip by pasting small engravings of important buildings she visited during her travels into the book.

[23] Elizabeth Cady Stanton's Commonplace Book, Rare Books Department, Boston Public Library. For Thirza Lee, see *Emma Willard and her pupils, or, Fifty years of Troy Female Seminary: 1822-1872*, p. 199.

[24] Kern, *Mrs. Stanton's Bible*, p. 42-43.

[25] Stanton, *80Y*, p. 43.

[26] For Kern's research, see *Mrs. Stanton's Bible*, p. 237 n 74. Elizabeth Stanton's

description of Finney, *80Y*, pp. 42-43. Henry Stanton's, *RR*, pp. 41-42.

[27] Kern, *Mrs. Stanton's Bible*, p. 237 n 81.

[28] "Who Was Elizabeth Cady Stanton?" Margaret Stanton Lawrence, no date, Part 1, pp. 9-11. Alma Lutz Collection, Vassar College.

[29] Elizabeth Cady Stanton's Commonplace Book, Rare Books Department, Boston Public Library, no page number, entry signed, "Susan Anthony" and dated, "Battenville, Jan. 17th, 1834."

[30] For Daniel Cady, see Ida Husted Harper, *Life and Work of Susan B. Anthony*, Vol. I, pp. 19-22 and Stanton, *80Y*, pp. 157- 162.

[31] Harper, *Life and Work of Susan B. Anthony*, Vol. I, p. 12.

CHAPTER FOUR: "FANATICS AND LUNATICS"

[1] From Lyman Beecher's lecture on oratory at Lane Seminary, quoted in Stanton, *RR*, p. 46.

[2] J. L. Tracy to Theodore Weld, November 24, 1831 in Gilbert H. Barnes and Dwight L. Dumond, eds., *Letters of Theodore Dwight Weld, Angelina Grimké Weld and Sarah Grimké, 1822- 1844*, II vols. Gloucester, Mass.: Peter Smith, 1965, 1:56-58. Also quoted in Robert H. Abzug, *Passionate Liberator: Theodore Dwight Weld & the Dilemma of Reform*, New York: Oxford University Press, 1980, p. 74.

[3] Charles Stuart to Theodore Weld, March 26, 1831 in Barnes and Dumond, eds., *Letters of Theodore Dwight Weld, Angelina Grimké Weld and Sarah Grimké, 1822-1844*, 1:42-44.

[4] Theodore Weld to James G. Birney, September 27, 1832 in William Birney, *James G. Birney and His Times: The Genesis of the Republican Party with Some Account of Abolition Movements in the South before 1828*, D. Appleton and Company, 1890; reprint, (New York: Negro Universities Press, 1969), 1:26-29. Emphasis as written.

[5] Stanton, *RR*, p. 43. Henry and Robert failed to notify the First Presbyterian Church in Rochester that they were moving to Ohio. On May 29, 1832 the brothers were dismissed from the congregation and were noted as being "at large." Records of the First Presbyterian Church of Rochester, NY, Local History Division, Rochester Public Library.

[6] Lawrence Thomas Lesick, *The Lane Rebels: Evangelicalism and Antislavery in Antebellum America*, Metuchen, NJ: The Scarecrow Press, 1980, p. 73.

[7] Ibid., p. 43.

[8] Stanton, *RR*, pp. 46-47.

[9] Lesick, *The Lane Rebels: Evangelicalism and Antislavery in Antebellum America*, p. 73.

[10] Barnes and Dumond, eds., *Letters of Theodore Dwight Weld, Angelina Grimké*

Weld and Sarah Grimké, 1822-1844, 1:111. Out of her six surviving adult children, Susanna lost her youngest child, Joseph, in 1832, George in 1833 and her eldest child, Susan, in 1836.

[11] Lesick, *The Lane Rebels: Evangelicalism and Antislavery in Antebellum America*, p. 74.

[12] Weld to Lewis Tappan, March 18, 1834 in Barnes and Dumond, eds., *Letters of Theodore Dwight Weld, Angelina Grimké Weld and Sarah Grimké, 1822-1844*, p. 1:132.

[13] Quoted from Finney's 1831 sermon "Sinners Bound to Change Their Own Hearts," as quoted in Lesick, *The Lane Rebels: Evangelicalism and Antislavery in Antebellum America*, p. 85.

[14] Ibid.

[15] Barnes and Dumond, eds., *Letters of Theodore Dwight Weld, Angelina Grimké Weld and Sarah Grimké, 1822-1844*, p. 1:120.

[16] Lesick, *The Lane Rebels: Evangelicalism and Antislavery in Antebellum America*, p. 79.

[17] H. B. Stanton, "Anti-Slavery in the Great Valley," March 10, 1834 as printed in the *American Anti-Slavery Reporter*, April 1834, p. 52 and *A Statement of the Reasons Which Induced the Students of Lane Seminary to Dissolve Their Connection with That Institution* (Cincinnati, 1834), p. 8.

[18] Robert Brewster Stanton, "Notes from My Note Books."

[19] Theodore Weld to Elizur Wright, January 24, 1834, Abolitionist Collection, 1834-1884, Manuscripts and Rare Books Department, Swen Library, College of William and Mary.

[20] H. B. Stanton, "Anti-Slavery in the Great Valley," March 10, 1834 as printed in the *American Anti-Slavery Reporter*, April 1834, p. 52.

[21] Ibid.

[22] Ibid.

[23] The *American Antislavery Reporter*, May 1834, pp. 76-77; the *Liberator*, April 12, 1834 and Lesick, *The Lane Rebels: Evangelicalism and Antislavery in Antebellum America*, p. 89.

[24] *New York Evangelist*, May 17, 1834. See also, the *Liberator* of the same date.

[25] *First Annual Report of the American Anti Slavery Society*. New York: Dorr & Butterfield, 1834, esp. pp. 34-36.

[26] Lucretia Mott to James Miller McKim, May 8, 1834 in Beverly Wilson Palmer, ed. *Selected Letters of Lucretia Coffin Mott*, Urbana, IL: University of Illinois Press, 2002, pp. 25-27.

[27] Huntington Lyman to Theodore D. Weld, November 16, 1891, Weld-Grimké Papers, Clements Library, University of Michigan.

[28] See Arthur H. Rice, "Henry B. Stanton as a Political Abolitionist," Columbia University, 1968, p. 46. Hereafter, Rice-*HBS*.

[29] Theodore Weld to James G. Birney, July 14, 1834 in Dwight L. Dumond, ed. *Letters of James Gillespie Birney (1831-1857)*, New York: D-Appleton-

Century Company, 1938, p. 1:127.

[30] [James Hall], "Education and Slavery," *Western Monthly Magazine*, 2, May 1834. Quoted in Lesick, *The Lane Rebels: Evangelicalism and Antislavery in Antebellum America*, p. 91.

[31] Weld's response is printed in its entirety in Barnes and Dumond, eds., *Letters of Theodore Dwight Weld, Angelina Grimké Weld and Sarah Grimké, 1822-1844*, pp. 1:136-46. See also, Lesick, *The Lane Rebels: Evangelicalism and Antislavery in Antebellum America*, pp. 91-92.

[32] Lesick, *The Lane Rebels: Evangelicalism and Antislavery in Antebellum America*, pp. 92-93.

[33] *Fifth Annual Report of the Trustees of the Cincinnati Lane Seminary: together with the Laws of the Institution and a Catalogue of the Officers and Students, November 1834*, (Cincinnati: Corey & Fairbank, 1834) p. 36.

[34] Quoted in Lesick, *The Lane Rebels: Evangelicalism and Antislavery in Antebellum America*, p. 92.

[35] Ibid., p. 94.

[36] Ibid., pp. 126-29.

[37] Theodore Weld to James G. Birney, October 6, 1834. Dumond, ed. *Letters of James Gillespie Birney (1831-1857)*, pp. 1:132-40.

[38] HBS to James A. Thome, September 11, 1834. Quoted in Lesick, *The Lane Rebels: Evangelicalism and Antislavery in Antebellum America*, p. 129.

[39] Ibid., pp. 129-30.

[40] Henry Stanton's speech at Lane was already in print by the time he left the seminary. See classified in *Liberator*, June 14, 1834, p. 95.

[41] Minutes of Lane Colonization Society printed in the *New York Observer and Chronicle*, July 26, 1834. For Stanton and Lincoln see Stanton, *RR*, pp. 50-51 and 234. For Robert's return to Lane, see Lesick, *The Lane Rebels: Evangelicalism and Antislavery in Antebellum America*, p. 199.

[42] Lesick, *The Lane Rebels: Evangelicalism and Antislavery in Antebellum America*, p. 137.

[43] Rice-*HBS*, p. 52. Lesick, *The Lane Rebels: Evangelicalism and Antislavery in Antebellum America*, p. 132.

[44] Lesick, *The Lane Rebels: Evangelicalism and Antislavery in Antebellum America*, p. 132 and S. Wells to Theodore Weld, December 15, 1834 in Barnes and Dumond, eds., *Letters of Theodore Dwight Weld, Angelina Grimké Weld and Sarah Grimké, 1822-1844*, pp. I:178-79.

CHAPTER FIVE: IN-LAWS AND OUTLIERS

[1] Susan Stanton, daughter of Susanna Brewster and Joseph Stanton, requested and received a dismission from the First Church Griswold on October 13,

1822 (*Records of the First Congregational Church of Griswold*, Vol. 2) and married Samuel C. Baldwin in Riga, NY, on December 13, 1823. *Rochester Telegraph*, December 30, 1823. Baldwin served with Henry Stanton on the corresponding committee at the Monroe County Republican meeting of those "friendly to the present National Administration" in May 1828. *Rochester Album*, May 27, 1828. No other joint reform efforts between the two men is known. The Baldwin family often attended local and state antislavery meetings, and Samuel Sr. signed the town's antislavery petition in 1838 as did Frances Avery and Susanna Stanton. "Slavery in the District of Columbia, February 14, 1838." NARA, Records of the 25th Congress.

[2] Records of the First Presbyterian Church, Rochester, NY. Typed transcript, Local History and Special Collections, Rochester Public Library. Birth year from Mt. Hope Cemetery Records, Rochester, New York.

[3] Theodore Dwight Weld, *American Slavery as It Is: Testimony of a Thousand Witnesses*, New York: American Anti-Slavery Society, 1839, p. 44-45. Ibid., p. 172. Emphasis as printed. See also William Goodell, *The American Slave Code in Theory and Practice*, New York: American and Foreign Anti-Slavery Society, 1853, pp. 148 and 216.

[4] *Rochester Album*, n.d., circa February 5, 1828.

[5] *Lyons* [New York] *Republican*, n.d.

[6] Avery's baptism is recorded in the Records of the First Presbyterian Church, Rochester, NY. Local History and Special Collections, Rochester Public Library. For the Stanton-Avery marriage, see the *Rochester Republican*, February 1, 1831.

[7] "Records of the Rochester Female Charitable Society," Special Collections, Rush Rhees Library, University of Rochester. Susanna also served on the board in 1836 and both Susanna and Frances paid dues from their joining the organization in 1833 until the 1840s. In her monograph about the early years of Rochester's benevolent women, Nancy Hewitt did not mention Susanna Stanton's work in charitable and antislavery associations, perhaps because she did not recognize the connection between Susanna and Henry or between Susanna and Elizabeth Cady Stanton. Frances M. Avery, Henry's sister, is only mentioned in passing, and she is not identified as Henry's sister. Nancy A. Hewitt, *Women's Activism and Social Change: Rochester, New York 1822-1872*, Ithaca: Cornell University Press, 1992, p. 152.

[8] Theodore Weld to James G. Birney, July 8, 1834 in Dumond, ed. *Letters of James Gillespie Birney (1831-1857)*, p. I:124.

[9] [Buffalo, New York] *Literary Inquirer*, July 23, 1834.

[10] Receipts of the American Antislavery Society as printed in the *American Anti-Slavery Reporter*, August 30, 1834, p. 128. Susanna and Frances (listed as Mrs. G. A. Avery) each made a $5.00 donation in their own names. The more prosperous George Avery sent $25.00.

[11] This letter was eventually given to her daughter-in-law, Elizabeth Cady

Stanton. Elizabeth mentioned the letter being in her possession in an 1850 letter to Theodore Weld. Elizabeth's mention of Susanna in this letter is the only time she referenced her mother-in-law in surviving correspondence. See Ann D. Gordon, ed. *The Selected Papers of Elizabeth Cady Stanton and Susan B. Anthony: In the School of Anti-Slavery 1840-1866*, Vol. I New Brunswick, NJ: Rutgers University Press, 1997, p. 1:173.

[12] The society's constitution and listing of officers and managers was published in the *Rochester Daily Democrat* on September 24, 1835. A handwritten copy of the constitution and a list of five signatures survive in the Porter Collection at the University of Rochester, Rush Rees Library, Special Collections. These handwritten notes do not include the names of all of the officers or managers, but the constitution, as printed in the *Rochester Daily Democrat* is the same. Historian Nancy Hewitt perhaps did not compare the handwritten and published listings of officers, and she incorrectly identified the third directress as Mrs. Selah Mathews and not Susanna Stanton. Mrs. Mathews served as the first secretary of the group. Hewitt, *Women's Activism and Social Change: Rochester, New York 1822-1872*, p. 83.

[13] Constitution of the Rochester Ladies Anti-Slavery Society as printed in the *Rochester Daily Democrat*, September 24, 1835.

[14] List of Officers of the Rochester Ladies Anti-Slavery Society as printed in the *Rochester Daily Democrat*, September 24, 1835. Samuel D. Porter was active in the local Liberty Party efforts and the Porter home was an active stop on the Underground Railroad.

[15] Although the official records of the Bethel Free Church note that it was formally established in August 1836, Theodore Weld wrote in April that he lectured there, indicating the congregation had left their other churches but had not yet drawn up their official documents. See Weld to Lewis Tappan, April 5, 1836 in Barnes and Dumond, eds., *Letters of Theodore Dwight Weld, Angelina Grimké Weld and Sarah Grimké, 1822-1844*, p. I:288.

[16] Records of Bethel Free Church, Washington Street Church, Central Presbyterian Church and Central Presbyterian Church Sunday School, p. 1. Copied by Lois Badger, Rochester, NY, 1948. Local History Division, Rochester Central Library. See also Strong, *Perfectionist Politics: Abolitionism and the Religious Tensions of American Democracy*, esp. pp. 91-115.

[17] Ibid., pp. 236-239. See also "The Semi-Centennial at the Central Church, Rochester," *New York Evangelist*, January 13, 1887, p. 3.

[18] Elizur Wright, ed. *Quarterly Anti-Slavery Magazine, Volume I*. New York: American Anti-Slavery Society, 1836, p. 95. This publication also notes that since its inception in December 1833, membership had grown from 44 members to 476 in two and a half years. Henry Stanton was also at this meeting, listed as a delegate from Ohio.

[19] Defensor, *The Enemies of the Constitution Discovered or, an Inquiry into the Origin and Tendency of Popular Violence. Containing a Complete and*

Circumstantial Account of the Unlawful Proceedings at the City of Utica, October 21st, 1835; the Dispersion of the State Anti-Slavery Convention, New York: Leavitt, Lord & Co., 1835, p. 181.

[20] Milton C. Sernett, *North Star Country: Upstate New York and the Crusade for African American Freedom*, Syracuse: Syracuse University Press, 2002, p. 181. See also William J. Switala, *Underground Railroad in New Jersey and New York*, Mechanicsburg [Penn.]: Stackpole Books, 2006, p. 116. Source notes for both of these monographs do not refer to the original source for Avery's participation; however, because George Avery is not a well known figure to modern scholars, his addition to the group of "safe houses" in the Rochester area was likely correct. The Department of the Interior's "Historic Resources Associated with the Freedom Trail in Central New York, 1820-1870," p. 41, (n.d., n.p.) contains the same information with the same unrelated source as Sernett.

[21] *The Colored American* [New York, NY], November 10, 1838.

[22] *Liberator*, January 1, 1841.

[23] Bailey (1807-1859) was also converted to the abolitionist cause by the Lane debates, and he spent the remainder of his life as an antislavery newspaper editor working first with James G. Birney on the *Philanthropist* and later as editor of the *National Era* [Washington, DC].

[24] Gilbert Hobbs Barnes, *The Antislavery Impulse 1830-1844*, New York: D. Appleton-Century Company, 1933, pp. 74-77. See also Rice-*HBS*, p. 52-53.

[25] HBS to Charles Finney, January 10, 1835, Charles Finney Papers, Oberlin College. Quoted in Rice-*HBS*, pp. 53-54.

[26] Barnes, *The Antislavery Impulse 1830-1844*, pp. 76-77.

[27] Theodore Weld to Lewis Tappan, March 9, 1836 in Barnes and Dumond, eds., *Letters of Theodore Dwight Weld, Angelina Grimké Weld and Sarah Grimké, 1822-1844*, pp. I:270-74.

[28] *Proceedings of the Ohio Anti-Slavery Convention, held at Putnam, on the twenty-second, twenty-third, and twenty-fourth of April, 1835*. Beaumont and Wallace [n.d., n.p.] Rare Books, Manuscript and Special Collections Library, Duke University. See also Rice-*HBS*, pp. 54-55.

[29] *Liberator*, May 16, 1835 and Ibid., p. 56.

[30] *Liberator*, June 6, 1835.

[31] Rice-*HBS*, pp. 60-61.

[32] A young men's antislavery group in New York City sought to raise a salary of $800.00 for Weld in 1835. Elizur Wright to Weld, May 26, 1835. Barnes and Dumond, eds., *Letters of Theodore Dwight Weld, Angelina Grimké Weld and Sarah Grimké, 1822-1844*, p. 221. Weld suffered long periods of illness due to poor traveling conditions and continued vocal projections. See also Rice-*HBS*, pp. 61- 62.

[33] HBS to Amos A. Phelps, December 18, 1835. Boston Public Library, Anti-Slavery Collection, Amos A. Phelps Papers. For the "gag rule" in the United

States House of Representatives, see William Lee Miller, *Arguing About Slavery: John Quincy Adams and the Great Battle in the United States Congress*, New York: Vintage Books, 1995.

[34] For example, Henry was a frequent speaker as the Providence Female Juvenile Anti-Slavery Society was organizing, and the group noted in their first annual report that their "beloved friend [Henry B. Stanton]" provided both "good advice and encouragement." *Liberator*, December 26, 1835.

[35] As reprinted in the *Liberator*, March 5, 1836. The editor of the *Woonsocket Advocate* noted that the "noble man" referred to was H. B. Stanton.

[36] HBS to Amos A. Phelps, December 18, 1835. Boston Public Library, Anti-Slavery Collection, Amos A. Phelps Papers. Stanton wrote to Phelps asking him to come to Rhode Island to help before the convention, offering to reciprocate in aiding Phelps' efforts in Connecticut. Phelps was unable to leave, but Charles Burleigh joined Henry in Rhode Island in January 1836– the month before the state convention. See also Rice-*HBS*, pp. 63-64.

[37] HBS to Amos A. Phelps, December 18, 1835. Boston Public Library, Anti-Slavery Collection, Amos A. Phelps Papers. The minutes of the meeting were recorded in "Proceedings of the Rhode-Island Anti-slavery Convention," Providence: H. H. Brown, 1836. Rare Book, Manuscript and Special Collections Library, Duke University.

[38] The two representatives from Providence were George Curtiss and Thomas W. Dorr. See William Goodell, *Slavery and Anti-Slavery; a History of the Great Struggle in Both Hemispheres; with a View of the Slavery Question in the United States*, William Harned, 1852; reprint, New York: Negro Universities Press, 1968, p. 420.

[39] Alvan Stewart and Theodore Weld to William Goodell, February 14, 1836. Special Collections & Archives, Hutchins Library, Berea College.

[40] Stanton to Phelps, March 5, 1836, Boston Public Library, Anti-Slavery Collection, Amos A. Phelps Papers.

[41] "Letter from H. B. Stanton, March 2, 1836" in the *Liberator*, March 12, 1836.

[42] HBS to Amos Phelps, April 13, 1836. Boston Public Library, Anti-Slavery Convention, Amos A. Phelps Papers.

[43] See *Rochester Republican*, April 26, 1836 and HBS to Amos Phelps, April 13, 1836. Boston Public Library, Anti-Slavery Convention, Amos A. Phelps Papers.

[44] *Livingston Democrat* (Geneseo, NY), April 26, 1836, May 31, 1836 and HBS to Amos Phelps, April 13, 1836. Boston Public Library, Anti-Slavery Convention, Amos A. Phelps Papers.

[45] See Stanton, *RR*, p. 50-51 and Henry Wilson, *Rise and Fall of the Slave Power in America*, James R. Osgood & Co., Boston, 1872, Vol. I p. 293.

[46] *Third Annual Report of the American Anti-Slavery Society*, New York: William S. Dorr, 1836, p. 22.

[47] Ibid., p. 29.

[48] Rice explores this idea further. Rice-*HBS*, pp. 80-90. See also Miller, *Arguing About Slavery: John Quincy Adams and the Great Battle in the United States Congress*, pp. 145-47. A similar situation occurred in the 1840s as notions of "free labor" ideology spread.

[49] Ibid., p. 30.

[50] *Lynn Record*, n.d., reprinted in the *Liberator*, May 28, 1836.

[51] HBS to Mary Grew, July 2, 1836. Philadelphia Female Anti-Slavery Society Papers, Historical Society of Philadelphia. Thanks to Dr. Anne Derousie for a copy of this letter.

[52] Diary of Lewis Tappan, July 6-8, 1836. Lewis Tappan Papers, Library of Congress. Tappan also wrote that he exchanged watches with Weld, noting, "he wished him to have a better one than the one he wore three years ago." Both timepieces were gifts of Tappan, the first valued at $21 and the replacement at $45.

[53] Diary of Lewis Tappan, July 24, 1836. Lewis Tappan Papers, Library of Congress. The announcement was also printed in the *Liberator* on August 13, 1836 and the *Emancipator* on August 25, 1836.

[54] *Emancipator*, August 25, 1836.

[55] Deborah Weston to Caroline Weston, June 6, 1836. Weston Family Papers, Boston Public Library.

[56] *Liberator*, June 11, 1836.

[57] *Liberator*, September 10, 1836.

[58] *Emancipator*, September 15, 1836.

[59] *United States Telegraph*, Washington, DC, November 30, 1836.

[60] Deborah Weston to Caroline Weston, October 21, 1836, Boston Public Library, Weston Family Papers.

[61] HBS to Anne W. Weston, [April 27, 1836], Boston Public Library, Weston Family Papers.

[62] Deborah Weston to Anne W. Weston, n.d. [1836?] Boston Public Library, Weston Family Papers.

[63] For a detailed discussion of the necessity for the restructuring, see Rice-*HBS*, p. 94.

[64] Elizur Wright to his parents, July 20, 1837, Wright Papers, Library of Congress. Quoted in Ibid., p. 95.

[65] Henry B. Stanton, *Remarks of Henry B. Stanton in the Representatives Hall on the 23d and 24th of February, 1837, before the Committee of the House of Representatives of Massachusetts, to Whom Was Referred Sundry Memorials on the Subject of Slavery*, Boston: Isaac Knapp, 1837, p. 12 and 29.

[66] Ibid., pp. 51-53.

[67] Angelina Grimké, Sarah Grimké and Mrs. Theodore Dwight to Jane Smith, February 1837. Box 3, Weld-Grimké Papers, Clements Library, University of Michigan. The Representative's Hall in Boston, the site of Henry Stanton's

1837 address, is located in the current Massachusetts State House, and the room is currently the meeting place of the State Senate.

[68] HBS to "friend Dearborn," Boston, April 27, 1837, author's collection; and Stanton, *RR*, pp. 49-50. Stanton's printed speech also became part of the AAS's pamphlet library and was sold at antislavery meetings.

[69] "Movements of Mr. Stanton," in the *Liberator*, April 28, 1837.

[70] See "Resolutions Adopted at the Last Anniversary," *Philanthropist*, June 16, 1837 and *Fourth Annual Report of the American Anti-Slavery Society with the Speeches Delivered at the Anniversary Meeting Held in the City of New York on the 9th May, 1837*, New York: William S. Dorr, 1837, pp. 17, 19, 23 and 27.

CHAPTER SIX: HOW QUESTIONS ABOUT WOMEN...

[1] *Formation of the Massachusetts Abolition Society*. No date/publication information, pg. 18 from Samuel May Anti-Slavery Collection, Cornell University.

[2] Catherine H. Birney, *The Grimké Sisters: Sarah and Angelina Grimké the First American Women Advocates of Abolition and Women's Rights*, New York: Lee and Shepard, 1885. See also, Carol Berkin, *Civil War Wives: The Lives and Times of Angelina Grimké Weld, Varina Howell Davis and Julia Dent Grant*, New York: Vintage Books, 2009, p. 41.

[3] From "Minutes of the Agency Committee," American Anti-Slavery Society, July 13, 1836 as quoted in Barnes, *The Antislavery Impulse 1830-1844*, p. 154.

[4] Some question exists as to whether or not Angelina was, in fact, an official agent of the AAS. Gilbert Hobbs Barnes, who discovered the Weld-Grimké papers and was the historian who rescued Weld from historical obscurity, claimed that she was formally appointed. However, articles in the *Liberator* (for example, H. C. Wright's response to the "Pastoral Letter," August 4, 1837) and individual correspondence seems to indicate that the arrangement was not a formal one and not an issue that should have worried the AAS.

[5] Sarah and Angelina Grimké attended the annual meeting of the New England Anti-Slavery Society, but the minutes did not record any mention of the sisters. Barnes and Dumond, eds., *Letters of Theodore Dwight Weld, Angelina Grimké Weld and Sarah Grimké, 1822-1844*. p. 1:409.

[6] Barnes, *The Antislavery Impulse 1830-1844*, p. 155.

[7] Birney, *The Grimké Sisters: Sarah and Angelina Grimké the First American Women Advocates of Abolition and Women's Rights*, p. 179.

[8] Berkin, *Civil War Wives: The Lives and Times of Angelina Grimké Weld, Varina Howell Davis and Julia Dent Grant*, p. 49.

[9] Theodore Weld to Sarah and Angelina Grimké, August 15, 1837 in Barnes and Dumond, eds., *Letters of Theodore Dwight Weld, Angelina Grimké Weld and*

Sarah Grimké, 1822-1844, p. 1:425.

[10] John Greenleaf Whittier to Sarah and Angelina Grimké, August 14, 1837 in Ibid., pp. 1:423-24.

[11] Angelina Grimké to Jane Smith, August 10, 1837 in Weld-Grimké Papers, Clements Library, University of Michigan.

[12] Ibid.

[13] Quoted in Barnes, *The Antislavery Impulse 1830-1844*, p. 157. Written 45 years after the event, the *History of Woman Suffrage* claimed Whittier had a very different reaction in 1837, and that he held a position that speaks to the issue of politics as being aligned with women's rights, and not with Garrisonian non-resistance: "On reading the 'Pastoral Letter,' our Quaker poet, John Greenleaf Whittier, poured out his indignation on the New England clergy in thrilling denunciations. Mr. Whittier early saw that woman's only protection against religious and social tyranny could be found in political equality. In the midst of the fierce conflicts in the Anti-Slavery Conventions of 1839 and '40, on the woman question *per se*, Mr. Whittier remarked to Lucretia Mott, "Give woman the right to vote, and you end all these persecutions by reform and church organizations." Elizabeth Cady Stanton, Susan B. Anthony, and Matilda Joslyn Gage, eds., *History of Woman Suffrage*, Vol. I New York: Fowler & Wells, 1881, 1:83-84. See Barnes and Dumond, eds., *Letters of Theodore Dwight Weld, Angelina Grimké Weld and Sarah Grimké, 1822-1844*, p. I:xxvi.

[14] Mayer, *All on Fire: William Lloyd Garrison and the Abolition of Slavery*, p. 167.

[15] Wendell Phillips Garrison and Francis Jackson Garrison, *William Lloyd Garrison, the Story of His Life, Told by His Children*, IV vols., Vol. I, New York: The Century Co., 1885, pp. 348-80. See also Mayer, *All on Fire: William Lloyd Garrison and the Abolition of Slavery*, pp. 151-65.

[16] Mayer, *All on Fire: William Lloyd Garrison and the Abolition of Slavery*, p. 170.

[17] See Lawrence B. Goodheart, *Abolitionist, Actuary, Atheist: Elizur Wright and the Reform Impulse*, Kent, Ohio: The Kent State University Press, 1990, esp. pp. 40-44 and Bertram Wyatt-Brown, *Lewis Tappan and the Evangelical War against Slavery*, Cincinnati, Ohio: Case Western Reserve University Press, 1969, pp. 85-89.

[18] Wyatt-Brown, *Lewis Tappan and the Evangelical War against Slavery*, p. 89.

[19] Mayer, *All on Fire: William Lloyd Garrison and the Abolition of Slavery*, p. 172-74.

[20] Declaration of Sentiments, American Anti-Slavery Society as reprinted in the *Emancipator*, May 2, 1839.

[21] Anna David Hallowell, ed. *James and Lucretia Mott. Life and Letters.* Boston: Houghton Mifflin Company, 1884, pp. 111-15. The other women who attended were: Lydia White, Esther Moore, and Sydney Ann Lewis.

[22] Quoted in Mayer, *All on Fire: William Lloyd Garrison and the Abolition of*

Slavery, p. 225.

[23] See Wendell Phillips Garrison and Francis Jackson Garrison, *William Lloyd Garrison: The Story of His Life as Told by His Children,* IV vols., Vol. II 1835-1840, New York: The Century Co., 1885, pp. 145 and 90-204.

[24] John Greenleaf Whittier to Sarah and Angelina Grimké, August 14, 1837. Barnes and Dumond, eds., *Letters of Theodore Dwight Weld, Angelina Grimké Weld and Sarah Grimké, 1822- 1844,* pp. 1:423-24.

[25] Ibid.

[26] "Seventh Annual Report of the Board of Managers of the Mass. Anti-Slavery Society," Boston, January 24-26, 1839.

[27] The meeting of the New England Antislavery Society convened in Boston on May 30, 1838. Walter M. Merrill and Louis Rucharnes, eds., *The Letters of William Lloyd Garrison, Volume II: A House Dividing against Itself, 1836-1840,* Cambridge, MA: Belknap Press, 1971, p. 367n5. "Seventh Annual Report of the Board of Managers of the Mass. Anti-Slavery Society," p. 32. Ibid., p. 16.

[28] HBS to James G. Birney in Dumond, ed. *Letters of James Gillespie Birney (1831-1857),* p. I:482.

[29] Rice-*HBS,* pp. 165- 67.

[30] Garrison to George W. Bensen, March 26, 1939. Garrison and Garrison, *William Lloyd Garrison: The Story of His Life as Told by His Children,* p. 285.

[31] Maria Weston Chapman, *Right and Wrong in Massachusetts,* Boston: Dow and Jackson, 1839, pp. 102-04.

[32] HBS to Elizur Wright, January 26, 1839. Elizur Wright Papers, Library of Congress. Reprinted from the 1838 report in the *Massachusetts Abolitionist,* March 26, 1840 (emphasis as printed.)

[33] Chapman, *Right and Wrong in Massachusetts,* pp. 102-04. See also Garrison and Garrison, *William Lloyd Garrison: The Story of His Life as Told by His Children,* p. 273.

[34] HBS to James G. Birney in Dumond, ed. *Letters of James Gillespie Birney (1831-1857),* p. 481.

[35] "Seventh Annual Report of the Board of Managers of the Mass. Anti-Slavery Society," p. iv.

[36] HBS to Elizur Wright, January 26, 1839. Elizur Wright Papers, Library of Congress. See also HBS to James G. Birney in Dumond, ed. *Letters of James Gillespie Birney (1831-1857),* pp. I:481-83.

[37] All antislavery petitions sent to Congress were immediately tabled from May 1836 (24th Congress) to December 1844 (28th Congress). The so-called "gag rule" was vehemently opposed by John Quincy Adams. See Miller, *Arguing About Slavery: John Quincy Adams and the Great Battle in the United States Congress.*

[38] For a thorough discussion of this fear, see Rice-*HBS,* p. 149. See also Larry E. Tise, *Proslavery: A History of the Defense of Slavery in America, 1701- 1840,* Athens, GA: The University of Georgia Press, 1987, concerning

the solidification of proslavery arguments in response to Garrison and the increasing visibility of the abolitionists in the North.

[39] HBS to James G. Birney in Dumond, ed. *Letters of James Gillespie Birney (1831-1857)*, p. I:482. See also HBS to Elizur Wright, January 26, 1839. Elizur Wright Papers, Library of Congress.

[40] HBS to James G. Birney in Ibid., pp. I:481-83.

[41] Garrison and Garrison, *William Lloyd Garrison: The Story of His Life as Told by His Children*, p. 238.

[42] Ibid., p. 239.

[43] HBS to Elizur Wright. January 26, 1839. Elizur Wright Papers, Library of Congress. Wright edited the paper for just under a year.

[44] Garrison's salary was $1,200, while Whittier received only $1,000 for editing the *Pennsylvania Freeman*. HBS to Elizur Wright, April 11,1839. HBS to Amos A. Phelps [n.d, n.p.] [January 1839]. Elizur Wright Papers, Library of Congress. Two years later, in 1841, Lydia Maria Child became the editor of the *National Anti-Slavery Standard*, the new official paper of the AAS, at a salary of $1,000 per year and on par with Whittier. Alma Lutz, *Crusade for Freedom: Women of the Antislavery Movement* Boston: Beacon Press, 1968, p. 176.

[45] *Friend of Man*, Utica, New York. February 6, 1839. HBS to Elizur Wright, February 4, 1839. Elizur Wright Papers, Library of Congress.

[46] Rice-*HBS*, p. 160.

[47] HBS to Elizur Wright. February 9, 1839. Elizur Wright Papers, Library of Congress.

[48] William A. Stanton, *A Record, Genealogical, Biographical, Statistical, of Thomas Stanton of Connecticut and His Descendants, 1635-1891*, Albany, NY: Joel Munsell's Sons, 1891, p. 462. Douglass lived with the Johnsons from September 1838 through much of 1839.

[49] *Sixth Annual Report of the Executive Committee of the American Anti-Slavery Society, with the Speeches Delivered at the Anniversary Meeting Held in the City of New York, on the 7th of May, 1839*, New York: William S. Dorr, 1839; reprint, New York: Kraus Reprint Co: 1972, pp. 28-29.

[50] It is possible that other women voted might also have voted "no" because most of the first names were recorded as initials only. Others of note: James McCune Smith, voted no, while Waterloo, NY resident and husband of future Seneca Falls Convention organizer, Richard P. Hunt, voted yes. Ibid., pp. 28-30.

[51] *Sixth Annual Report of the Executive Committee of the American Anti-Slavery Society, with the Speeches Delivered at the Anniversary Meeting Held in the City of New York, on the 7th of May, 1839*, New York: William S. Dorr, 1839; reprint, New York: Kraus Reprint Co: 1972, p. 34.

[52] Ibid.

[53] Ibid., pp. 42-43.

[54] Ibid., p. 45. See also, the *Emancipator*, May 23, 1839, p. 14.

[55] Ibid.

[56] *Emancipator*, May 23, 1839, p. 14.

[57] See *Symmes' Theory of Concentric Spheres, By a Citizen of the United States*, Cincinnati: Morgan, Lodge and Fisher, 1826.

[58] *Friend of Man*, Utica, New York, May 29, 1839.

[59] See *Emancipator*, May 30, 1839.

[60] HBS to Elizur Wright, April 2, 1839. Elizur Wright Papers, Library of Congress.

[61] Rice-*HBS*, pp.170-71.

[62] HBS to Amos Phelps, June 18, 1839, Elizur Wright Papers, Library of Congress. See also Garrison and Garrison, *William Lloyd Garrison: The Story of His Life as Told by His Children*, p. 306. Phelps resigned his post on the Board of Managers of the MAS on April 30, 1839. Phelps to F. C. Jackson, April 30, 1839, typed copy in Elizur Wright Papers, Library of Congress.

[63] Calls were usually printed in all antislavery publications. See *Friend of Man*, Utica, New York, May 29, 1839.

[64] *Emancipator*, August 15, 1839.

[65] Orange Scott of Albany. *Emancipator*, August 15, 1839.

[66] *Emancipator*, August, 15, 1839.

[67] Garrison and Garrison, *William Lloyd Garrison: The Story of His Life as Told by His Children*, p. 309.

CHAPTER SEVEN: THE WHIRLWIND AND THE SUN FLOWER

[1] Annual Report of the Massachusetts Antislavery Society, 5th Annual Meeting, xiii. Speech delivered January 25, 1837.

[2] HBS to Elizabeth Cady, January 1, 1840. The poem was written by Sir Thomas Moore, a longtime favorite of the Stantons. As quoted in Gordon, ed. *The Selected Papers of Elizabeth Cady Stanton and Susan B. Anthony: In the School of Anti- Slavery 1840-1866*, p. 1.

[3] HBS to Gerrit Smith, September 22, 1840. Gerrit Smith Papers, Special Collections Research Center, Syracuse University Library.

[4] Stanton, *80Y*, p. 60. See also Lutz, *Created Equal: A Biography of Elizabeth Cady Stanton 1815-1902*, p. 18.

[5] Lutz, *Created Equal: A Biography of Elizabeth Cady Stanton 1815-1902*, p. 19. Stanton, *80Y*, p. 58.

[6] Elizabeth Cady to Peter Smith, January 27, [1836] Gerrit Smith Papers, Special Collections Research Center, Syracuse University Library.

[7] Patricia Carley Johnson, "Sensitivity and Civil War: The Selected Diaries and Papers, 1858-1866, of Frances Adeline [Fanny] Seward." Ph.D. dissertation, University of Rochester, 1964, pp. 670-671.

[8] Elizabeth Cady to Elizabeth Smith, July 20 [1839]. Alma Lutz Collection, Vassar College.

[9] Elizabeth Cady to Elizabeth Smith, September 11, [1839], Alma Lutz Collection, Vassar College.

[10] *Liberator*, October 11, 1839.

[11] Lutz, *Created Equal: A Biography of Elizabeth Cady Stanton 1815-1902*, p. 19.

[12] Stanton, *80Y*, pp. 59-60.

[13] ECS's quote about Henry, Elizabeth Cady Stanton Papers, Library of Congress. The poem in Elizabeth's commonplace book, *Song of the Irish Peasant Wife*, was written by Caroline Norton, a British social reformer. Long after the poem was written in Elizabeth's commonplace book, Norton divorced her husband due to his infidelity, and she became an active early feminist. Norton helped to push several important bills through Parliament, including bills concerning child custody, divorce and married women's property bills.

[14] *The Emancipator*, September 19, 1839 and November 7, 1839.

[15] Stanton, *80Y*, p. 61.

[16] *Emancipator*, November 14, 1839.

[17] *Emancipator*, November 14, 1839. See also Elizur Wright, *Myron Holley; What He Did for Liberty and True Religion*, Boston: The Author, 1882, pp. 254-55.

[18] *Massachusetts Abolitionist*, November 7, 1839, p. 150.

[19] *Liberator*, December 6, 1939, p. 195.

[20] Gerrit Smith to Ann Smith, December 11, 1839. Gerrit Smith Papers, Special Collections Research Center, Syracuse University Library.

[21] Ibid.

[22] Daniel Cady to Gerrit Smith, December 14, 1839, Gerrit Smith Papers, Special Collections Research Center, Syracuse University Library.

[23] HBS to Gerrit Smith, December 25, 1839. Gerrit Smith Papers, Special Collections Research Center, Syracuse University Library. Ann Smith to Elizabeth Smith, December 20-21, 1839. Gerrit Smith Papers, Special Collections Research Center, Syracuse University Library.

[24] Lucretia Mott to James Miller McKim, December 29, 1839. Palmer, ed. *Selected Letters of Lucretia Coffin Mott*, p. 69.

[25] HBS to Elizabeth Cady, January 1, 1840 in Gordon, ed. *The Selected Papers of Elizabeth Cady Stanton and Susan B. Anthony: In the School of Anti-Slavery 1840-1866*, pp. 1-3.

[26] Stanton-Blatch, *Letters*, pp. II:4-5.

[27] *Friend of Man*, Utica, New York, May 29, 1839.

[28] With the possible exception of the Massachusetts clergy.

[29] HBS to Elizur Wright, no date, likely end December 1839. Elizur Wright Papers, Library of Congress.

[30] *Massachusetts Abolitionist*, April 9, 1840. See also the *Emancipator* of the

same date.

[31] For Daniel Cady's opposition to the marriage, see Gerrit Smith to Ann Smith, December 12, 1839 and Daniel Cady to Gerrit Smith, December 14, 1839. Gerrit Smith Papers, Special Collections Research Center, Syracuse University Library. For the end of the engagement, see Elizabeth Cady to Ann Smith, March 4, 1840 in Gordon, ed. *The Selected Papers of Elizabeth Cady Stanton and Susan B. Anthony: In the School of Anti-Slavery 1840-1866*, pp. 4-6.

[32] Stanton, *80Y*, p. 71.

[33] HBS to Gerrit Smith, February 27, 1840. Gerrit Smith Papers, Special Collections Research Center, Syracuse University Library.

[34] See for example, Griffith, *In Her Own Right: The Life of Elizabeth Cady Stanton*, pp. 23-24 and 31. The story was first reported by Lutz in 1940. Lutz, *Created Equal: A Biography of Elizabeth Cady Stanton 1815-1902*, pp. 16-19.

[35] Elizabeth wrote to a friend a few months later about her observations of a French delegate she met at the World's Anti- Slavery Convention, Francois Guizot. Elizabeth noted that "her brother [in-law] used to get his strongest arguments against immediate abolition" from Guizot's works. As noted by Ann Gordon, "her brother" probably refers to Bayard (who had been mentioned earlier in the same letter) as Elizabeth's last surviving brother had died in 1826 and Guizot's work was not published until 1828. See ECS to Sarah M. Grimké and Angelina Grimké Weld, June 25, 1840. Gordon, ed. *The Selected Papers of Elizabeth Cady Stanton and Susan B. Anthony: In the School of Anti-Slavery 1840-1866*, p. 11 and p. 15 n. 17.

[36] HBS to Gerrit Smith, February 27, 1840. Gerrit Smith Papers, Special Collections Research Center, Syracuse University Library.

[37] Ibid.

[38] Ibid.

[39] Quoted in Lutz, *Created Equal: A Biography of Elizabeth Cady Stanton 1815-1902*, p. 21.

[40] See editorial note in Gordon, ed. *The Selected Papers of Elizabeth Cady Stanton and Susan B. Anthony: In the School of Anti-Slavery 1840-1866*, p. 8.

[41] HBS to Gerrit Smith, April 17, 1840. Gerrit Smith Papers, Special Collections Research Center, Syracuse University Library.

[42] Ibid.

[43] Barnes and Dumond, eds., *Letters of Theodore Dwight Weld, Angelina Grimké Weld and Sarah Grimké, 1822-1844*, p. II:828. Weld's letter is dated April 10, 1840 and within the document, Weld mentions that he attempted to make Stanton's request in person to Tappan "last Monday" (April 6) but Tappan was not at his office. Weld likely received word from Henry shortly before the 6th of April. Henry's letter to Weld did not survive.

[44] Ibid.

[45] HBS to Amos A. Phelps, April 7, 1840. Amos Phelps Papers, Boston Public

Library.

[46] Ibid. Portions of this letter are also quoted in Griffith, but Griffith assumed the letter's date was April 17 due to a later pencil notation of that date. The letter's postmark shows the 7th, and Stanton also wrote to Phelps on the 11th and referenced items within this letter. Griffith, *In Her Own Right: The Life of Elizabeth Cady Stanton*, pp. 32-33; Stanton, *80Y*, p. 71.

[47] Stanton, *80Y*, p. 71.

[48] See Ibid., p. 71. See also Daniel Webster and Edward Everett, *The Works of Daniel Webster*, vol. II Boston: Charles C. Little and James Brown, 1851, p. 344 and Charles McCarthy, *The Antimasonic Party: A Study of Political Antimasonry in the United States, 1827-1840*, American Historical Association Washington, D. C.: Government Printing Office, 1903, p. 414.

[49] Barnes and Dumond, eds., *Letters of Theodore Dwight Weld, Angelina Grimké Weld and Sarah Grimké, 1822-1844*, pp. 678-79. The Weld's marriage certificate survives in the Weld-Grimké Papers, Clements Library, University of Michigan, and the document was signed by those in attendance including Henry and the Averys. Although historians have long noted the confusion surrounding the actual date of the Stanton's marriage, it appears that the confusion resulted purely from Elizabeth's autobiography. Elizabeth (or a printer's error) stated the date as May 10, but Henry's *Random Recollections* (all three editions) as well as newspaper accounts (*Liberator*, May 15, 1840; *Emancipator*, May 15, 1840 and the *Massachusetts Abolitionist*, June 4, 1840) are consistent with the May 1 date. The *Abolitionist* likely missed inserting the announcement in the previous issue as it mentions the "1st inst."

[50] Lutz, *Created Equal: A Biography of Elizabeth Cady Stanton 1815-1902*, p. 35.

[51] Harriot Stanton Blatch to Alma Lutz, May 16, 1930 (typed transcript). Alma Lutz Collection, Vassar College.

CHAPTER EIGHT: A WHOLE NEW WORLD

[1] Stanton, *80Y*, p. 81.

[2] HBS to Gerrit Smith, February 27, 1840. Gerrit Smith Papers, Special Collections Research Center, Syracuse University Library.

[3] H.C.H. to W.L. Garrison, April 24, 1840, as printed in the *Liberator*, May 15, 1840.

[4] Rice-*HBS*, p. 200.

[5] William L. Garrison to Lucretia Mott, April 28, 1840, Merrill and Rucharnes, eds., *The Letters of William Lloyd Garrison, Volume II: A House Dividing against Itself, 1836-1840*, p. 592. Kraditor, *Means and Ends in American Abolitionism: Garrison and His Critics on Strategy and Tactics, 1834-1850*, p. 9.

[6] *Seventh Annual Report of the Executive Committee of the American Anti-Slavery Society*, New York: William S. Dorr, 1840; reprint, Kraus, 1972, p. 9.

[7] Ibid., p. 10.

[8] William L. Garrison to Helen E. Garrison, May 15, 1840. Merrill and Rucharnes, eds., *The Letters of William Lloyd Garrison, Volume II: A House Dividing against Itself, 1836-1840*, p. 611.

[9] *Seventh Annual Report of the Executive Committee of the American Anti-Slavery Society*, p. 67. Emphasis as printed.

[10] "Statement of the Executive Committee of the American and Foreign Anti-Slavery Society," *Emancipator*, February 25, 1841. Emphasis as printed.

[11] *Massachusetts Abolitionist*, May 28, 1840.

[12] Formed in 1839. *Emancipator*, March 29, 1839.

[13] Rice-*HBS*, pp. 200.

[14] Birney, *James G. Birney and His Times: The Genesis of the Republican Party with Some Account of Abolition Movements in the South before 1828*, pp. 365-66.

[15] Stanton and Blatch, *Letters*, p. II:6.

[16] Merrill and Rucharnes, eds., *The Letters of William Lloyd Garrison, Volume II: A House Dividing against Itself, 1836-1840*, p. 381.

[17] *Emancipator*, March 28, 1839.

[18] *Proceedings of the General Anti-Slavery Convention, Called by the Committee of the British and Foreign Anti-Slavery Society, and Held in London, from Friday, June 12th, to Tuesday, June 23rd, 1840*, London: Johnston and Barrett, 1841, p. 8.

[19] See Minutes of the Meeting of the British and Foreign Anti-Slavery Society, August 30, 1839. Rhodes House Antislavery Papers, Oxford University. Included in this collection are the queries sent to the various slave-holding nations, including a separate query for Texas. Douglas H. Maynard, "The World's Anti-Slavery Convention of 1840," *The Mississippi Valley Historical Review* 47, no. 3 (Dec. 1960): p. 452. See also, Louis Filler, *Crusade against Slavery: Friends, Foes, and Reforms, 1820-1860*, Algonac, MI: Reference Publications, Inc., 1986, p. 70. Barnes and Dumond, eds., *Letters of Theodore Dwight Weld, Angelina Grimké Weld and Sarah Grimké, 1822-1844*, p. II:858.

[20] Henry Stanton wrote Gerrit Smith on the inside and back cover of the second call. Letter from Stanton to Smith dated April 17, 1840. Gerrit Smith Papers, Special Collections Research Center, Syracuse University Library. See also HBS to Amos Phelps, letter also written on a copy of the February 15 call (n.d. [March 28, 1840]), Amos Phelps Papers, Boston Public Library.

[21] William L. Garrison to Helen E. Garrison, May 19, 1840 in Merrill and Rucharnes, eds., *The Letters of William Lloyd Garrison, Volume II: A House Dividing against Itself, 1836-1840*, p. 616.

[22] William L. Garrison to Helen E. Garrison, May 19, 1840 in Ibid.

[23] *Liberator*. Quoted in Garrison and Garrison, *William Lloyd Garrison: The Story of His Life as Told by His Children*, p. 352.

[24] Stanton, *80Y*, p. 53.

[25] Sarah Grimké to Elizabeth Pease, November 15, 1840. Garrison Papers, Boston Public Library. The Rhodes House Anti-Slavery Papers contain correspondence of note from many Americans during this time period. See also Annie Heloise Abel and Frank J. Klingberg, eds., *A Side-Light on Anglo-American Relations, 1839-1858: Furnished by the Correspondence of Lewis Tappan and Others with the British and Foreign Anti-Slavery Society*, Lancaster, PA: Lancaster Press, 1927.

[26] *Emancipator*, May 1, 1840 and *Liberator*, May 8, 1840.

[27] Lewis Tappan to Theodore Weld, May 4, 1840. Barnes and Dumond, eds., *Letters of Theodore Dwight Weld, Angelina Grimké Weld and Sarah Grimké, 1822-1844*, p. II:834 and n. 2.

[28] "Mr. Stanton and the Woman Question," *National Anti-Slavery Standard*, October 22, 1840 and "Mr. Stanton and the Woman Question," as reprinted in the *Liberator*, December 4, 1840.

[29] See Palmer, ed. *Selected Letters of Lucretia Coffin Mott*, p. 75.

[30] Frederick B. Tolles, ed. *Slavery And "The Woman Question": Lucretia Mott's Diary of Her Visit to Great Britain to Attend the World's Anti-Slavery Convention of 1840*, Supplement No. 23 to the *Journal of the Friends' Historical Society* Haverford, PA: Friends' Historical Association, 1952, p. 22.

[31] Minutes of the Meeting of the British and Foreign Anti-Slavery Society, June 11, 1840. Rhodes House Antislavery Papers, Oxford University. Although James G. Birney was not listed as a visitor at this meeting, his vote is recorded as seconding the motion appointing Thomas Clarkson as president of the meeting.

[32] Minutes of the Meeting of the British and Foreign Anti-Slavery Society, June 11, 1840. Rhodes House Antislavery Papers, Oxford University, resolution 281. The protest by Sarah Pugh was also included in Lucretia Mott's diary; the text differs slightly, but not materially between the two. See Tolles, ed. *Slavery And "The Woman Question": Lucretia Mott's Diary of Her Visit to Great Britain to Attend the World's Anti-Slavery Convention of 1840*, p. 28. A resolution from the same meeting added Henry Stanton's name to the roster of secretaries of the convention.

[33] *Proceedings of the General Anti-Slavery Convention, Called by the Committee of the British and Foreign Anti-Slavery Society, and Held in London, from Friday, June 12th, to Tuesday, June 23rd, 1840*, p. 23.

[34] Ibid., 333. See also Donald R. Kennon, "An Apple of Discord: The Woman Question at the World's Anti-Slavery Convention of 1840," *Slavery & Abolition* 5, no. 3 (1984): p. 251. Kennon did not examine the Minutes of the Meeting and relied on the Garrisonian controlled *National Anti-Slavery Standard* for his information.

[35] Kennon, "An Apple of Discord: The Woman Question at the World's Anti-Slavery Convention of 1840," p. 251.

[36] Wendell Phillips to the *Liberator*. Garrison and Garrison, *William Lloyd Garrison: The Story of His Life as Told by His Children*, pp. 368-69. Emphasis as printed.

[37] Kennon, "An Apple of Discord: The Woman Question at the World's Anti-Slavery Convention of 1840," p.250.

[38] *Proceedings of the General Anti-Slavery Convention, Called by the Committee of the British and Foreign Anti-Slavery Society, and Held in London, from Friday, June 12th, to Tuesday, June 23rd, 1840*, p. 45.

[39] Stanton, *80Y*, p. 79. See also Lutz, *Created Equal: A Biography of Elizabeth Cady Stanton 1815-1902*, pp. 28-29 and Stanton, Anthony, and Gage, eds., *History of Woman Suffrage*, p. 1:61.

[40] For Phillips, see "Mr. Stanton and the Woman Question," *National Anti-Slavery Standard*, October 22, 1840, p. 78. Garrison, see W. L. Garrison to Helen Garrison, June 29, 1840 in Garrison and Garrison, *William Lloyd Garrison: The Story of His Life as Told by His Children*, pp. 381-84.

[41] James G. Birney to Lewis Tappan, August 29, 1840 in Dumond, ed. *Letters of James Gillespie Birney (1831-1857)*, p. II:596.

[42] "Mr. Stanton and the Woman Question," *National Anti-Slavery Standard*, October 22, 1840, p. 78.

[43] *Proceedings of the General Anti-Slavery Convention, Called by the Committee of the British and Foreign Anti-Slavery Society, and Held in London, from Friday, June 12th, to Tuesday, June 23rd, 1840*, p. 563.

[44] Tolles, ed. *Slavery And "The Woman Question": Lucretia Mott's Diary of Her Visit to Great Britain to Attend the World's Anti- Slavery Convention of 1840*, p. 44.

[45] Stanton, *80Y*, pp. 82-83.

[46] Griffith, *In Her Own Right: The Life of Elizabeth Cady Stanton*, p. 34.

[47] See for example, ECS to Elizabeth J. Neall, January 25, 1841 in Gordon, ed. *The Selected Papers of Elizabeth Cady Stanton and Susan B. Anthony: In the School of Anti-Slavery 1840-1866*, pp. 18-19.

[48] ECS to Sarah M. Grimké and Angelina Grimké Weld, June 25, 1840 in Ibid., pp. 8-11.

[49] Ibid.

[50] Lucretia Mott to ECS, March 16, 1855 in Palmer, ed. *Selected Letters of Lucretia Coffin Mott*, p. 236.

CHAPTER NINE: THE EMANCIPATION OF ELIZABETH CADY

[1] Stanton, *80Y*, p. 110.

[2] Date from Gordon, Vol. 1, p. 20 n. 2 and a letter from HBS to Gerrit Smith. Henry wrote that the Stantons arrived in Johnstown "yesterday" on January 8,

1841. Gerrit Smith Papers, Special Collections Library, Syracuse University. Griffith wrote that the Stantons spent the Christmas holiday with Elizabeth's sister Harriet Eaton before traveling to Johnstown, but her sources do not include this information. *In Her Own Right*, p. 40. Elizabeth wrote that they stayed in New York City for two weeks. ECS to Elizabeth J. Neall, January 25 [1841] in Gordon, ed. *The Selected Papers of Elizabeth Cady Stanton and Susan B. Anthony: In the School of Anti-Slavery 1840-1866*, pp. 18-20.

[3] Ibid.

[4] See ECS to Elizabeth Smith, March 17, [1841] Elizabeth Cady Stanton Papers, Library of Congress.

[5] Records of Mt. Hope Cemetery, Rochester, New York.

[6] Elizabeth Neall to Elizabeth Whittier, August 16, 1841. Quoted in Andrea Constantine Hawkes, "The Life of Elizabeth McClintock Phillips, 1821-1896: A Story of Family, Friends, Community, and a Self-Made Woman." University of Maine, Ph.D. Diss., 2005, p. 148.

[7] ECS to Elizabeth Neall, January 25, [1841] in Gordon, ed. *The Selected Papers of Elizabeth Cady Stanton and Susan B. Anthony: In the School of Anti-Slavery 1840-1866*, p. 19.

[8] ECS to Elizabeth Smith, March 17, [1841] Elizabeth Cady Stanton Papers, Library of Congress.

[9] Lutz, *Created Equal: A Biography of Elizabeth Cady Stanton 1815-1902*, p. 35. Gerrit Smith to Theodore Weld, March 14, 1841. Barnes and Dumond, eds., *Letters of Theodore Dwight Weld, Angelina Grimké Weld and Sarah Grimké, 1822-1844*, pp. II:862- 64.

[10] Rice-*HBS*, p. 243.

[11] *Emancipator*, March 11, 1841. Likely, a contributing factor to Birney's resignation was his impending marriage to Gerrit Smith's sister-in-law, Elizabeth Fitzhugh, on March 25, 1841. The couple made Peterboro their home for several years. See Gerrit Smith to Theodore Weld, March 14, 1841 in Barnes and Dumond, eds., *Letters of Theodore Dwight Weld, Angelina Grimké Weld and Sarah Grimké, 1822-1844*, p. II:862.

[12] Lucretia Mott to Richard and Hannah Webb, February 25, 1842 in Palmer, ed. *Selected Letters of Lucretia Coffin Mott*, p. 111. Mott wrote that, "she [ECS] has lately made her debut in public—in a Temperance speech...she infused into her speech a homeopathic dose of Womans Rights." See also Gordon, ed. *The Selected Papers of Elizabeth Cady Stanton and Susan B. Anthony: In the School of Anti-Slavery 1840-1866*, p. 25 dated November 26, 1841. Henry Stanton noted in a letter to a fellow Liberty Party organizer on September 3, 1841, that his lecture schedule included talks on both antislavery and temperance in central New York. (author's collection)

[13] ECS to Elizabeth Neall, November 26 [1841] in Gordon, ed. *The Selected Papers of Elizabeth Cady Stanton and Susan B. Anthony: In the School of Anti-Slavery 1840- 1866*, p. 25.

[14] Ibid.

[15] Rice-*HBS*, p. 244.

[16] Quoted in Gordon, ed. *The Selected Papers of Elizabeth Cady Stanton and Susan B. Anthony: In the School of Anti-Slavery 1840- 1866*, Vol. I, p. 32 n. 10, from the *Emancipator*, February 24 and March 4, 1842.

[17] From the *Emancipator and Free American*, Boston, March 3, 1842, quoted in Rice-*HBS*, p. 244.

[18] HBS to ECS, [June 23, 1842] Elizabeth Cady Stanton Papers, Library of Congress.

[19] Lori D. Ginzberg, *Elizabeth Cady Stanton: An American Life*, New York: Hill and Wang, 2009, p. 51. Chris Dixon, *Perfecting the Family: Antislavery Marriages in Nineteenth-Century America*, Amherst, Mass.: University of Massachusetts Press, 1997, p. 90 and Griffith, *In Her Own Right: The Life of Elizabeth Cady Stanton*, p. 80.

[20] A further consequence of Ginzberg, Dixon, Griffith and others incorrectly stating that HBS was not at home during the births of his children is that it also suggests that not only did Elizabeth bear the burden of having seven children, but also that in an era when childbirth was an especially dangerous time for women, Henry was not even concerned enough about her welfare to be at home. On a research trip to our nation's capital, I visited the Sewall-Belmont house. During the tour, the docent emphatically claimed that Henry Stanton was not there for the birth of any of his children—this at a museum primarily dealing with the 20th century women's suffrage movement. While this is anecdotal, it shows the wide reach that this kind of "evidence" touches, and it speaks to the persistent theme of explaining the origins of the women's rights movement through the victimization of its founding mothers beyond their lack of political and civil rights.

[21] Elizabeth mentions she was attended by only a nurse and one female friend during Margaret's birth in 1852. ECS to Lucretia Mott, October 22, 1852 in Gordon, ed. *The Selected Papers of Elizabeth Cady Stanton and Susan B. Anthony: In the School of Anti-Slavery 1840-1866*, pp. 212-13. Lutz cites a letter to Elizabeth Smith Miller wherein Elizabeth states she was attended by a nurse and Amelia Willard. Lutz, *Created Equal: A Biography of Elizabeth Cady Stanton 1815-1902*, p. 81.

[22] Lutz wrote that in 1844 when Henry, Jr. was born Henry was "busy with his law practice" presumably in Boston (p. 39). In 1851 when Theodore was born, Henry was in Albany (p. 61) and in 1852 when Margaret was born, she includes a letter written by ECS to Elizabeth Smith Miller stating Henry was in Syracuse. Lutz, *Created Equal: A Biography of Elizabeth Cady Stanton 1815-1902*, p. 81.

[23] Gordon, ed. *The Selected Papers of Elizabeth Cady Stanton and Susan B. Anthony: In the School of Anti-Slavery 1840-1866*, Vol. 1, p. 37 n. 1. Rice-*HBS*, pp. 246-47. Fletcher (1788-1869) would also serve on the Massachusetts

State Supreme Court (1848-1853) and Sewall (1799-1888) was an active reformer in the abolition and women's rights movements in Massachusetts. See *Boston Evening Transcript*, December 21, 1888, p. 3.

[24] See *Whig & Courier*, June 28, 1844 and *Bolles Family in America*, Henry W. Dutton & Son, Boston, 1865, p. 28 and Edward H. Redstone, Massachusetts State Librarian, to Alma Lutz, September 1, 1932, Alma Lutz Papers, Vassar College. *Virginia Law Register*, Vol. 7, No. 8 (December 1901) pp. 591.

[25] *Emancipator and Free American*, November 3, November 10, and December 15, 1842.

[26] Bruce Laurie, *Beyond Garrison: Antislavery and Social Reform*, New York: Cambridge University Press, 2005, pp. 58-59.

[27] *Emancipator and Free American*, August 25, 1842, p. 67.

[28] Ibid.

[29] *Emancipator and Free American*, January 13, 1842.

[30] ECS to Elizabeth Pease, February 12, [1842] in Gordon, ed. *The Selected Papers of Elizabeth Cady Stanton and Susan B. Anthony: In the School of Anti-Slavery 1840- 1866*, p. 30.

[31] Ibid.

[32] Hoffman's *Albany Directory*, 1844-1845. The law office was located at 44 State Street, and from appearances, the building still survives. The site of the Cady townhome is now a pump house for the City of Albany.

[33] See for example, ECS to Elizabeth Smith, [1843], Typed transcript, Theodore Stanton Collection, Douglass Library, Rutgers University.

[34] HBS to ECS, March 30 [1844]. Elizabeth Cady Stanton Papers, Library of Congress.

[35] Tryphena-Edward Bayard, see Griffith, *In Her Own Right: The Life of Elizabeth Cady Stanton*, p. 227. Harriet Cady and Daniel Cady Eaton, *New York Spectator*, December 31, 1830. Catherine Cady and Samuel Wilkeson, *Schenectady Reflector*, June 25, 1841. Margaret Cady and Duncan McMartin, *Portrait and Biographical Record of Jasper, Marshall and Grundy Counties, Iowa*, Chicago: Biographical Pub. Co., 1894, pp. 371-372.

[36] Griffith, *In Her Own Right: The Life of Elizabeth Cady Stanton*, pp. 42-43.

[37] Hoffman's *Albany Directory*, 1844-45 and the *Buffalo Courier*, December 3, 1889.

[38] See for example, "Daniel Cady. Biographical Sketch of the late Judge Cady & Outline of his Professional Career," signed, "H.B.S." *Schenectady Cabinet*, February 6, 1855 also printed in *New York Times*, January 31, 1855. The word "late" in the title refers to Cady's retirement and not his death. Will of Daniel Cady, November 11, 1859, Fulton County Surrogate's Court.

[39] HBS to James G. Birney, Albany, April 19, 1843 in Dumond, ed. *Letters of James Gillespie Birney (1831-1857)*, II:735.

[40] HBS to James G. Birney, August 11, 1845 in Ibid., p. II:959.

[41] Griffith, *In Her Own Right: The Life of Elizabeth Cady Stanton*, pp. 43-44.

See also ECS to Elizabeth Smith [1843], Typed Transcript in Theodore Stanton Collection, Douglass Library, Rutgers University, and HBS to Elizabeth Cady Stanton, June 11 [1844], Elizabeth Cady Stanton Papers, Library of Congress.

[42] ECS to Elizabeth J. Neall, February 3, 1843 in Gordon, ed. *The Selected Papers of Elizabeth Cady Stanton and Susan B. Anthony: In the School of Anti-Slavery 1840–1866*, p. 41. Neall was visiting the McClintocks of Waterloo, NY, and this letter was addressed to her there. Although ECS spent "two winters" in the area, she makes no mention in her letter of any acquaintance with the Thomas McClintock or his family, suggesting that she had not yet made the acquaintance of a family that will figure prominently in the early years of the women's rights movement. Stanton, *80Y*, p. 128.

[43] The Liberty vote totals are only available for the gubernatorial vote. Table in Laurie, *Beyond Garrison: Antislavery and Social Reform*, p. 75.

[44] Rice-*HBS*, pp. 247- 48.

[45] HBS to Gerrit Smith, August 4, 1843. Gerrit Smith Papers, Syracuse University.

[46] See Rice-*HBS*, pp. 249-50. See also Johnson, *The Liberty Party, 1840–1848; Antislavery Third-Party Politics in the United States*, pp. 41-43.

[47] HBS to Gerrit Smith, November 12, 1844. Gerrit Smith Papers, Syracuse University.

[48] Ibid.

[49] Ibid. Henry received 1,498 votes. See HBS to Gerrit Smith, November 23, 1844. Gerrit Smith Papers, Special Collections Library, Syracuse University. ECS's biographer Elisabeth Griffith, while citing this letter, misstated what Henry actually wrote to Smith about the votes he received. Griffith wrote: "He had turned down the Liberty party's congressional nomination in 1844 because he thought he could not win it." Griffith, *In Her Own Right*, p. 46. However, the letter says nothing of the kind. Henry wrote: "Mr. Cady is, I suppose, greatly distressed at my running for Congress. To console him, you may tell him, that I have never accepted any nomination—that I positively declined to accept—but that in spite of all my opposition, I was nominated, & 1500 voted from me without asking me whether I was willing they should do so—an evidence of the strong hold I have upon the affections of the people of Essex South!!"

[50] HBS to Gerrit Smith, November 23, 1844. Gerrit Smith Papers, Syracuse University.

[51] *Trial of B. W. Williams and Others, Editor and Printers of the Dew Drop, Taunton Mass., for an Alleged Libel Against William Wilbar, a Rumseller of Taunton, containing the libelous article entitled "A Dream," The Evidence in the Case, The Argument of H. B. Stanton, Esq. and the Charge of His Honor, Judge Hubbard,* Hack & King, Taunton, Mass., 1846.

[52] Stanton, *A Record, Genealogical, Biographical, Statistical, of Thomas Stanton of*

Connecticut and His Descendants, 1635-1891, p. 460.

[53] *Boston Daily Post*, August 10, 1844. Thanks to Patricia Cline Cohen for this article. For Elizabeth's study see Lucretia Mott to Elizabeth Cady Stanton, March 23, 1841 and editor's note 9. Gordon, ed. *The Selected Papers of Elizabeth Cady Stanton and Susan B. Anthony: In the School of Anti-Slavery 1840-1866*, pp. 22- 23.

[54] HBS to Gerrit Smith, Boston, September 18, 1845. Gerrit Smith Papers, Special Collections Library, Syracuse University. It is impossible to know why this letter has been consistently overlooked by ECS' biographers. The letter is located in the same repository as the majority of surviving correspondence between Henry and Gerrit Smith, and despite being in the same collection, from the same time period, and in the same folder as other letters that were utilized, this letter was consistently overlooked. Also, as stated, there is no evidence to substantiate Henry's absence at the birth of most of the couple's children.

[55] HBS to Gerrit Smith, December 18, 1845. Gerrit Smith Papers, Syracuse University.

[56] "Address of the Committee Appointed By A Public Meeting, Held At Fanenil [*sic*] Hall, September 24, 1846, for the purposes of considering the recent case of Kidnapping From Our Soil, and of taking measures to prevent the recurrence of Similar Outrages," Boston, White & Potter, 1846.

[57] Irving H. Bartlett, "Abolitionists, Fugitives and Imposters in Boston, 1846-1847," *The New England Quarterly* 55, no. 1 (Mar., 1982): p. 97.

[58] The committee was also the forerunner of the Boston Vigilance Committee that became very active after the passage of the Fugitive Slave Law of 1850. Ibid.

CHAPTER TEN: PERFECTIONISM AND PRAGMATISM

[1] Marcus T. Reynolds, Esq., quoted in Stanton, *RR*, p. 139.

[2] Johnson, *The Liberty Party, 1840-1848; Antislavery Third-Party Politics in the United States*, pp. 291, 94-95.

[3] Eleventh Annual Report, Presented to the Massachusetts Anti-Slavery Society, by its Board of Managers, January 25, 1843, pp. 90-91, 94.

[4] Lucretia Mott to Maria W. Chapman, May 5, 1845. Unknown repository. Letter transcribed from original image posted on eBay Live auction of the Henry E. Luhrs Collection, October 25, 2007.

[5] *Emancipator and Free American*, January 11, 1844. While acknowledging Liberty's use of the term, Eric Foner mentions it only in passing. Eric Foner, *Free Soil, Free Labor, Free Men: The Ideology of the Republican Party before the Civil War*, New York: Oxford University Press, 1970; reprint, 1995, p. 92.

[6] *Emancipator and Free American*, January 11, 1844. See also, Rice-*HBS*, p. 250-52.

[7] *The Boston Daily Atlas*, October 29, 1844. Quote from a report of an address by HBS given on October 27, 1844. An excellent summary of their work can be found in Ibid., pp. 252- 62.

[8] HBS to Gerrit Smith, December 18, 1845. Gerrit Smith Papers, Syracuse University.

[9] Ibid.

[10] Editorial attributed to Henry Stanton in the *Emancipator*, February 24, 1847 quoted in Rice-*HBS*, p. 267.

[11] Michael F. Holt, *Rise and Fall of the American Whig Party: Jacksonian Politics and the Onset of the Civil War*, New York: Oxford University Press, 1999, p. 249.

[12] Rice-*HBS*, p. 268.

[13] Ibid., p. 269.

[14] James G. Birney to Lewis Tappan, September 12, 1845. Dumond, ed. *Letters of James Gillespie Birney (1831-1857)*, pp. II:970-71.

[15] Rice-*HBS*, p. 271.

[16] "Address of the Macedon Convention by William Goodell; and Letters of Gerrit Smith," Albany: S. W. Green, 1847, p. 3.

[17] Ibid., p. 4.

[18] The Liberty League is frequently described in similar fashion as the Garrisonians during the 1839-1840 schism. The League is praised for its moral high ground and referred to as the party of the "radicals." In many ways, this parallel corresponds with an overall characterization of those abolitionists engaging within the political system as being opportunists or somehow not as devoted to the cause as their perfectionist counterparts. As with the Garrisonians, Gerrit Smith's perfectionism is usually depicted in much the same way. This is not to minimize Smith's contributions to abolition or his long record of philanthropy and devotion to reform causes; however, the historiographical exclusion of the political abolitionists tends to overstate the contributions of the perfectionists by obscuring and minimizing the practical wisdom and meaningful successes of the more pragmatic reformers. For example, Gerrit Smith's most recent biographer states: "[The Liberty League] was the more radical wing of the Liberty Party, and it eventually became the Radical Abolition Party in the mid-1850s." However, despite the author's concession that Smith did not endorse the Free Soil Party, he nonetheless credits Smith with the "birth" of the Republican Party, while ignoring the contributions of the pragmatic politicians who engineered the coalition that created the new party. The early Republican platforms were not abolitionist, but followed the free soilers on the issue of slavery. Ibid., pp. 6-7, and Dann, *Practical Dreamer: Gerrit Smith and the Crusade for Social Reform*, pp. 327-28.

[19] HBS to Salmon P. Chase, August 6, 1847, American Historical Association,

"Annual Report of the American Historical Association for the Year 1902. Sixth Report of Historical Manuscripts Commission: With Diary and Correspondence of Salmon P. Chase," Washington: Government Printing Office, 1903.

[20] Hugh Davis, *Joshua Leavitt: Evangelical Abolitionist*, Baton Rouge, LA: Louisiana State University Press, 1990, pp. 234-35 and 41. See also Rice-*HBS*, pp. 271-72.

[21] Rice-*HBS*, p. 274.

[22] HBS to John P. Hale, July 6, 1847. John P. Hale Papers, New Hampshire Historical Society, Concord, NH.

[23] HBS to Salmon P. Chase, August 6, 1847, American Historical Association, "Annual Report of the American Historical Association for the Year 1902. Sixth Report of Historical Manuscripts Commission: With Diary and Correspondence of Salmon P. Chase."

[24] Tappan, Leavitt, Stanton, Willey, Whittier and Cleveland to John P. Hale, July 26, 1847. John P. Hale Papers, Special Collections, Dartmouth College Library.

[25] Henry Brewster to John P. Hale, March 17, 1848, John P. Hale Papers, New Hampshire Historical Society.

[26] HBS to Salmon P. Chase, August 6, 1847, American Historical Association, "Annual Report of the American Historical Association for the Year 1902. Sixth Report of Historical Manuscripts Commission: With Diary and Correspondence of Salmon P. Chase."

[27] Today, this corner is home to four different parking lots, and not too far from the landmark Hotel Lafayette. Rice-*HBS*, pp. 277-78.

[28] The *Daily Courier* [Buffalo], October 22, 1847. See also, Ibid., p. 279.

[29] HBS to John P. Hale, Seneca Falls, October 30, 1847. Hale-Chandler Papers, Dartmouth University.

[30] HBS to Gerrit Smith, December 20, 1843. Gerrit Smith Papers, Syracuse University.

[31] Griffith, *In Her Own Right: The Life of Elizabeth Cady Stanton*, p. 46. Sallie G. McMillen, *Seneca Falls and the Origins of the Women's Rights Movement*, New York: Oxford University Press, 2008, p. 83. Judith Wellman, *The Road to Seneca Falls: Elizabeth Cady Stanton and the First Woman's Rights Convention*, Urbana, IL: University of Illinois Press, 2004, p. 164.

[32] HBS to Gerrit Smith, December 20, 1843. Gerrit Smith Papers, Syracuse University.

[33] HBS to Gerrit Smith, May 20, 1844. Gerrit Smith Papers, Syracuse University.

[34] Ibid.

[35] Barbara A. Yocum, "The Stanton House Historic Structure Report, Women's Rights National Historical Park, Seneca Falls, New York," Lowell, Mass.: National Park Service, Department of the Interior, 1998, pp. 15-16.

See also: Griffith, *In Her Own Right: The Life of Elizabeth Cady Stanton*, p. 48. As Griffith notes, technically until the passage of the Married Women's Property Act the following year, the property legally belonged to Henry.

[36] Alma Lutz Collection at Vassar College. Interview transcript dated August 1931, entitled "Blatch."

[37] Elizabeth Cady Stanton to Rebecca R. Eyster, [1847? May? 1?], Typed transcript, Theodore Stanton Collection, Douglass Library, Rutgers University. A shorter version of the letter appears in Stanton and Blatch, *Letters*, II:15-16. Although the date of this letter and its original content cannot be known for certain because only the typescript remains, the content seems consistent with the historical record and the date proposed by Rutgers is likely a close one. For the Eysters, see Rev. J. C. Jensson, *American Lutheran Biographies*, Milwaukee, Wis.: Franklin Book Store, 1890, pp. 208-11.

[38] This letter is mentioned or quoted by Wellman (p. 168), McMillen (p. 143) and Griffith (p. xx), however, neither Wellman, McMillen or Griffith included the very clear sentence about the nature of the Stanton marriage. Wellman suggests that the letter to Eyster is from the 1859-1860 period because of Elizabeth's concern with married women's use of their husband's names during this era. However, Elizabeth also discusses this very issue at the Rochester Women's Rights Convention in August 1848. Further, by 1859, the Eysters had moved to Gettysburg. The precise date of this letter is not nearly as important as the sentiments it conveyed.

[39] Wellman, p. 170.

[40] Stanton, *80Y*, p. 144.

[41] *Liberator*, March 10, 1848. See also Davis, *Joshua Leavitt: Evangelical Abolitionist*, p. 236 and the *National Era*, August 26, 1847, p. 2. Henry's surviving letters from this time period are dated from Seneca Falls, in contrast to the dates of his move to Seneca Falls in Wellman and Gordon. Compare Wellman, *The Road to Seneca Falls: Elizabeth Cady Stanton and the First Woman's Rights Convention*, p. 165: "Elizabeth began a year of life as a single parent." Ann Gordon wrote that Henry stayed in Boston until December, but spent a month in Seneca Falls, beginning in mid-October. It's unclear why she did not consider it the other way around—that he moved to Seneca Falls in mid-October, but returned to Boston to conclude pending legal cases. Gordon, ed. *The Selected Papers of Elizabeth Cady Stanton and Susan B. Anthony: In the School of Anti-Slavery 1840-1866*, p. 63-64 n. 3.

[42] ECS to Elizabeth Smith Miller, [15? April 1847], in Gordon, ed. *The Selected Papers of Elizabeth Cady Stanton and Susan B. Anthony: In the School of Anti-Slavery 1840- 1866*, pp. 62-63.

[43] Supreme Court appointment announcement printed in the *National Era*, February 17, 1848. For legal cases see, HBS to John P. Hale, January 9, 1848 and January 20, 1848, Hale-Chandler Papers, Dartmouth University.

[44] Henry B. Stanton to the *Emancipator*, March 1, 1848 and reprinted in the

Liberator, March 10, 1848. See also Rice-*HBS*, pp. 284-85. Stanton, *RR*, pp. 158-59.

[45] HBS to John P. Hale, Johnstown, March 2, 1848. John P. Hale Papers, New Hampshire Historical Society.

[46] Herbert D. A. Donovan, *The Barnburners: A Study of the Internal Movements in the Political History of New York State and of the Resulting Changes in Political Affiliation, 1830-1852*, New York: New York University Press, 1925, p. 7.

[47] For a thorough discussion of the debates surrounding these two issues, see Ibid., pp. 14-20.

[48] Ibid., p. 22.

[49] Ibid., pp. 32 and 33.

[50] Ibid., pp. 55-56. See also Rice-*HBS*, pp. 287-88. Stanton, *RR*, p. 157-58.

[51] Donovan, *The Barnburners: A Study of the Internal Movements in the Political History of New York State and of the Resulting Changes in Political Affiliation, 1830-1852*, p. 87.

[52] Ibid., p. 88.

[53] Ibid., pp. 93-95. Stanton, *RR*, pp. 159-61.

[54] *Albany Argus*, October 17, 1847. Quoted in Donovan, *The Barnburners: A Study of the Internal Movements in the Political History of New York State and of the Resulting Changes in Political Affiliation, 1830-1852*, p. 94.

[55] See Rice-*HBS*, p. 293- 94. Donovan, *The Barnburners: A Study of the Internal Movements in the Political History of New York State and of the Resulting Changes in Political Affiliation, 1830-1852*, pp. 103-05. See also Henry B. Stanton to [Amos Tuck], May 13, 1848, John P. Hale Papers, New Hampshire Historical Society.

[56] HBS to [Amos Tuck], May 13, 1848, John P. Hale Papers, New Hampshire Historical Society.

[57] Salmon P. Chase to J. L. Trowbridge, March 10, 1864, Salmon P. Chase Papers, Library of Congress. Quoted in Rice-*HBS*, p. 295.

[58] *Emancipator*, February 24, 1847, quoted in Ibid., p. 293.

CHAPTER ELEVEN: THE MIGHTY VOTE

[1] Elizur Wright, "The Liberty Voter's Song." Philip Green Wright and Elizabeth Q. Wright, *Elizur Wright: The Father of Life Insurance* Chicago: University of Chicago Press, 1937, p. 100.

[2] Judy Wellman identified the Avery's daughter as Delia. Wellman, *The Road to Seneca Falls*, p. 170. Delia Avery was the name of George Avery's niece (daughter of his brother and Lane Seminary student, Courtland Avery) who died in 1851. Burial records at Mt. Hope Cemetery identify Frances and George's daughter as "Anna R. Avery," and her tombstone inscription is

"Anna Avery." The *Rochester Daily Democrat* listed the child's name as Delia Anna Blackford [Avery] (6/14/1848).

3 For Avery's financial losses, see *Rochester Daily Democrat*, January 22, 1845 and *Rochester Daily Advertiser*, November 26, 1845. Avery's Liberty run, see: *Rochester Daily Democrat*, February 10, 1841. The Canada Mission has escaped previous historical works. See *Liberator*, March 17, 1843 and June 19, 1846.

4 *Massachusetts Abolitionist*, February 11, 1841.

5 Burial records of Mt. Hope Cemetery, Rochester, New York. *Rochester Daily Democrat*, June 28, 1848. Unfortunately, the only reason this visit by the Averys to the Stanton home was documented was because of the death of little George Avery. Judy Wellman's discovery of this visit prompted my initial research into Henry's family. Wellman, *The Road to Seneca Falls: Elizabeth Cady Stanton and the First Woman's Rights Convention*, p. 170. As Judy Wellman noted, the loss of two children within her family circle might well have been the reason Elizabeth decided to be photographed with her two eldest sons. See also Martha Wright to Lucretia Mott, August 5, 1848, Garrison Papers, Smith College.

6 The *North Star* [Rochester, NY], July 21, 1848. Henry Stanton was the speaker at this large rally held at the Ontario County Courthouse.

7 *Rochester Daily Advertiser*, August 31, 1848.

8 Stanton, *80Y*, p. 145. Letter written by ECS to her son Theodore upon Henry's death in 1887. Quoted in Ann D. Gordon, *The Selected Papers of Elizabeth Cady Stanton & Susan B. Anthony, Vol. IV: When Clowns Make Laws for Queens, 1880-1887*, 2006, p. 543.

9 Strong, *Perfectionist Politics: Abolitionism and the Religious Tensions of American Democracy*, pp. 129-30.

10 Wellman, *The Road to Seneca Falls: Elizabeth Cady Stanton and the First Woman's Rights Convention*, 180-84.

11 Stanton, *80Y*, p. 148.

12 Wellman, *The Road to Seneca Falls: Elizabeth Cady Stanton and the First Woman's Rights Convention*, p. 189.

13 *Seneca Falls Courier*, June 13, 1848 and July 11, 1848. Judy Wellman expresses a similar idea in describing the Women's Rights call.

14 Dated from a letter from ECS to Elizabeth McClintock, July 14. Gordon, ed. *The Selected Papers of Elizabeth Cady Stanton and Susan B. Anthony: In the School of Anti-Slavery 1840-1866*, p. 69.

15 For example, see Phelps, ed. *Our Famous Women*, p. 613. Lutz, *Created Equal: A Biography of Elizabeth Cady Stanton 1815-1902*, p. 46. Wellman, *The Road to Seneca Falls: Elizabeth Cady Stanton and the First Woman's Rights Convention*, p. 193.

16 ECS to Elizabeth McClintock, July 14. Gordon, ed. *The Selected Papers of Elizabeth Cady Stanton and Susan B. Anthony: In the School of Anti-Slavery 1840-1866*, p. 69.

[17] Stanton, Anthony, and Gage, eds., *History of Woman Suffrage*, p. I:68.

[18] The complete Declaration, resolutions, and minutes of the convention are printed in Gordon, ed. *The Selected Papers of Elizabeth Cady Stanton and Susan B. Anthony: In the School of Anti-Slavery, 1840-1866*, pp. 75-88.

[19] Ibid., p. 77. Stanton, Anthony, and Gage, eds., *History of Woman Suffrage*, p. I: 72.

[20] Phelps, ed. *Our Famous Women*, pp. 603-23.

[21] The only author to attempt to answer the question of Henry's whereabouts is Wellman. She cites an article from the *New York Tribune* on July 19, 1848 stating that Henry was speaking in Canandaigua, NY during the Women's Rights Convention. Wellman, *The Road to Seneca Falls*, p. 277 n. 30. However, Wellman's source refers, instead, to a speech Henry delivered on July 13 (the week before the convention) in Warsaw, Wyoming County, NY.

[22] Harriot Stanton Blatch to Alma Lutz, [n.d.] Nyack, NY, Alma Lutz Collection, Vassar College. This letter was written to Lutz after Blatch received a draft of Lutz's manuscript. She also corrected Lutz on another matter concerning her father: "You say the Call of the Loyal League 'was definitely by Elizabeth.' I agree, but was not the idea of the League, my father's?" In a letter dated July 4, 1931, Blatch asked Lutz if she had a copy of "my father's *Random Recollections*," fearing Lutz was ignoring her father's work as a reformer. Lutz's replies were not retained. Alma Lutz Papers, Vassar College.

[23] Harriot Stanton Blatch to Alma Lutz, August 11, 1833, Alma Lutz Papers, Vassar College.

[24] Interestingly, Bullard and Lutz include the exact same quote from Lucretia Mott. Phelps, ed. *Our Famous Women*, p. 614. Lutz, *Created Equal: A Biography of Elizabeth Cady Stanton 1815- 1902*, p. 46. For Susan B. Anthony, see Phelps, ed. *Our Famous Women*, p. 615.

[25] Lutz, *Created Equal: A Biography of Elizabeth Cady Stanton 1815-1902*, pp. 45, 46.

[26] Stanton, Anthony, and Gage, eds., *History of Woman Suffrage*, p. I:73.

[27] For Warsaw see: *The National Era*, July 13, 1848 and July 27, 1848; the *Rochester Daily Advertiser*, July 17, 19, 21 and 22, 1848; the *New York Tribune*, July 19, 1848. For Varick, see the *Buffalo Daily Courier*, July 20, 1848. For July 15, see HBS to Charles Sumner, Seneca Falls, July 15, 1848, Charles Sumner Papers, Houghton Library, Harvard University, reel 6:257. For July 17: HBS to John P. Hale, July 17, 1848, Hale-Chandler Papers, Dartmouth University. For July 27: *Rochester Daily Advertiser*, July 22, 29, 1848. *New York Tribune*, August 1, 1848, *Seneca County Observer*, August 3, 1848, *National Era*, August 10, 1848. For July 31 and August 1 see, HBS to John Greenleaf Whittier, Seneca Falls, July 31, 1848 in John Albree, ed. *Whittier Correspondence from the Oak Knoll Collections, 1830-1892* Salem, Mass.: Essex Book and Print Club, 1911, pp. 102-04.

[28] For August 3, see *Seneca County Courier,* August 4, 1848. August 5, Martha Wright to Lucretia Mott, August 5, 1848, Garrison Papers, Smith College; August 15, *Seneca County Courier,* August 18, 1848.

[29] HBS to Charles Sumner, Seneca Falls, July 15, 1848. Charles Sumner Papers, Houghton Library, Harvard University, reel 6:257.

[30] HBS to John P. Hale, Seneca Falls, July 17, 1848. Hale-Chandler Papers, Dartmouth College.

[31] ECS to Rebecca R. Eyster, [1847? May? 1?], Typed transcript, Theodore Stanton Collection, Douglass Library, Rutgers University. Also, a shorter version of the letter appears in Stanton-Blatch, *Letters,* pp. II:15-16.

[32] Gordon, ed. *The Selected Papers of Elizabeth Cady Stanton and Susan B. Anthony: In the School of Anti-Slavery 1840-1866,* p. 1:106.

[33] See *Report of the Woman's Rights Convention Held at Seneca Falls, NY, July 19th and 20th, 1848,* Rochester: John Dick, 1848, p. 6. See Stanton, Anthony, and Gage, eds., *History of Woman Suffrage,* pp. 809-10 for a list of signers. See 80Y, p. 144-45 for Bascom's political background and women's rights sentiment. The surviving copy of the minutes of the Rochester Convention is held by Special Collections, Rush Rhees Library, University of Rochester.

[34] ECS to Amy Post, September 24, 1848. Harper Collection, HM10499, Huntington Library, San Marino, California.

[35] Quoted in Leslie Friedman Goldstein, "Morality & Prudence in the Statesmanship of Frederick Douglass: Radical as Reformer," *Polity* 16, no. 4 Summer (1984): p. 607.

[36] Lewis Tappan to John P. Hale, June 20, 1848. Hale-Chandler Papers, Dartmouth University. Tappan was particularly a concern at this time. Amos Tuck met with Tappan the same day that Tappan wrote to Hale, and Tuck's very lengthy letter was riddled with Tappan's fears. Amos Tuck to John P. Hale, June 21, 1848, John P. Hale Papers, New Hampshire Historical Society.

[37] Lewis Tappan to John P. Hale, July 3, 1848, Hale Chandler Papers, Dartmouth University.

[38] HBS to John P. Hale, Seneca Falls, July 17, 1848. Hale-Chandler Papers, Dartmouth University. For a more detailed examination of the thoughts of others, including Tappan and Whittier, see Rice-*HBS*, pp. 295-99.

[39] HBS to John Greenleaf Whittier, Seneca Falls, July 31, 1848 in Albree, ed. *Whittier Correspondence from the Oak Knoll Collections, 1830-1892,* pp. 102-04.

[40] Ibid.

[41] John P. Hale to Lewis Tappan, July 6, 1848. John P. Hale Papers, New Hampshire Historical Society.

[42] Johnson, *The Liberty Party, 1840-1848; Antislavery Third-Party Politics in the United States,* p. 85. See also Rice-*HBS*, p. 300. For women attendees see [unknown] to John P. Hale, August 19, 1848. John P. Hale Papers, New Hampshire Historical Society.

[43] Johnson, *The Liberty Party, 1840-1848; Antislavery Third-Party Politics in the*

United States, p. 85. Rice-*HBS*, p. 300.

⁴⁴ Rice-*HBS*, p. 301.

⁴⁵ Reinhard O. Johnson, in comparing the 1848 and 1844 Liberty platforms, considers claims that Liberty did, in fact, control the platform "questionable." However, Stanton, Leavitt and other Liberty men at the convention believed differently. See Johnson, *The Liberty Party, 1840-1848; Antislavery Third-Party Politics in the United States*, p. 86. See also: HBS to John P. Hale, August 20, 1848, John P. Hale Papers, New Hampshire Historical Society.

⁴⁶ Ibid., pp. 86-87. Rice-*HBS*, pp. 305-06 and Henry B. Stanton to John P. Hale, August 20, 1848, John P. Hale Papers, New Hampshire Historical Society.

⁴⁷ HBS to John P. Hale, August 20, 1848, John P. Hale Papers, New Hampshire Historical Society. Rice-*HBS*, pp. 305-06. Davis, *Joshua Leavitt: Evangelical Abolitionist*, pp. 247-66.

⁴⁸ Johnson, *The Liberty Party, 1840-1848; Antislavery Third-Party Politics in the United States*, p. 88. Lewis Tappan to HBS, September 25, 1848, Lewis Tappan Letterbook, Lewis Tappan Papers, Library of Congress.

⁴⁹ Van Buren came in second in Massachusetts, New York and Vermont. His totals in Wisconsin and Michigan were less, but he won close to 16% of the total electorate in those two states. On the local level, Ansel Bascom lost his race against Sackett. Vote totals: Sackett—2,044 votes to Bascom's 1,597. The Hunker Democrat, Bigelow, was last at 1,069 votes. Rice-*HBS*, p. 310. Johnson, *The Liberty Party, 1840-1848; Antislavery Third-Party Politics in the United States*, pp. 89-90. *Seneca Free Soil Union*, November 17, 1848.

EPILOGUE: A TRUE CONJUGAL UNION

¹ ECS's diary entry, November 12, 1880 as printed in Stanton-Blatch, *Letters*, p. II:177.

² Martha Wright to Lucretia Mott, March 5, 1849. Garrison Family Papers, Smith College.

³ See Rice-*HBS* p. 45 and HBS to Charles Sumner, Seneca Falls, November 8, 1849, Charles Sumner Papers, Houghton Library, Harvard University, reel 7:008.

⁴ For the date, see Gordon, ed. *The Selected Papers of Elizabeth Cady Stanton and Susan B. Anthony: In the School of Anti-Slavery 1840-1866*, p. 178 n.1. Griffith mistakenly notes that he was born the following day. Griffith, *In Her Own Right: The Life of Elizabeth Cady Stanton*, p. 66. Perhaps some of the confusion is due to Elizabeth's account of Daniel's (Neil) infancy. In *80Y*, Elizabeth devotes an entire chapter to "Motherhood," and within her recollections, she describes her frustrations with baby nurses, doctors, and

parental advice manuals. Within this chapter, Elizabeth relates a story of her son's dislocated collarbone and the way in which she devised—against doctor's orders—her own form of bandages. Stanton, *80Y*, pp. 108-27. This account flows from an earlier discussion of baby nurses, presumably from her experiences following Neil's birth, leading readers to assume that the two incidents referred to the same child. Complicating the matter, an incorrectly attributed date on a letter from Elizabeth to Henry published in the 1922 edition of Stanton's letters added to the confusion by placing the incident in 1842. Letter incorrectly dated March 16, 1842 published in Stanton-Blatch, *Letters*, p. II:8. The correct date is February 24, 1851. Elizabeth's account in her autobiography does not mention Henry at all, and the baby's dislocated collarbone is attributed to Neil by both Lutz and Griffith. Lutz, *Created Equal: A Biography of Elizabeth Cady Stanton 1815-1902*, pp. 36-37. Griffith, *In Her Own Right: The Life of Elizabeth Cady Stanton*, p. 69. However, from Henry's letters to Elizabeth during this time period, it is clear that there is a serious inconsistency with these accounts. Following the birth of their fourth son, Theodore Weld Stanton in 1851, there are several existent letters relating to Henry's concern about his son's dislocated collarbone. In an attempt to reassure Elizabeth one letter pointedly states, "I have often heard of the limbs of children being dislocated at birth & they are never thought serious." HBS to ECS, Albany, NY, February 20, 1851, Elizabeth Cady Stanton Papers, Library of Congress. Had this been their second child with a dislocated collarbone, surely Henry would have reminded Elizabeth that Neil's bones had been successfully mended. As further evidence, in the incorrectly dated letter, Elizabeth mentions a character from a Dickens novel that was not published until 1846, making it impossible for the child in question to have been Neil who was born in 1842.

[5] ECS to HBS, Seneca Falls, [February 27,] 1851. Elizabeth Cady Stanton Papers, Vassar College, Poughkeepsie, New York.

[6] *Journal of the Senate of the State of New York at Their Seventy-Fourth Session*, Albany: Charles Van Benthuysen, 1851, p. 175.

[7] HBS to ECS, Albany, February 15, 1851. Elizabeth Cady Stanton Papers, Library of Congress.

[8] Ibid.

[9] *Journal of the Senate of the State of New York at Their Seventy-Fourth Session*, p. 175.

[10] Although the petitions did not survive the Albany fire, from surviving information, it is possible that the petitions introduced by Henry and one of those introduced later in the session by Sen. Stone were from men. The *Journal of the Senate* noted that Henry's petitions were from "inhabitants" of his district, while the second of Sen. Stone's petitions were from "ladies." Ibid., p. 331.

[11] Martha Wright to Lucretia Mott, December 9, 1850, Garrison Family

Papers, Smith College.

[12] Martha Wright to Lucretia Mott, Dec? 1841? typed transcript in Garrison Family Papers, Smith College and reprinted in Cott, *Roots of Bitterness*, pp. 165-166. For suffrage petition, Martha Wright to Lucretia Mott, December 13, 1853, typed transcript, Garrison Family Papers, Smith College. David Wright was also opposed to women's equal pay. In 1846, Martha questioned him as to why the family seamstress made half that of the caretaker. David claimed that paying them the same would be a "curse to the community" because it would "raise the price of labor and set people by the ears." Martha Wright to Lucretia Mott, May 13, 1846, Garrison Family Papers, Smith College.

[13] *Journal of the Senate of the State of New York at Their Seventy-Fourth Session*, p. 269 and p. 331.

[14] Ibid., pp. 600-602.

[15] Ibid., p. 603. See also Stanton, *RR*, pp. 167-68.

[16] *Journal of the Senate of the State of New York at Their Seventy-Fourth Session*, pp. 607 and 611.

[17] "One of the Renegades in a Fix," *Seneca County Courier*, May 15 1851. See also *Seneca County Courier*, May 22, 1851.

[18] [Geneva, NY] *Gazette*, May 10, 1851.

[19] Harriot Stanton Blatch and Alma Lutz, *Challenging Years: The Memoirs of Harriot Stanton Blatch*, New York: G. P. Putnam's Sons, 1940, p. 35.

[20] *Seneca County Courier*, May 15, 1851.

[21] ECS to Elizabeth Smith Miller, Seneca Falls, June 4, 1851 in Stanton-Blatch, *Letters*, pp. II:28-31.

[22] Ibid., p. 29.

[23] Ibid., p. 30.

[24] Ibid., p. 29.

[25] Oswego *Daily Times*, June 6, 1851. Blatch and Lutz, *Challenging Years: The Memoirs of Harriot Stanton Blatch*, p. 35.

[26] Henry's *RR* states that he won by five votes. However, official state documentation shows Stanton victorious by four votes. See also, *Seneca County Courier*, June 5, 1851. Stanton, *RR*, p. 168. For the 1849 totals, see HBS to Charles Sumner, Seneca Falls, November 8, 1849, Sumner Papers, Houghton Library, Harvard University, 7:008.

[27] Ibid., p. 167.

[28] Stanton-Blatch, *Letters*, p. II:27.

[29] *Documents of the Senate of the State of New York, Seventy-Fourth Session*, 3 vols., Vol. 3 Albany: Charles Van Benthuysen, 1851, Document No. 85. 15 pages.

[30] Ibid., Document No. 85, page 4.

[31] *Journal of the Senate of the State of New York at Their Seventy-Fourth Session*, p. 772.

[32] Stanton, *RR*, p. 170.

[33] Stanton, *80Y*, p. 163. *Liberator*, May 30, 1851.

[34] Gordon, ed. *The Selected Papers of Elizabeth Cady Stanton and Susan B. Anthony: In the School of Anti-Slavery 1840-1866*, pp. 182-184.

[35] *Lily*, April 1, 1852 and *Rochester Daily Democrat*, April 21, 1852.

[36] The *Carson League*, May 19, 1853.

[37] *Frederick Douglass' Paper*, April 15, 1852 and November 3, 1854.

[38] *Frederick Douglass' Paper*, September 4, 1851 and October 16, 1851.

[39] January meeting, *Frederick Douglass' Paper*, January 22, 1852. February meeting held at Mrs. S.D. Porter's home, *Frederick Douglass' Paper*, February 5, 1852. The May 7th meeting at the Avery home, *Frederick Douglass' Paper*, April 29 and May 13, 1852. The November meeting, *Frederick Douglass' Paper*, November 5, 1852. Douglass' speech printed as "*Oration, Delivered in Corinthian Hall, Rochester, by Frederick Douglass, July 5th, 1852*." Lee, Mann & Co., American Building, Rochester, 1852.

[40] Burial records, Mt. Hope Cemetery, Rochester, New York. See also, 1860 US Federal Census, Oberlin, Ohio, page 67. Frances' body was brought back to Rochester for burial. The three Avery daughters surviving to adulthood are buried elsewhere. The Avery's eldest daughter, Frances Maria Avery married a nephew and namesake of the famous Daniel Boone. Susan, the middle daughter had an unhappy and abusive marriage, ultimately resulting in divorce. Elizabeth Cady Avery never married, and lived in Cleveland until her death on December 2, 1922 at the age of 83.

[41] Robert B. Stanton, "Notes from My Note Books." New York Public Library. Robert Brewster Stanton's father (and Henry's brother), Robert Lodowick Stanton, is often confused with Henry and Elizabeth's youngest son due to inaccurate cataloging in the 20th century. Robert Lodowick's name is often incorrectly written as Robert Livingston Stanton. Henry's brother Robert, was given his middle name after their father, Lodowick. The Library of Congress and WorldCat corrected this mistake in 2008, but many reprints of Robert Lodowick's book still persist in giving him an incorrect name. The Livingston name comes from Elizabeth's family. Henry's *Random Recollections* is correct (in index) and Robert Lodowick Stanton's baptismal records still exist at the Preston [Connecticut] Town Hall showing his correct name.

[42] Ibid.

[43] *Rochester Daily Democrat*, November 1, 1853, and *Rochester Daily Advertiser*, November 1, 1853.

[44] For an enlightening and thorough discussion of ECS as a historical figure, see Ellen Carol DuBois, *Harriot Stanton Blatch and the Winning of Woman Suffrage*, New Haven: Yale University 1997, pp. 242-78.

[45] The only surviving mention of Susanna in Elizabeth's letters concerns a letter written by Theodore Weld in 1834 that Susanna gave to Elizabeth as a keepsake. See p. 207-208 n. 11.

[46] Gordon, ed. *The Selected Papers of Elizabeth Cady Stanton and Susan B. Anthony: In the School of Anti-Slavery 1840-1866*, p. 608.

[47] Blatch and Lutz, *Challenging Years: The Memoirs of Harriot Stanton Blatch*, p. 35.

[48] Stanton, *A Record, Genealogical, Biographical, Statistical, of Thomas Stanton of Connecticut and His Descendants, 1635-1891.*, pp.461-62.

[49] HBS to ECS, Willard Hotel, Washington, DC, January 28, 1857, Elizabeth Cady Stanton Papers, Library of Congress.

[50] HBS to Margaret Livingston Stanton, Washington, DC, January 16, 1857. Courtesy of Coline Jenkins/Elizabeth Cady Stanton Trust. My sincere thanks to Coline Jenkins for sharing this wonderful family letter with me.

[51] HBS to ECS, Washington, DC, February 14, 1858, Elizabeth Cady Stanton Papers, Library of Congress.

[52] HBS to ECS, Washington, DC, [February 17, 1859], Elizabeth Cady Stanton Papers, Library of Congress.

[53] Martha Wright to Susan B. Anthony, August 29, 1858. Garrison Family Papers, Smith College.

[54] See Gordon, ed. *The Selected Papers of Elizabeth Cady Stanton and Susan B. Anthony: In the School of Anti-Slavery 1840-1866*, p. 444.

[55] "Mrs. Stanton and The 'Wide-Awakes'," *National Anti-Slavery Standard*, October 10 1860.

[56] Susan B. Anthony to Henry B. Stanton, Jr. and Gerrit S. Stanton, Seneca Falls, September 27, 1860, in Gordon, ed. *The Selected Papers of Elizabeth Cady Stanton and Susan B. Anthony: In the School of Anti-Slavery 1840-1866*, pp. 441-44.

[57] Ibid., p. 443 and Rice-*HBS*, p. 371.

[58] Ibid., p. 384.

[59] Ibid., pp. 405, 13-15.

[60] ECS to Lillie Devereux Blake, Washington, DC, January 6, 1879, Theodore Stanton Collection, E. C. Stanton Papers, Douglass Library, Rutgers University.

[61] ECS to Rebecca R. Eyster, [1847? May? 1?]. Typed transcript, Theodore Stanton Collection, Douglass Library, Rutgers University.

[62] Stanton-Blatch, Vol. 2, pp. 353-354.

INDEX

Made in the USA
San Bernardino, CA
19 July 2016